THE AMERICAN MAIL

The American Mail

Enlarger of the Common Life

Wayne E. Fuller

THE CHICAGO HISTORY OF AMERICAN CIVILIZATION
Daniel J. Boorstin, EDITOR

THE UNIVERSITY OF CHICAGO PRESS
Chicago and London

THE UNIVERSITY OF CHICAGO PRESS, CHICAGO 60637
THE UNIVERSITY OF CHICAGO PRESS, LTD., LONDON

© 1972 by The University of Chicago
All rights reserved. Published 1972
Printed in the United States of America

International Standard Book Number: 0–226–26884–5 (clothbound)
Library of Congress Catalog Card Number: 72–78254

FOR BILLIE

Contents

Editor's Preface

For much of American history, the mail was our main form of organized communication. Americans wanting to know the state of the world, the health of a friend, or the fate of their business anxiously awaited the mail. To advise a distant relative, to order goods, to pay a bill, to express views to their congressman or love to their fiancée, they used the mail. No American institution has been more intimately involved in daily hopes and fears. Nor has any institution been more effective in cementing community or more essential to the function and growth of a democratic government.

Yet from American historians the mail has not received its due. And our national myopia is betrayed in the fact that the abundant new courses in "communications" in schools and colleges, preoccupied with radio and television, allow us to forget the central role of the mail in the history of American life.

This book should help rescue the subject and help give it a deserved dignity and prominence in our thinking about our whole past. Mr. Fuller reminds us of the continuity of our institutions, showing us how new techniques, instead of simply displacing the old, have a way of transforming them into surprising new roles. When the telephone first came into use, observers predicted that it would virtually abolish the mail, and the coming of radio brought prophecies of the demise of the telephone and the phonograph. But each of these actually produced new uses for old techniques and institutions. The new apparatus of American communications in the later twentieth century—the telephone, the phonograph, photography, radio, and television—have all stirred surprising new uses for the "post offices and post roads" (art. 1, sec. 8) given into the power of Congress by the framers of the Constitution in 1787.

One peculiarity of the mail is that documents and objects which record its past have become raw material for a universal and increasingly popular hobby. "Philately" (which came into the language only in 1865)—the collection and study of postage stamps, postmarks, and related materials, popularly known as "stamp collecting"—has engaged the interest of people of all ages. In this way many have received their first (and sometimes their best) lessons in geography and political history. The enthusiasm, the expertise, and the competitive passions of philatelists have become proverbial.

Not only for students of American civilization, then, but for all these millions, Mr. Fuller's book provides a new, lively, and scholarly path into all American history. He performs the magic of the best historians, transmuting little-noted facts into touchstones of our whole experience. Through the story of the mail, he shows the progress of technology (the impact of the railroad, the automobile, and the airplane), he recounts the debates over innovation (over the postage stamp, free home delivery,

Editor's Preface

RFD, parcel post, and airmail), and he reminds us of the changing standards for what is educational, decent, or obscene. We witness the scramble for mail contracts and for the political patronage of post office jobs. We see how the demands of special groups—country-store owners, mail-order houses, retailers, publishers, farmers, and others—have been shaped by American conditions and have shaped an American standard of living. Mr. Fuller carries his story through the transformation of the United States Mail into the United States Postal Service in 1971.

In all these ways, Mr. Fuller admirably fulfills the purpose of the "Chicago History of American Civilization," which aims to make each aspect of our culture a window to all our history. The series contains two kinds of books: a chronological group, which provides a coherent narrative of American history from its beginning to the present day, and a topical group, which deals with the history of varied and significant aspects of American life. This book is one of the topical group, which includes, among others, John F. Stover's *American Railroads*, John B. Rae's *The American Automobile*, and Carl F. Condit's *American Building*.

DANIEL J. BOORSTIN

Prologue

For almost three hundred years, the postal system was virtually the only means widely scattered Americans possessed for communicating with one another and with relatives in the lands of their birth. Indeed, even as late as World War I the postal service, as the inscription on the old Washington, D.C., post office had it, was still, for most Americans, the principal

Messenger of Sympathy and Love
Servant of Parted Friends
Consoler of the Lonely
Bond of the Scattered Family
Enlarger of the Common Life
Carrier of News and Knowledge
Instrument of Trade and Industry
Promoter of Mutual Acquaintance
Of Peace and Good Will among Men and Nations.

In all those years, the American postal system became inextricably interwoven into the fabric of American civilization.

Prologue

Like the family album whose photographs record the growth and changes of the family, the history of the American mail service reflects the nation's progress and development. Where the American people went as they spread across the continent, there went the mails; and the frontier line itself, as it moved from year to year and decade to decade, can be traced in the postal records. So too, in the statistics on the increasing volume of mail may be read the story of the nation's growing population and burgeoning industry. The changes in transportation that marked the American advance from horseback to stagecoach, from canal to steamboat, and from railroads to automobiles and airplanes are revealed in the voluminous postal papers preserved in the National Archives. Few, in fact, are the aspects of the American past—military, religious, social, political, economic —with which the postal system has not been connected in one way or another.

But the nation's postal service was more than a mirror reflecting the nation's progress. As much a promoter of that progress as an index of it, it had much to do both directly and indirectly with the spread of the country's early stagecoach lines, the building of roads, and the development of steamboats, railroads, and the merchant marine. Newspapers and periodicals relied upon it for their survival, as did countless businessmen whose transactions and advertisements were carried largely by mail. Even democracy itself and the welding of sections into one mighty Union owed something to this omnipresent arm of the national government. "Of all existing departments," Senator Charles Sumner said in 1870, "the post office is most entitled to consideration for it is the most universal in its beneficence. . . . There is nothing which is not helped by the post office."

By the time the first real postal system began in English

Prologue

America in the late seventeenth century, the western world had already experienced some two thousand years of postal service, and most of the postal principles Americans would adopt were borrowed from their European ancestors who had worked them out across the years. Not that the American Post Office was a replica of others, for it was not. Still, it is somewhat astonishing to observe how much was derivative and how little was really new in the American postal system of the nineteenth century.

Organized postal systems sprang not from the desire of separated friends to communicate with one another, but from the needs of leaders of government. For in the ancient world—where postal services originated—no less than in the modern, the control of communication and the control of government went hand in hand. Among the first to grasp this principle were the rulers of ancient Persia, whose great empire stretched in 500 B.C. from India across the Hellespont to Macedonia. Here, upon a royal road extending from Susa near the Persian Gulf to Sardis in Asia Minor, the Persian rulers built a string of stations at fourteen-mile intervals, stocked them with fleet-footed horses to bear the royal messengers from post to post, and so established the first real postal service known to the western world. "Nothing mortal travels so fast as these Persian messengers," wrote Herodotus, the Greek historian, and so it must have seemed to the ancients, for the fifteen-hundred-mile journey was completed in little more than seven days.

An even greater model of speed and efficiency in the ancient world was the Roman postal system, the *cursus publicus*. Like the Persians, the Romans used the relay system and by the time of Augustus had built stations along the network of highways that connected Rome with all parts of the empire. The Romans called their stations *posts* from the Latin *positus*, meaning placed.

3

Prologue

Through these they relayed messages and even passengers across the empire, and so slow were changes in transportation that not for almost nineteen hundred years was there a faster postal system than the *cursus publicus.*

Owned and operated by the government for the purposes of government, these two ancient postal services established the principle of government ownership of postal systems. However, as a rule neither carried private letters such as those the Apostle Paul wrote to the churches he had founded in Asia Minor and elsewhere, and before this practice was established governments had to wage a lengthy battle with private postal systems.

This struggle might have been shorter had the Roman Empire endured. In time, the *cursus publicus* would probably have carried private letters and eliminated the necessity of private messengers. But with the collapse of the empire came the end of its postal system, and one interesting measure of the bleakness of European life after the empire's decline was that for some six hundred years, except for the royal couriers who served Charlemagne, there is almost no record of a postal system in Europe.

But just as the disappearance of the postal service revealed the decline of the Roman civilization, its reappearance in the late Middle Ages signaled the reawakening of Europe's commerce and the rebirth of its learning. By the thirteenth century, so far had Europeans progressed from the doldrums of the earlier years and so great was the need for communication that enterprising men had established their own private postal systems, and their messengers, carrying poles for fording streams, knives for protection, and small metal bags from which the term "mail" originated, could be seen trekking about the continent. The monks, whose growing intellectual interests made intermonastery communication desirable, the students at the rising European universities, who found it necessary to write home for money and reassurance, the merchants, like those who had formed the Hanseatic League, whose business ventures depended for success upon a far-flung system of communication —all these established their own postal services. The monastery at Cluny, France, for example, kept up a correspondence with monasteries in Spain as well as with those of Hungary and Poland. And the messenger service at the University of Paris served students for more than four hundred years. But the most famous private postal system of all time, perhaps, was that organized by Franz and Johann von Taxis.

This famous family, known as von Taxis in Germany and Tasso in Italy, operated its huge postal system throughout parts of Europe with varying degrees of fortune for more than four hundred years. First authorized to carry the mail through the Holy Roman Empire in the late fifteenth century, the family eventually arranged a contract with Charles V, who was both king of Spain and Holy Roman Emperor, to extend their postal system throughout Charles's realm. To do this they blanketed much of central Europe and the lowlands with relay stations, equipped them with fine horses, established regular schedules for their postriders, and made their post a model of efficiency and speed. A letter sent the one thousand miles from Rome to Brussels by the von Taxis postal service reached its destination, according to one account, in ten and a half days in summer and twelve in winter. And this letter might have been a private as well as an official communication of the government, for the von Taxis system carried them both and in doing so built up a princely fortune for the family.

Prologue

The von Taxis family postal business was only one of a number of private posts that developed in the sixteenth and seventeenth centuries to take care of the expanding postal business, but by the seventheenth century the trend against private posts had begun. As the power of Spain and the Holy Roman Empire declined, so did the fortunes of the von Taxis postal system. Elsewhere the growth of strong national states doomed the private posts, and what happened in England was characteristic of what eventually befell the postal systems in other national states.

The English postal system, like that which King Louis XI of France established in 1477, dates back at least as far as the late fifteenth century when, during England's Wars of the Roses, Edward IV established a post northward to Scotland. But this post and other government mail systems that followed it over the next few years were makeshift affairs, to be used mostly in times of emergency. They carried only the official communications of the government, and private correspondence, mostly that of monks and businessmen, was taken by private posts. By the time Henry VIII ascended the throne in 1509, however, private posts were carrying the letters of the government as well as those of private persons.

But at a time when no one's throne was secure, official mail was too important to trust to private carriers. Early in the sixteenth century, mainly to protect and convey the government's dispatches, Henry VIII appointed Sir Brian Tuke master of the posts and authorized him to establish a royal post. Henry did not prohibit private postal services, but he did begin a trend toward creating a government postal monopoly, and successive rulers, in order to control communication and prevent subversion, enlarged the government's control over the postal service by placing new restrictions on private posts. Elizabeth—confronting the intrigues surrounding Mary Queen of Scots, who secretly received and sent letters hidden in beer kegs—King James I, Oliver Cromwell, and Charles II all had reason to fear the uncontrolled private posts, and all tightened the government's monopoly over the mail.

To thwart foreign conspiracies, in 1609, the year of Virginia's "starving time," James I ordered all letters to be sent through the royal mail. Nearly half a century later, in 1657, Cromwell had Parliament enact England's first complete postal law, which strengthened the government's monopoly of the service, not only to promote trade but to prevent, as he said, "many dangerous and wicked designs . . . against the peace and welfare of this Commonwealth, the intelligence whereof cannot well be communicated but by letters of escript." Moreover, under Charles II government officials opened and resealed suspicious-looking letters and made this practice a fine art when one of the king's postal agents built a miraculous machine that could break a letter's seal so keenly that it could not be detected.

Yet even as the government strengthened its monopoly of the mails, private posts continued to exist, principally because of the poor but costly service offered by the royal mail. So numerous were those who carried letters outside the mails that a small directory was published in 1637 entitled *The Carriers' Cosmography; or, A Brief Relation of the Inns, Ordinairies, Hosteleries, and other lodgings in and near London; where the Carriers, Waggons, Foot-posts and Higglers do usually come from any parts . . . of the Kingdom of England . . . ,"* to suggest where people might go to mail their letters. "The Carriers of Abingdon do lodge at the George in Broad street," ran a typical entry in the directory. "They do come on Wednesdays, and go away on Thursdays."

As was to be the case with the American mail, all this invasion of the government's postal monopoly by private business was really a boon to the mail service, for it forced the government to improve its postal system. After 1680, for example, when a London merchant named William Dockwra organized and successfully operated a private post to deliver letters in and around London for a penny apiece, the government eventually took it over, as it was to do with other successful postal innovations. Furthermore, in the late seventeenth and early eighteenth centuries, private competition helped force the government to expand its postal service to serve all the people. Although postage rates, established in the 1630s and based upon the number of sheets in a letter plus the distance the letter traveled, were raised in the early 1700s when the government sought to make money from the post office, still the mail schedules were improved, a by-post system developed virtually covering England with mail service, and attempts were made to speed up the mails.

In Elizabeth's England, a law had provided that postriders must travel at seven miles an hour in summer and five in winter, and some two hundred years later the mail was moving no faster. In fact, at the close of the seventeenth century the mails were estimated to be traveling on the average at the rate of five miles an hour. To improve this situation an express, somewhat resembling the modern registered-letter service, was established by employing mounted messengers to speed urgent messages to their destination. About the same time, the government's adoption of William Dockwra's idea of postmarking letters to indicate the time of their mailing forced postmasters to push letters through their post offices as fast as possible lest a delay in a postmarked letter be traced to them. And finally, in the late eighteenth century, at the suggestion of John Palmer, a merchant at Bath, the British government began to send mail by coach, not only to protect the mail but primarily to make the speed of the mails comparable to that of travelers.

In attempting to speed up the mails, the government was acting in accordance with the oldest postal tradition. "My days are swifter than the post," lamented Job in biblical days, noting the association between the mails and speed, and so closely has speed been associated with the mails that much of the world's postal history can be written around the attempts to send mail faster each day than it went the day before.

In part this was because postal systems were developed to carry government messages which had to travel as swiftly as possible to avoid some impending catastrophe. Most American schoolboys know, of course, that if the mails had been airborne in 1812, or if there had been a "hot line" between Washington and London so Congress could have known on 18 June, when it declared war on England, that England had taken steps two days before to end her attack upon American shipping, there might have been no War of 1812. And even if there had been a war, no bloody battle at New Orleans would have been fought had it been known in America that two weeks before the battle, the treaty ending the war had been signed in faraway Ghent. As it was, news of the Peace of Ghent and the Battle of New Orleans reached Washington, D.C., at about the same time.

But the constant efforts to hurry the mails along cannot be completely explained by the importance of either government or business letters. The search for faster and faster ways of carrying the mail has gone on continuously regardless of the urgency of its contents and seems to have been inspired by demands that were perhaps partly emotional. Unimportant words reduced to writing, enclosed in a stamped envelope or even sealed with a wafer, and mailed somehow assumed for both sender and receiver a quality of urgency out of all proportion to their significance in ordinary conversation. Perhaps it was the magic of the message by which, as Voltaire wrote, "the absent becomes present," that led Englishmen in the late sixteenth and early seventeenth centuries to write "haste, post, haste, for thy life, life, life," on their letters and sparked demands for faster mail delivery.

Whatever the reason, speed became the symbol of postal systems around the world. The ancient Greeks had endowed their messenger god with winged feet, and the Chinese postmen carried feathers in their hats. Artistic conceptions of the postal service almost always depicted a sense of rapid motion— prancing horses attached to a stagecoach or a postrider galloping across the prairies. There was even a reflection of speed and urgency about the coiled golden horn emblazoned on the arms of the von Taxis family, which represented the horns their postriders blew when approaching towns or meeting travelers along the roads.

But for all the efforts to carry the mails more swiftly, the incredibly long drought of inventions in the field of transportation prevented any real advance in the speed of the mails for more than two millennia. About 500 B.C. Persian postriders were carrying messages a distance of fifteen hundred miles in little more than seven days. In 1861, 2,361 years later, the famous Pony Express riders in the United States carried President Abraham Lincoln's first inaugural address sixteen hundred miles in seven days and eighteen hours. And aside from its express service, the fastest the British postal service was able to transport the mails by the late eighteenth century, even with the careful planning that went into developing John Palmer's stagecoach service, was about nine miles an hour.

But if the British, at the time they were colonizing America, had yet to revolutionize the speed with which their mails were carried, by the early eighteenth century they had at least grappled with a significant number of postal problems. They had not yet completely won the battle with private enterprise, but they had established the principle of government monopoly of the mails. They had accepted the idea that the postal service was to be used by the people as well as the government and were in the process of extending the service over the entire kingdom. Postage rates had been established according to the number of sheets in a letter plus the distance the letter was to travel, and, somewhat to the detriment of the service, the idea that the postal service should produce a revenue for the treasury had been adopted. A delivery system had been worked out for London, letters with postage prepaid were sometimes sent, though prepayment was not obligatory, and postmarks were in use.

The British, then, after more than two centuries of experience, had produced a rich store of postal knowledge, much of which was to be passed on to their countrymen in the new world in the succeeding years.

I

The Colonial Post Office

"April 28, 1625—Loving and Kind friends, etc. I know not whether this will ever come to your hands, or miscarrie, as other my letters have done; yet in regard of the Lord's dealing with us hear, I have had a great desire to write unto you, knowing your desire to bear a parte with us, both in our joyes, and sorrows, as we do with You."

So wrote Roger White, member of a group of Separatists in Holland, to William Bradford, leader of the Pilgrims who had left Holland five years before to build a home in the new world. That the letter turned up in William Bradford's history of the Plymouth Plantation was proof that, unlike the others, it had reached its destination. It was indicative, too, of the yearning of friends an ocean apart to communicate with one another and of the difficulties of doing so.

Because they were Englishmen in America, not Americans, the early English colonists in the new world were bound by ties of memory and love to those in the land they had left rather than to those in the scattered communities they were building in America. For this reason their first mail routes, if routes they were, stretched east and west, not north and south, and lay across the ocean separating them from England rather than upon the land dividing their isolated settlements. And just as their first mail routes were water routes, so the first mail carriers were either passengers or captains of the ships that plowed the waters between the new world and the old.

This mail system was informal and completely unpredictable, although it worked reasonably well in England. Letters to and from England found their way to their destinations first through the coffeehouses along the wharves where they were both received and sent, and later, in the 1660s, through the English post offices. But in the settlements it was a different story. In none of the plantations in the early 1630s was there an authorized place for ship captains either to gather letters bound for England or to deposit those they brought to the new world. To distribute the letters they brought, it was necessary either to find the persons to whom they were addressed or to leave them at someone's home in the hope that somehow they might eventually be given to the rightful owners.

As the colonial population increased, so did the letters addressed to the settlers. So too, no doubt, did the number of missed connections, and it was probably this miscarriage of letters that prompted the establishment of the first post office in the English colonies. In November 1639 the Massachusetts General Court, displaying that passion for order and organization so typical of the Puritans, created a post office of sorts by ordering that all letters brought from overseas be deposited at Richard Fairbanks's house. Fairbanks, whose house was apparently used for other public services as well, was to act as a kind of postmaster whose duty it was to see that the letters from the old world were delivered to their addresses and those going abroad were sent according to direction. For this he was to receive a penny per letter, but he was to have no monopoly of the business. No one, according to the law, was required to send his letters overseas through Fairbanks's post office.

Such as it was, this was the colonists' first organized postal system, and aside from a similar arrangement established by the Dutch at New Amsterdam in 1652, the only postal service established by law in the colonies along the seaboard for almost two decades.

Not that there was no other system of communication in the colonies. On the contrary, as the older colonies grew and new ones were founded, as children matured and left their homes to build others in the wilderness, as trade increased and dangers of one kind or another threatened, a surprisingly large number of letters were exchanged among the settlers, particularly in New England. Their mail carriers were those who took passage on the ships that sailed from colony to colony along the coast, the ship captains, or special messengers employed for carrying urgent letters. But however letters went, chance usually determined when they would go. The sudden arrival of a ship, the occasional visit of a stranger, or the departure of an acquaintance for another colony afforded opportunities for sending and receiving letters. The Dutch at Fort Amsterdam, for example, first wrote to the settlers at Plymouth in 1627, when a handful of them accidentally encountered some Indians who lived near the Plymouth colony and offered to carry a letter to the Pilgrims.

Obviously such haphazard arrangements were unsatisfactory for a growing population, but it was not until the middle of the seventeenth century that more formal postal systems began to be established by colonial legislatures. In 1657 the Virginia House of Burgesses established the "tobacco post," making each plantation owner responsible for passing official messages and letters on to the next plantation. A planter's failure to do so could result in his forfeiting one hogshead of tobacco.

More than a decade later, both Massachusetts and Connecticut, concerned because the cost of sending public messages was high and unregulated, enacted legislation establishing wages for the carrying of such messages and setting the maximum prices that the postman could be charged for his expenses. In Massachusetts, the letter carrier was to receive three pence a mile for his work, and innkeepers were to charge him no more than two shillings for a bushel of oats or four pence for hay for his horse. The Massachusetts General Court also appointed John Haywood postmaster, first at Boston in 1677, where the merchants were complaining about lost letters, and later for the entire colony. Finally, in 1683, shortly after the founding of Pennsylvania, William Penn established a mail service that bore letters from Philadelphia to the falls of the Delaware River for three pence, to Chester for two pence, and into Maryland for six pence.

Although these developments had taken place within the colonies by the 1680s, the fact that no permanent intercolonial postal service had yet been established reflected the continued absence of common interests among the colonies. Still Englishmen in America instead of Americans, the colonists' interests outside their own colonies remained primarily in England.

True, three attempts at developing an intercolonial postal system had been made by 1690. In 1672, Governor Francis Lovelace of New York, a man of vision and enterprise, prompted by

The Colonial Post Office

Charles II's desire that his American subjects correspond with one another—possibly to ward off a Dutch threat to New York—tried to develop a postal service between New York and Boston. The following decade, in 1684, the pressure of the French and Indians upon the New England colonies and New York led New York's governor, Thomas Dongan, to suggest the building of posthouses from Canada to the Carolinas as a way of tying the colonies together in the face of the enemy. And then in the late 1680s a third attempt was made when the New England colonies, the Jerseys, and New York were lumped together in the Dominion of New England.

All these attempts ended in failure. With great expectations, Governor Lovelace sent a postman off to Boston in 1673 with a number of mailbags, each designated for a particular town along the way, and a letter to Massachusetts's governor, John Winthrop. "I herewith present you with two rarities," he wrote, "a packquett of the latest inteligence [*sic*] I could meet withal, and a post—by the latter you will meet with a monthly fresh supply."

The governor was more optimistic than realistic. There was no road between New York and Boston, and one of Lovelace's recommendations, apparently ignored, was that Winthrop consult the ablest woodsmen about cutting a way through the forest which could in time become the king's highway. Moreover, Bostonians apparently had no great compulsion to write to New Yorkers. When New York was temporarily retaken by the Dutch in 1673, at the very time when Lovelace was in Connecticut trying to stir up enthusiasm for his post, the postal service collapsed, and though postmasters were subsequently appointed in both cities, there was little communication between them.

The Colonial Post Office

Governor Dongan's system fared no better. Permitted by the British government to establish such a service, he did manage to get the mails started between Boston and New York, but the system was never effective. Neither was that which was operated under the Dominion of New England. Probably no more popular with Americans than the Dominion itself, this service collapsed with the Dominion in 1689, so that by 1690, after nearly a century in the wilderness, the colonies were still without an intercolonial postal system.

But change was on the way. In England, William and Mary had replaced James II on the throne after his overthrow in the "glorious revolution" of 1688, and when the dust of the revolution had settled and the Dominion of New England had fallen, the British government made plans to establish an intercolonial post office in America.

By this time, almost unnoticed, the English colonies had grown remarkably. By 1690 all the major colonies on the American mainland except Georgia had been established, and nearly 200,000 persons lived along the coast from Maine to South Carolina. Virginia alone contained almost 60,000 inhabitants, and Massachusetts had 50,000. Boston was a city of some 7,000 persons, New York City 5,000, and Philadelphia and its environs nearly 12,000. Yet these people had no systematic means of communication with one another which could be used to promote trade among themselves and help protect them from the menace of the French and Indians poised upon their borders.

Whether this situation entered into the British government's determination to establish a colonial postal system is uncertain. That decision, at least, was no part of any scheme to reorganize the whole colonial empire, and it may have been made largely to please a court favorite who believed that it was now possible to make money from an American post office. However it was, in 1691 the British government authorized Thomas Neale to establish a postal service in the colonies from Virginia to Canada. This grant was to last for twenty-one years and gave Neale a monopoly of the postal business in America.

Thomas Neale had a gambler's spirit. As groom porter to both Charles II and William III it had been his duty, among other things, to provide cards and dice for the kings and their friends and to act as a judge when disputes arose over the games. He had been instrumental in arranging lotteries to raise money for the government, had once been in charge of licensing gaming-houses in the realm, and, according to report, had gambled away two fortunes in his life. In short, Neale's public career seems to have been associated in one way or another with games of chance, and perhaps he viewed the colonial post office as another such game which, if played right, might yield a fortune.

Neale never came to America, but authorized the governor of New Jersey, Andrew Hamilton, to establish the post office. The choice was a good one, for Hamilton, a Scotchman who had come to America in 1686, was a man of great tact and enterprise. To secure the cooperation of the independent-minded colonial legislatures, he submitted for their approval a draft bill which included suggested postal rates, rules for the appointment of postmasters, confirmation of Neale's monopoly, and such other regulations as might be necessary for the successful operation of the system.

Two colonies, Maryland and Virginia, refused to join the Neale postal system, possibly because they did not have a draft of Neale's bill before them, or perhaps simply because they resented being asked to join by the crown rather than by Hamilton. Five colonies, however—New Hampshire, New York, Pennsylvania, Connecticut, and Massachusetts—did enact the proposed legislation with certain reservations. A concession was made, for example, to postmaster-innkeepers in both New York and New Hampshire. In neither place were they to be taxed for the ale and liquor they kept in stock. And in Massachusetts, the general court, with typical Yankee shrewdness, granted Hamilton the postal monopoly only on the condition that the mail service be efficient. To ensure its efficiency, the Massachusetts law required that each letter be marked to show the day of the month and the year it was received for mailing. This was the first provision for postmarking letters in America, but legally it never went into effect, for the Massachusetts law was rejected by the postal authorities in England.

Why this law, the only one of those enacted by the colonies, was disallowed is not exactly clear. It may have been, as was said, that the restrictions Massachusetts attached to the operation of the service were a threat to Neale's postal monopoly; but more than likely the British government's growing distrust of Massachusetts and her independent ways had something to do with it. In any event, the Massachusetts General Court so resented the discrimination that when some time later a new postal law was drawn up by British authorities and submitted to the general court, it was huffily ignored. But it did not really matter, for the postal system, like so many things in colonial Massachusetts, operated without the law.

The Neale post office began in 1693, and soon mails were dispatched weekly on routes that ran from Portsmouth, New Hampshire, to Boston, New London, New Haven, New York,

The Colonial Post Office

Perth Amboy, Burlington, and Philadelphia, and on to New Castle in Delaware. It seemed a promising beginning, and all things considered this first real postal system in English America worked as well as could be expected. But, alas, as a money-making venture it was a failure. After four years of operation, Postmaster General Hamilton wound up with a deficit of more than two thousand pounds, for reasons not too difficult to explain.

In the first place, the postage rates were too high to attract many letters. Besides, the rates lacked uniformity, since each colony had fixed its own. The postage on a letter going from New York to Boston, for example, was twelve pence, but from Boston to New York it was nine. Nor was Neale's monopoly really secure. Many letters traveled outside the mails, thereby paying no postage at all, and even the ship captains, in violation of the law, would not always take the letters they brought to the new world to the post offices where postage could be collected.

In New York, moreover, the service was injured because the assembly had refused to extend Neale's monopoly along the Hudson River, where most of the people lived and where most of the postal business was done. Then, too, the first four years of the postal service, 1693 to 1697, coincided with King William's War in the colonies, which doubtless affected the postal revenues adversely. This was suggested by the fact that in 1699, two years after the war had ended, the service was paying all its expenses except Postmaster General Hamilton's salary and seemed to be approaching the time when it would actually make a profit.

Still, changes seemed necessary, and that same year, 1699,

Hamilton joined Neale in London to plead for a strengthening of the postal monopoly in America to prevent so many letters from being sent outside the mails. But the government, unwilling to strengthen the monopoly unless it controlled the service, made virtually no changes, and the post office limped into the eighteenth century. In 1704, according to one account, the mail service went no farther east than Boston and no farther west than Philadelphia, and Lord Cornbury, governor of New York, complained that year that if he wanted to send a letter to Maryland or Virginia it must go either by special messenger —or express as this was called—or by a traveler going that way. "The least I have known any express to take hence to Virginia has been three weeks," he wrote.

By this time, both Neale and Andrew Hamilton were dead and the postal monopoly had passed into other hands. Three years later, in 1707, the British government, acting on recommendations made in 1699, purchased the owners' rights to the monopoly of the American postal system, took control over the colonial post office, and appointed Colonel John Hamilton, Andrew's son, postmaster general.

So ended Thomas Neale's private postal system in America. Financial failure though it was, it had made an important contribution to colonial life. During King William's War and the early part of Queen Anne's War, this intercolonial postal system had carried official dispatches back and forth among the colonies free of charge and, as Andrew Hamilton wrote, contributed "much toward putting the Kings subjects in security in time of Warr by ye frequent Conveyance of Intelligence when allarms happen, for want of wch. many familys have been cutt off before the settling of the Post." Even more important, this early postal service had taught the colonists a lesson in cooperation, fostered intercolonial intercourse, and so helped the colonists move a step toward unity.

For a time the British government operated the American Post Office much as Hamilton had done. But after 1711, it was regulated by the provisions of Queen Anne's Act, which Parliament had enacted the previous year. By this act the postal system throughout the entire empire was made a monopoly of the British government, deputy postmasters general were appointed in Edinburgh, Dublin, New York, and the West Indies, and new postage rates—based as they had been in the seventeenth century on the number of sheets in a letter and the distance the letter was going—were established throughout the empire, thereby eliminating the old postage rates set by the colonial legislatures.

Drawn primarily as a revenue measure to finance Queen Anne's War, the act of 1710 was accepted without murmur in all the English colonies except Virginia. There, in 1717, almost fifty years before the Stamp Act controversy, Virginians raised the cry of "no taxation without representation" when the new postage rates were announced and set about thwarting the law. Knowing the law provided that all letters accompanying and pertaining to merchandise were to go free, they claimed that all their letters were of this nature and refused to pay postage on any of them. Not content with this, the Virginia assembly enacted a law providing that any postmaster who demanded postage on any letter that did in fact accompany merchandise would be fined five pounds. Had this law been allowed to stand it would have meant that no postmaster would have dared to demand postage on any letter coming from overseas, since he could never be sure which letters in the ship captain's mailbag did indeed pertain to merchandise and which did not. As it was, the law was vetoed, but the Virginia colonists won their point in the end. The British government did not attempt to establish the postal system in Virginia until 1732.

In the North, however, particularly on the old routes between Boston, New York, and Philadelphia, pioneered by the Neale post office, the mails moved with reasonable dispatch. In 1715, the mail left Philadelphia for New York every Friday and reached there on Saturday night. Mail going on to Boston lay over in New York until Monday, when it began its journey to Boston by the way of Long Island and New Haven. On Thursday, the postriders from New York and Boston met at Saybrook and exchanged mails, and the Boston rider returned to his city with the mail that had left Philadelphia more than a week before. There the mail was taken to the post office, whose postmaster, with Yankee foresight, had once posted the following notice: "This is to give Notice, that when the Street Door is shut and no Light Candle and Lanthorn is seen hanging up in the Postoffice Entry at Boston on the Post nights coming in: Then all persons concerned may be assured without knocking or inquiring that there is no Post yet come in; and before Candle lighting if no Post be come in; the same is to be seen on a little Board hanging out at the Post-Office Window."

After 1721, the American Post Office no longer needed the British postmaster general's financial support, but at the same time it did not produce a revenue for the British treasury. Because of the high rate of postage, Americans, as they did with other imperial laws they did not like, paid little attention to the postal laws. They sent their letters outside the mails when they had a chance, and the royal officials in the colonies were as powerless to enforce the postal monopoly as they were the navigation laws controlling colonial trade.

In a way, the colonists were not entirely to blame for their evasion of the postal law, for the post office in America had gone on for years with scarcely any improvement in the service. Between 1711 and 1753, only Alexander Spotswood, deputy postmaster general from 1730 to 1739, made significant improvements. This one-time lieutenant-governor of Virginia brought Virginia into the postal system in 1732, and although the service to Virginia and to the rest of the South remained sporadic, the extension nonetheless helped to draw the southern and northern colonies closer together. However, Spotswood was perhaps remembered less for this achievement than for his appointment of Benjamin Franklin as the postmaster at Philadelphia in 1739.

Benjamin Franklin could scarcely have taken the Philadelphia postmastership in the hope of making money from it directly. Indeed, local postmasters in colonial days were lucky if they did not lose money. Since prepayment of postage was the exception, not the rule, those to whom letters were addressed paid the postage if they could. If they could not, and this was often the case, the postmasters often gave their patrons their letters on the promise to pay. But promises to pay were apparently honored no more in colonial days than today, and the overdue notices postmasters placed in the newspapers were a sad commentary on the failure of the policy. "This is to give notice to all persons in Town and Country that are indebted to Andrew Hay, Postmaster at Perth Amboy," ran one such notice, "for the postage of letters to Pay the same or they may expect t[r]ouble; some having been due near four years."

The Colonial Post Office

But Franklin, like so many postmasters of that day, was a newspaper editor, and it was for this reason he wanted the postmastership. At this time, newspapers were not allowed in the mails, but editor-postmasters could, by special arrangements, send their newspapers with their mail carriers and at the same time prevent their competition from doing so. In fact, Franklin's competitor in Philadelphia had done this very thing to Franklin's newspaper, and when Franklin became postmaster he, in effect, returned the favor for a time. That the post office proved valuable to him, Franklin admitted in his *Autobiography*. "I accepted it [the postmastership] readily, and found it a great advantage," he wrote; "for, tho' the salary was small, it facilitated the correspondence that improv'd my newspaper, increas'd the number demanded, as well as the advertisements inserted, so that it came to afford me a comfortable income. My old competitor's newspaper declin'd proportionately."

Franklin, however, was no ordinary editor-postmaster. Always fascinated by the small yet practical ways of improving man's lot—stoves, spectacles, and libraries, for example—Franklin saw in the post office a rather simple way to better colonial life, to speed communications among men with scientific and philosophical interests, to enhance the position of Philadelphia as the hub of the colonies, and possibly even to strengthen the ties among the colonies, and by midcentury he had grown interested in becoming deputy postmaster general.

Learning in 1751 that the incumbent deputy postmaster general, Eliot Benger, was "thought to be near his end," as he put it, Franklin wrote with unseemly haste that year asking a friend to support him for the position when Benger died. Nearly two years later, in 1753, Benger did die, and the anxious Franklin became deputy postmaster general. But the office was now divided, and Franklin had to share the deputy postmaster generalship first with William Hunter and then, after Hunter's death, with John Foxcroft.

When Franklin and his colleague assumed control of the colonial postal system, the mail was being carried from Falmouth, Maine, to Charleston, South Carolina, but only with great irregularity. Service from Philadelphia to Williamsburg, Virginia, operated only when enough letters had accumulated to make a trip necessary. Below Williamsburg and on to Charleston the mails were still more uncertain. But even in the North the service was no model of speed and regularity. In winter the mails from Philadelphia to Boston went only once in a fortnight, and to send and receive a letter took six weeks.

But Franklin wasted little time bemoaning the condition of the service he had inherited. Apparently acting on the assumption that "lost time is never found," as he wrote in *Poor Richard's Almanac*, he threw himself into a thorough reform of the post office. Since postage rates had been set by Queen Anne's Act and he could do nothing to lower them, his aim was to speed up the service, improve its regularity, and make it so attractive and valuable it would draw the support of those who were inclined to send their letters outside the mails. To do this he made an inspection of the post routes and increased both the speed of the mail carriers and the frequency of their trips. The round trip between Philadelphia and Boston was cut to three weeks, and the mails between Philadelphia and New York were made three times a week. Mail carriers left the two cities each Monday, Wednesday, and Friday morning and arrived at their destinations thirty-three hours later. By the early 1770s the mails had been so improved that New York City had six mails each week—three from Philadelphia which came each Monday, Wednesday, and Friday, two from Boston, on Wednesday and Saturday, and on Tuesday one from Quebec by way of Albany.

Besides all this, Franklin laid out new post routes—incidentally extending the circulation of his newspaper as he did—established a penny-post delivery system in Philadelphia, began the practice of admitting newspapers in the mails at fixed postage rates, and eventually, after Canada was taken from the French in 1763, helped extend the mail service from Canada to New York.

The results of these improvements revealed the wisdom of Franklin's philosophy, for the postal revenues increased so dramatically that in 1761 the colonial post office for the first time not only showed a profit but sent its surplus to the post office in England, where it was entered in the account with a notation that this was "the first remittance ever made of its kind."

Franklin's wizardry, however, was helped along by the British government's creation in 1755 of a regular mail boat service between England and the colonies. Aside from a temporary packet service begun in the early years of the century, no such service had yet been established. Northern mails, it was true, had been sent with the mast fleet that left New England on schedule, and in the South the mails could go with the tobacco fleet. But these fleets sailed so infrequently that they were of little value as mail boats. Most of the time letters had to be sent to England by whatever merchant ships happened along.

Some colonies obviously fared better than others under this arrangement. Ships came frequently to Massachusetts, New York, and Virginia, and as early as the middle of the seventeenth century a sizable amount of correspondence passed among business families scattered throughout the mainland colonies, the West Indies, and England. But even in these colonies uncertain sailings diminished the effectiveness of the mail service, which in turn added to England's burden in governing her colonies. Official correspondence was months traveling between the Board of Trade in London and the royal governors, and in such places as North Carolina and Connecticut, whose shores ships rarely touched, years sometimes intervened before the Board of Trade would hear from its governors. In June 1745, for instance, the Board of Trade wrote Governor Matthew Johnson of North Carolina that it had had no letter from him in three years! A year and a half later, in January 1747, Johnson wrote the board that he had just received its letter dated 19 July 1744.

Such service was the subject of much complaint by both the Board of Trade and the royal governors in America. It accounted for much of the inefficient political control England exercised over her colonies and helps explain why His Majesty's subjects in America were so long unhampered by British restrictions. But with the gathering of forces for the great contest with France in America in the 1750s, the time for better communications between England and her American colonies had come. In a rare spirit of cooperation, the governors of New York, Virginia, Massachusetts, and Nova Scotia asked for a regular mail service between England and the colonies in 1755, and after General Braddock's defeat in the forests of Pennsylvania that year, the British government was more or less frightened into establishing the new service. In September of that year, the British postmaster general established a monthly mail service between Falmouth, England, and New York.

The service was costly but popular, and when the French and

Indian War was over in 1763, England not only continued the mail packets but, after establishing a southern postal district for all colonies below Virginia in 1765, inaugurated another packet line from Falmouth to Charleston, South Carolina.

By the late 1760s, then, not one but three packet lines ran from England to America—one to New York, one to the West Indies, and one to Charleston. At the same time, the inland mail service stretched from Canada to Charleston. It had been greatly improved throughout the New England and middle colonies, but below Virginia only one mail route, extending from Charleston to Suffolk, Virginia, and from Suffolk to New York, connected the southern district with the northern.

While all this mail service, both up and down the coast and between England and America, helped make the American Post Office a financial success by the 1760s, the postal system itself had an importance beyond its monetary surplus. It was both a sign and, in its own way, a cause of the growing unity among the English colonies in America. The rapidly swelling number of intercolonial marriages, intercolonial business arrangements, and intercolonial educations, so noticeable by this time, not only were reflected in the larger flow of mail among the colonies, but were themselves in part made possible by the improved postal service.

Moreover, the newspapers, which Franklin had admitted to the mails and safeguarded with equal postage rates for all, were moving by way of the improved postal system to areas farther and farther away from their places of publication to smash old barriers, substitute an American view for local prejudices, and so help convert Englishmen into Americans. In 1762 the New York *Mercury* boasted that besides New York, it circulated through "ev'ry Town and Country Village," in Connecticut, Rhode Island, and New Jersey. No more than a decade before, such a circulation of one newspaper would have been impossible.

Benjamin Franklin's improved postal service also enhanced England's ability to govern her colonies. For the system that sped American letters back and forth among the colonists did the same for the official correspondence among the crown's officials, both in America and between England and America. As it happened, this occurred at a fortuitous time for the mother country, for it was just at the time when the mail service became most effective that she sought to impose restrictions upon her American daughters. Thus, ironically, the mails which through the years had helped foster an American view of things could now be used to help suppress that view. But in the 1760s the American Post Office was even more directly involved in the incipient quarrel between England and the colonies than this, and it was the British officials themselves who first raised the issue.

Having emerged from the colonial wars in 1763 with a heavy debt and a huge new empire to police, the British government was anxious to share the burden of her empire with her American colonies and so, among other things, imposed a stamp tax upon them in 1765. The colonists met this act, as every American knows, with the famous cry, "no taxation without representation," and forced its repeal in 1766. But before the repeal, Benjamin Franklin, then living in London as he had been for some time, was called before a committee of the House of Commons to explain the American attitude toward taxation. This, at least, was the committee's ostensible purpose, but what it really wanted, apparently, was to show that the colonial Post Office furnished a precedent for taxing the colonists without representation.

The committee's position was a strong one, for postage rates in America were high and had been, it was true, established by Parliament to raise a revenue without the consent of the colonists. And yet, with the exception of Virginia, no colony had then protested. Furthermore, since the postal service was a government monopoly, it appeared that Americans had no choice but to pay the postage, or tax, if they wanted their letters sent. And finally, the postal surpluses themselves, of which Franklin was so proud, implied taxation, since had the people had not been paying more for postage than the service cost, there would have been no surpluses.

When questioned, Franklin, of course, rejected the comparison between the stamp tax and postage and made two points: first, that postage, unlike the stamp tax, was paid for a service rendered and, second, that a tax imposed by Parliament without the consent of the colonists was unconstitutional if it could not be avoided. Postage, he said, could be avoided in spite of the postal monopoly, for people could send their letters by private messengers.

Franklin's answers were not altogether satisfactory. His assertion that postage could be avoided by sending letters by private messenger, while legally correct, was scarcely realistic. Few Americans could pay for such messengers; nor could they wait, if they were businessmen, for some acquaintance to take their letters when he journeyed to the next town and beyond. Moreover, they could not send letters by anyone who made regular trips from town to town, such as stagecoach drivers, because that would have violated the monopoly. So the committee did, perhaps, win the argument. But what was won in England was lost in America. For the committee had introduced the idea that the Post Office taxed the people, something only a handful of Americans had seen before, and as time passed more and more of them came to regard postage as a tax and the Post Office as an instrument of British tyranny.

The consequences were that Americans, with their considerable ingenuity for such things, began to undermine the Post Office. Sons of Liberty forced ship captains to take their letters to the coffeehouses for distribution rather than to the post offices, where postage would have to be paid on them. Others, taking advantage of the postal laws permitting letters accompanying merchandise to go free, attached their letters to some article of merchandise, no matter how ridiculous, to avoid paying postage. Hugh Finlay, surveyor of the post office, was informed in New Haven in 1773 that "sometimes a small bundle of chips, straw or old papers accompanys a seal'd packet or large letter, and the riders insist that such letters are exempted from postage."

Besides this, more and more letters were carried outside the mails at reduced rates by regular postriders, who developed such large private businesses that there were, in some places, two post offices—the regular one and the one at the postrider's home. "It is common," wrote Finlay from Newport, Rhode Island, of an old postrider named Mumford, "for people who expect letters by Post finding none at the Post Office to say 'well there must be letters, we'll find them at Mumford's.'"

So from the time of the Stamp Act controversy on, Americans bypassed the Post Office while the king's officials stood by helplessly. "It is virtually impossible to put a stop to this practice in the present universal opposition to every thing connected with Great Britain," wrote Finlay. "Were any Deputy Post Master to do his duty, and make a stir in such matter, he would draw on himself the odium of his Neighbors and be mark'd as the friend of Slavery and oppression and declar'd enemy to America."

The Colonial Post Office

But the time came, even before "the shot heard round the world" was fired, when it was no longer enough merely to evade the old Post Office. In 1774, responding to the Boston patriots' destruction of a favorite English beverage, Parliament closed the Boston port to all trade, placed restraints upon Massachusetts's government, and by other measures roused American wrath throughout the colonies. In the turbulence that followed these "Intolerable Acts," as the colonists called them, the more radical Americans who, besides sending letters outside the mail, were also using the postal service to stir up resistance to British policies, began to fear that postmasters loyal to the king would open their letters and curb the distribution of their incendiary papers. And so a movement was undertaken to replace the old post office with what the Americans, who were fast becoming experts in propaganda, called a "constitutional post."

A disgruntled newspaper publisher named William Goddard led the movement and developed plans to establish a kind of "do-it-yourself" post office controlled by postal committees in each colony who would regulate the postal system, appoint local postmasters, and help select the postmaster general. To win support for his post office, Goddard attacked the old one with the argument that it was unconstitutional because it raised a tax without American consent and was being used, as he thought, to stop the "channels of publick Intelligence."

It was serious business, this first attempt to overthrow an institution of the old order, and early in February 1774 Goddard left Baltimore headed for Pennsylvania, New York, and New England to enlist support for his scheme. Besides the committees of correspondence who feared, as one man wrote, that the postmaster general could "open all letters from the Committees of Correspondence in this country," and the editors who worried about the possible rejection of their newspapers in the mail, Goddard was helped immeasurably by the British government's dismissal of Benjamin Franklin from the postal service in January 1774. By this act the British had foolishly severed an important link between the old Post Office and the Americans, who were now less reluctant to erect their "Constitutional Post Office" on the wreckage of the old one than they might otherwise have been.

But even if Franklin had not been removed, no doubt the results would have been the same. For Goddard's cause was popular and was heralded by the frenetic patriot press. "How cheerfully," said the New York *Gazette*, "will every well wisher to his Country lay hold of the Opportunity to rescue the Channel of Public and Private Intelligence out of the Hands of a Power, openly inimical to its Rights and Liberties."

And, in fact, well-wishers did rally to the Constitutional Post. Throughout that year, while resolutions against the Intolerable Acts were being adopted and plans were laid for the first Continental Congress, money was being subscribed for the new system, post offices were established, and postriders were hired, so that by the time the Second Continental Congress met in May 1775 the new postal service was already in operation from Maine to Williamsburg, Virginia. Indeed, it is more than likely that the gale that swept from the North in the spring of 1775 bringing to Patrick Henry's ears the "clash of resounding arms" was carried along by the Constitutional Post.

But the Constitutional Post was short-lived. Acutely aware of the importance of the Post Office to its efforts to resist British authority, the Second Continental Congress took control of Goddard's postal system in July 1775, appointed Benjamin

Franklin postmaster general, made Goddard surveyor of the posts, and prepared to extend the service all the way to Georgia, where it had not gone before. Six months later, Christmas 1775, a royal postal official in New York, noting that no mail had come through the royal postal service for some time, formally closed the British Post Office in America, thereby leaving the field to the patriot postal service.

Administered from 1776 to 1782 by Richard Bache, Franklin's son-in-law, who was appointed postmaster general when Franklin became the American minister in Paris, the Post Office was Congress's indispensable agent throughout the war years. Just as it had been an instrument for nurturing an American mind and encouraging resistance to the British, so now it was used to unite Americans in a common cause. At great cost and at great hazard, postriders carried letters and documents of one kind or another between a frequently moving government and its armies in the field as well as between soldiers and their families.

Not all the mail got through, of course. Often it was seized by the British, and the stolen letters, oddly enough, were published in Loyalist newspapers. In the spring of 1781, John Sullivan, New Hampshire's delegate to Congress, first learned of a letter addressed to him when he read of it in the Loyalist newspaper the *Royal Gazette*. "I observed in Rivington'[s] paper [the *Royal Gazette*]," wrote Sullivan to the president of New Hampshire, "a letter from you informing me that I might draw upon you for two hundred pounds State money, which Letter was intercepted in the mail taken at Clove and Rivingtons [*sic*] publication of it was the first Intelligence I have had respecting money for my support for Six months past. I am unwilling," he continued, "to say much respecting money or other affairs lest this might fall into Enemy hands."

The Colonial Post Office

Still, many more letters got through the American postal system than were stolen, and the six volumes of the collected *Letters of the Members of the Continental Congress* attest to the revolutionary government's great dependence upon the postal service.

All the letters of the members of Congress went free through the post, as did those of the officers and soldiers of the Continental Army, and with free letters composing the bulk of the mail, the Post Office, like the government, ran into debt. "The expense [of the Post Office] is very high," wrote John Adams in 1776, when his own letters to his beloved Abigail were numerous, "and the Profits, (so dear is everything and so little Correspondence is carried on, except in frank'd letters), will not support the office." Since the Post Office could not support itself, Congress had either to appropriate money for it or see it disappear; one measure of its importance to the government was the vast sum of money—$163,000 in 1780 alone—Congress poured into it to keep it afloat.

That Congress realized the Post Office would be as important in peace as in war was made clear in 1782. By then the war was all but over, and Congress, noting that "the communication of intelligence . . . from one part to another of the United States is essentially requisite to the safety as well as the commercial interest thereof," wrote a detailed postal law carefully defining the rules and regulations for the operation of the postal service throughout the thirteen states. It also replaced Richard Bache with Ebenezer Hazard as postmaster general.

Like so many men who were associated with the Post Office, Hazard had been a publisher in New York in 1775 when Goddard had proposed his Constitutional Post, and had helped organize that postal service in New York. In 1776 he became surveyor general of the Continental Post Office, and by 1782 was perhaps better prepared than anyone in the new nation to direct the Post Office through the troubled days of the Confederation.

Just as the British victory over the French in 1763 had weakened the ties between England and her colonies, who no longer needed the mother country's protection, so the American victory over the British loosened the bonds among the thirteen states. No longer confronted by a common enemy, jealous of their own particular powers, and bound together under the Articles of Confederation in a loose federation that safeguarded their individual sovereignties, the states tended to go their own ways as thirteen separate nations. At the same time, the economic depression that struck the nation in the aftermath of the war placed additional strains on the relations between the states and brought unrest within them. The scarcity of hard money, which forced them either to issue paper money or to raise taxes, only aggravated the problems Americans had in adjusting to their new situation.

Not surprisingly, the Post Office suffered with the nation and reflected its problems. For one thing, Congress had attempted to give the Post Office a monopoly of the letter-carrying business in its law of 1782. But high postage rates, the depression, and the scarcity of hard money made it inevitable that private citizens would send their letters outside the mails either by friends or by itinerants wandering through the countryside. This, of course, meant a loss of revenue, but Congress was powerless to prevent the evasion.

This helplessness, in turn, was partly the result of Congress's uncertain postal power. Because the states had been so fearful of the central government's interference within their borders, the Articles of Confederation had given Congress the power to regulate the postal service between, but not necessarily within, the states, an ambiguity that added to Postmaster General Hazard's difficulties in administering the service. The Maryland legislature, for example, thought the postal power so weak that it once considered a bill to appoint its own postmaster general and employ postriders to carry the mail within its borders, contending that Congress had been given the right to regulate the Post Office from state to state but not to establish post offices within a state except upon the Main Post Road.

Surely this uncertainty over its postal power also enlarged the problem of securing the privacy of the mails. The British had repeatedly seized and opened American mails during the Revolution, and perhaps for this reason Congress was especially sensitive about this violation. But fearful of being unable to enforce harsh penalties, it included in the postal law of 1782 only fines for those who opened other people's mail. Of course this was not enough to keep postmasters, innkeepers, and postriders from having a look at someone else's letters, and the complaints on this score were numerous. Madison and Jefferson, to name but two, not only complained but customarily sent their most important messages to one another in cipher.

The scarcity of hard money that plagued the states was another source of trouble, for as paper money was issued, Postmaster General Hazard had to decide whether to accept it in payment for postage or not. The decision was not an easy one. On the one hand, the Post Office could not pay mail contractors with paper money, for they would not accept it. Yet paper money was legal tender in states like Rhode Island and North Carolina, and to refuse to accept it in payment for postage was a slap in the face of the paper-money states.

Nevertheless, Postmaster General Hazard opted for hard

money. Congress backed him up, but the decision brought its share of trouble. In Edenton, North Carolina, where dollars were "as scarce as hen's teeth," as the saying went, and paper money was rapidly becoming worthless, a postal official was almost mobbed in 1786 when he ordered the postmaster there to receive nothing but hard money for postage. The next year, the year of Captain Shay's rebellion in Massachusetts, the postmaster at Newport, Rhode Island, was harassed by a band of paper-money men when he refused to receive a letter for mailing from the governor without prepayment of postage. "The Reason I would not trust the State with Letters," he wrote, "is this: They owe me for a number, and my account has been lying before the Assembly Three Sessions, and they will not pay it without I will take Paper Money on par which passes 8 for 1."

At the same time that Americans insisted on using paper money of dubious value for postage, they complained loudly about the irregularity of the mail. That there was much to complain about was evident almost everywhere the mails ran, and at certain seasons of the year one could no more expect his mail to be on time than he could expect his letters to arrive unopened. Members of Congress were particularly upset when their mails were late, as they often were, and their letters were filled with uncomplimentary remarks about the irregular service. For this and other reasons they were often at odds with Postmaster General Hazard and frequently talked of replacing him. One member of Congress wrote in 1785 that his mail from Carolina to New York had been forty days on the road. "Congress," he added "disapprove of the Conduct of the officers who have superintendance of this department and will very soon take Measures for their better Regulation."

In the long run, however, it was much less significant that

letters were read before they reached their destinations or that the mails were irregular than that the postal service continued to operate in the face of all the problems that vexed the nation. And if men sometimes wryly suggested as they wrote to friends that they would "hazard a letter," they had at the same time much for which to thank Postmaster General Hazard. For throughout the years of the Confederation he, more than anyone else, was responsible for maintaining the postal service.

With immense energy, Hazard kept mails moving the length of the young Republic from Maine to Georgia. Over much of the Main Post Road the mails went with enough regularity to cause hundreds of Americans in the little villages along the way to look forward to "post day" when, with good luck, the news of the world would be brought to their communities. Beyond this, Hazard made contracts to have the mails carried by stagecoach on the most important routes, put the service on a paying basis, established cross post offices off the Main Road, and sent the mail into the interior of the country as far west as Pittsburgh. By the time the Constitution went into effect in 1789, the mails were being carried to seventy-five post offices over twenty-four hundred miles of post roads.

All this meant that the Post Office, as it had done throughout the colonial period, was performing a unique service for the new nation. Like the lands of the Northwest which were owned by all the states, the postal service, too, was the concern of all and strengthened the ties among them. It made possible a continuation of an American conversation among Americans from Georgia to Maine, but more than that, it forced Congress to deal with a problem of mutual concern; not many matters drew more attention than the mail service. Furthermore, the postal laws the Confederation enacted set precedents to be used by the new government for years, and the bureaucracy it established—the postmasters, the stagecoach contractors, the mail carriers—made the transition from the old government to the new with so little trouble that no new postal law was written until 1792, three years after the new government became effective.

II

The People's Post Office

The postal system that emerged from the Confederation period and matured in the nineteenth century was, in many ways, unique among the postal systems of the world. Like so many things American, it could be described in superlatives. It grew faster, became larger, hired more employees, transported more mail, and, of course, cost more than any mail service in the world. But its uniqueness was not so much in all these things as in the postal policy which governed its operations and accounted for the pattern of its development.

"The Congress," said the Constitution, "shall have the Power to Establish Post Offices and post Roads"; but for three years after the new government began in 1789, no one knew exactly how that power was to be used. Three times in that period, President Washington called Congress's attention to the need for postal legislation, and three times Congress responded by temporarily continuing the old Confederation Post Office in operation. Not until the postal act of 1792, reaffirmed and made permanent in 1794, did Congress finally create the nation's Post Office and disclose its interpretation of its power to establish post offices and post roads.

The Post Office Act of 1792 established the office of the post-master general, set the postage at rates ranging from six cents on a single-page letter going as far as 30 miles to twenty-five cents on one going more than 450 miles, and outlined the rules and regulations under which the Post Office was to operate. It also established three basic principles that were to govern the nation's postal policy throughout its history. The first was that the Post Office must be self-supporting; the second, that the Post Office make no profit, but use its surpluses to extend its services; and the third, that Congress, not the postmaster general, must establish the nation's post roads.

The first of these principles was the great commandment. Copied after the British system, it was to be the most warmly debated, the most often referred to, and ironically, the most often violated. About the second principle there was some confusion at first. The Post Office was attached originally to the Treasury Department as if it were expected, like the British Post Office, to make a profit, and until the 1820s, it did return more than a million dollars in postal surpluses to the Treasury. But in time, the Post Office was separated from the Treasury, and the idea of a nonprofit postal system was firmly established. The last of Congress's notable principles was the most difficult for members of Congress to agree upon and the principal reason why the permanent establishment of the Post Office was so long delayed.

At issue was the question whether Congress had the right to delegate its power to establish post offices and post roads to the postmaster general. The Senate saw no problem here and tried for two years to enact legislation delegating that power, first because it seemed logical to have the postmaster general, rather than an amorphous body like Congress, decide where mail routes were to run and post offices to be established, and, second, because this was the way the British had done it.

But the House of Representatives refused to recognize British postal practice as a proper guide for Americans. "There is no analogy between the United States and Great Britain, when the subject of the post roads and post offices are to be considered," remarked one congressman in a kind of private declaration of independence. Besides, following the British example might even "unhinge the government," and lead the nation down the road to monarchy. The principal argument in the House of Representatives, however, was that it would be unconstitutional for Congress to delegate its authority to establish post offices to the postmaster general.

Quarreling over the constitutionality of a given proposition was to become a national pastime in the years ahead, and as in this case so in the future the Constitution was almost always invoked to mask the congressmen's real interests. Had they really been concerned about the constitutionality of delegating their power to the postmaster general, congressmen would have refused him the power to establish post offices as well as post roads, but they never really argued this point and in the end did, in effect, delegate this power to him.

What concerned the congressmen was not the Constitution but their constituents, whose demands for mail routes, they felt, must be heard. Delegate the power to establish post roads to the postmaster general, they said, and the people's wishes might be ignored. But retain this power in Congress, and the people, who best knew over what roads the mails should be carried, would have a voice in their establishment. This was the nub of the argument, but the congressmen's ardent insistence upon giving the people a hearing in this matter was not without political inspiration. For no power of divination was necessary to foresee that post roads in the young Republic would not be simply two tracks through the wilderness. Whatever information must be exchanged between voters and their congressmen had to pass over the post roads, and along their paths must be established the post offices which might mean life or death to some tiny community trying to establish its identity in the wilderness. Post roads were, in short, too valuable to congressmen to be placed in the hands of an appointed official.

For good or ill, the House of Representatives won its point, and the principle that Congress must establish post roads, so different from the British scheme of things, had far-reaching effects upon the nation's postal service. It meant that the American people, both collectively and in special interest groups, would more than any other single factor shape the American mail system. Given a voice in postal affairs, they would make constant demands upon the Post Office Department. These demands, in turn, would bring post roads to town, village, and country across the land, establish post offices in cities and cross-roads country stores, help eventually to determine postage rates, and force the postmaster general to improvise, innovate, and reorganize the service from time to time, to add new services and speed up the old—all to keep abreast of the people's requests. In fact, because of this principle the people's Post Office became one of the nation's best examples of democracy at work.

The usual method by which the people made their demands known was the petition, and from the Republic's earliest years throughout the nineteenth century an endless stream of postal petitions filled the mails of congressmen and senators alike. So great was this outpouring that it is probably true to say that no other single matter, year in and year out, brought Congress so many petitions from the people before World War I.

Americans petitioned mostly for post roads, which meant, of course, mail routes. This, at least, was true in the nineteenth century, when from whatever point they settled on their westward march—the distant side of the Appalachian Mountains, the edge of the Mississippi and Missouri rivers, the Pacific, or the plains of Kansas and Nebraska—they demanded post routes to bring them their mail. And at session after session congressmen obligingly entered their petitions in the records of Congress, passed law after law establishing post roads for their constituents, and blithely handed the postmaster general the task of installing the postal service on routes they had created.

This was a revolutionary way to run a post office, and no doubt most postmasters general would have much preferred to have had the power to establish post roads delegated to them. Had they had that power, the growth of the postal service would likely have been more orderly, if slower, and the organization of the Post Office more businesslike. As it was, the postmasters general had little choice but to do Congress's bidding, and this, as it turned out, was a mammoth undertaking.

Perhaps few public officials in the young American republic worked harder than the early postmasters general. To install postal service on the post roads Congress created, they had to establish post offices at appropriate places along the roads, appoint postmasters to command them, and make innumerable contracts with those who would carry mail from post office to post office along the new routes. They had to supervise, insofar as this was possible, the work of mail contractors, and they especially had to make certain that the postmasters they appointed conducted their offices properly and returned the correct remittances—the postage taken in at their offices minus their commissions—to the Post Office. Besides all this, they had to keep voluminous records, worry over stacks of dead letters, and write hundreds of letters whose subjects for one day might range from scolding a postmaster for permitting an eleven-year-old boy to carry the mail to answering a congressman's demands for better mail service in his district.

Given the vast area over which the postal network spread, in the nation's early years it was impossible to manage this business efficiently, and the mail service Americans first knew was as primitive as the country itself. At first the mails were thrown into large portmanteaus and hauled from post office to post office. At each office the postmaster opened the portmanteau, removed the mail for his office, closed the bag, locked it, and sent it on its way. Later, as the amount of mail and the number of post offices increased, distributing post offices were created to which mail for certain areas was sent for sorting and for relaying to the final destination.

The distributing offices were a help, indeed an absolute necessity, but they did not greatly improve the actual handling of the mail. Letters and newspapers were often mangled beyond legibility or, even worse, lost in transit. All too often private letters were read by persons other than those for whom they were intended, a practice encouraged by the absence of envelopes. Until mid-century letters were simply folded over and sealed with wax or a wafer, and though they were postmarked they bore no postage stamp, nor was their postage likely to have been prepaid. Instead they were "rated up," as the expression went, at the post office of their origin and their postage fixed according to the number of pages and the distance they were going. This postage was then charged to the addressee at the post office of destination. To get their money's worth and to avoid paying for an extra page, thrifty Americans not only filled both sides of a sheet of paper but often wrote up and down as well as across the pages.

If by good fortune the mails were not lost on their travels, they were often late, as they had been in the Confederation period. And, of course, the farther they traveled, the later they usually were, so that letters and newspapers conveyed over the post roads along the frontier were as often late as on time. President Jackson's first inaugural address, for example, given 4 March 1829, was printed twenty days later in Saint Louis and twenty-six days later in New Orleans. Poor roads, unbridged rivers, and inclement weather were blamed for tardy mails, and not without reason, for good roads were as unfamiliar to Americans of the early nineteenth century as wagon roads are to their descendants. At the same time, careless contractors and indolent postmasters accounted for much of the trouble. And because the postal authorities could communicate with postmasters and contractors no faster than their own mail service would permit, failures in the mail service were not immediately known or offending officials quickly identified. Consequently, corrections were often delayed and sometimes never made.

But neither the tardy service nor incompetent postmasters and mail contractors slowed the Americans' demand for mail service, and if the Post Office Department could not improve the service, it could extend it. In fact, considering all that had to be done and the difficulties of doing it, the growth of the postal service was a minor miracle. In 1792, when the postal law was passed, less than 6,000 miles of post roads existed and no more than 195 post offices had been established. These, for the most part, were located along the main post road that ran from Wiscassett, Maine, to Savannah, Georgia. None was established farther west than Pittsburgh, and Vermont, Kentucky, Tennessee, and the old Northwest had none at all.

Throughout the 1790s, however, in the nation's temporary capital in Philadelphia, Postmaster General Timothy Pickering and his successor Joseph Habersham, the one from Massachusetts and the other from Georgia, were hard at work. By 1800 they had managed, with the help of only a handful of clerks, to establish 903 post offices and to install mail service over 20,817 miles of post roads. By the time the capital had been moved to the District of Columbia and Thomas Jefferson's postmaster general, Gideon Granger, had taken charge of the department, the mails had breached the Appalachian barrier and were being carried through Ohio, Kentucky, and Tennessee, south as far as Natchez, Mississippi, and west as far as Vincennes, Indiana.

But there was no pause. In 1803 came the purchase of Louisiana, opening a vast new territory for westering Americans, and mails were immediately sent to New Orleans in what was to become through the decades one of the Post Office's most expensive operations. That same year Ohio became a state, and even then Americans were already pushing into the new lands beyond the Buckeye state. And if the War of 1812 temporarily slowed western migration, its close signaled the beginning of the greatest rush west the nation had yet seen. "All old America seems to be breaking up and moving westward," wrote an observer of the movement, and it did appear so from the postal records. In 1812, the nation had 2,610 post offices and 39,378 miles of post roads. Eight years later, 4,500 post offices and 72,492 miles of post roads had been established. In one year alone, 1819, Postmaster General Return G. Meigs, who had replaced Granger in 1814, installed new mail service on more than 8,000 miles of post roads, and the next year he established 500 post offices.

The installation of postal service over so many miles of post roads in so short a time was a tribute to the energy of Postmaster General Meigs and his postal clerks, who in 1820 numbered twenty-one, and to the postal policy developed by Congress. Certainly the mails would never have moved westward with such rapidity had not members of Congress, prompted by the demands of their constituents, made post roads of so many forest trails and thus forced the postmaster general to extend mail service to them.

But trouble lay ahead. Many of the new post roads ran through unpopulated areas, and the postage collected upon them, as scanty as the population, was much too small to pay for the service. Moreover, these post roads were longer and often more costly to operate than those running through more thickly settled areas. Then, to make the Post Office's burdens greater, the land boom petered out in 1819, a financial panic ensued, and postal revenues diminished not only from the West and South but from all over the nation. The result of all this was that in 1820, the same year 500 new post offices had been created, and for four years following, the Post Office spent more money than it received, raising a perplexing question: Was the extension of the service to be sacrificed for the principle of the balanced postal budget or the balanced budget for the principle of the extension of the service?

Obviously the original expectation had been that mail routes would not be extended beyond the department's ability to pay for the service, and probably they would not have been had the postmaster general had control over the post roads. But once this power had been given to Congress, the conflict between the principles of service extension and pay-as-you-go became inevitable. Members of Congress, eager to give their constituents the mail service they demanded, established post roads helterskelter throughout the land as if the money to pay for them flowed from an artesian well. Financing the mail routes, they seemed to believe, was the job of the postmaster general.

This was, in fact, one of the postmaster general's duties. But he was in an unenviable position. He could, at the risk of rousing congressional wrath, delay the establishment of post roads for a time, and he could drive hard bargains with mail contractors to reduce the cost of the service. He could also limit the kind of mail service—daily, weekly, biweekly, and so on—to the least costly. Beyond this, he could do almost nothing to balance the postal budget. He could not prevent Congress from establishing new post roads, nor could he raise postage rates to cover the additional costs. And even after 1825, when he received the power to discontinue nonpaying post routes, it was so hedged about with qualifications that it was difficult to eliminate a route over which almost no mail was carried in an entire year!

So the inherent conflict in the nation's postal policy was uncovered in the 1820s, but members of Congress did not then want to face the problem of whether the extension of the mails or a balanced budget was to take precedence. Clearly, they wanted both, and their answer to the postal deficit in 1820 was to investigate the inefficiencies in the management of the Post Office.

The congressional investigation of the Post Office Department that began in 1821 was not the first. Two others had already been made, and in subsequent years they would become as much a part of the people's Post Office as mail contractors who were often the subject of investigation. Instigated usually either because of postal deficits or because of poor service, the investigations were extraordinarily useful in providing a way for Congress to control the people's business.

Doubtless improvements in the postal service would have been made by the postmaster general, as indeed they were, without the people's prodding and congressional investigations. But generally speaking the postmasters general were a conservative lot, and it is unlikely that postal progress would have been as rapid had there been no investigations. In fact, most major reforms in the service and the modernization of the whole system in the 1850s were in part products of postal investigations.

The investigation of Postmaster General Meigs in 1821, however, turned up nothing startling. Members of Congress found no corruption, if this is what they were looking for, but they did find inefficiency and carelessness in handling postal finances.

By modern standards the Post Office's management of its finances was appalling. The department handled all its own monies, kept its own accounts, wrote its own drafts, received either directly or through bank deposit slips remittances from local postmasters, and, except for the salaries of the postmaster general and his assistants, paid all its postmasters, mail contractors, and incidental expenses from its own revenues. But its financial records were a mass of confusion. Some records were simply noted on slips of paper without dates, and some, indeed, were kept in the head of one faithful postal clerk who served the department from 1799 to 1829. Remittances from postmasters were often overdue and some debts were so long outstanding that the department finally categorized them with fine distinction as "bad" and "desperate."

Not all this inefficiency could be blamed on Postmaster General Meigs. The nation's disorganized banking system, the difficulties of collecting remittances throughout the nation, and the awkward methods of paying mail contractors made it almost impossible for the left hand to know what the right was doing in keeping the Post Office accounts. Nevertheless, when Meigs resigned in 1823 because of ill health, his successor, John McLean, forced mail contractors into line, reorganized the work in the Post Office Department itself, carefully watched the expansion of post roads, and so wiped out the postal deficit by 1825.

Postmaster General McLean, former congressman from Ohio, won a national reputation for his management of the Post Office. His praises were on almost all lips, and his record was enviable. He was the first postmaster general to make an issue of spending the postal surplus to extend the service, and in so doing severed whatever ties remained between the Treasury Department and the Post Office. Moreover, in his six years in office he established over 2,000 new post offices, upgraded the existing service, installed new mail service over more than 30,000 miles of post roads, and still managed to balance the postal budget from 1825 to 1827.

But even Postmaster General McLean stubbed his toe on the nation's postal policy. For two years in a row, 1827 and 1828, largely because of his optimism about the excess of revenues over expenditures and his determination to use the surplus, Congress enacted bills increasing the number of post roads by some 400 and adding very suddenly more than 9,000 miles to their total length. This was an unprecedented extension, and it soon became obvious that McLean, for all his efficiency, was no miracle-worker. He too began to run a postal deficit, and his fame as an administrator rests partly on his good fortune in being elevated to the Supreme Court before the full effects of the postal deficits could be felt. What he had sown, however, was reaped by William Barry, his ill-starred successor.

Barry was a kindly man and was highly respected by those who knew him well. A Kentucky politician, he was the first postmaster general to sit in the president's cabinet, and like McLean he served six years. But where McLean had such success extending the service and balancing the budget, Barry, who also extended the service, ran into deficits which mounted yearly. By 1834, as near as anyone could tell, the postal surplus that had been accumulating in the Treasury had been used, the postal deficit was larger than it had ever been, and an irate Congress was once more investigating the Post Office.

How had it happened that the postal surplus could have been wiped out and so large a deficit incurred? Both the majority and the minority members of Congress's committee to investigate the Post Office eyed Postmaster General Barry critically. Barry, they agreed, had violated the spirit if not the letter of the postal law, failed to bargain properly with mail contractors, run a slipshod department, and for what was called "improved service" had in innumerable instances recklessly increased the pay of contractors above the sum stipulated in their original contracts and so extravagantly multiplied the department's expenses. These charges reverberated throughout the country in the 1830s, tarnishing Barry's reputation, and from that time on he has been known as one of the nation's most incompetent postmasters general. "The management of the post office had reached a high peak of efficiency under the dynamic energy of John McLean ... ," wrote one historian. "It was destined to fall to one of its lowest points under McLean's successor, William T. Barry."

Barry was no doubt more pliable than he should have been. Afraid to make enemies for the administration and at the same time sincerely desiring to extend the mail service to the common man in good Jacksonian tradition, he could say no neither to mail contractors who sought to improve their contracts nor to the people who demanded more and better mail service. Still, Barry was as much a victim of the nation's postal policy and of his predecessor's administration as he was of his own weakness, and his side of the story illuminates the tightwire that postmasters general walked in trying to heed Congress's demands for more postal service and at the same time make the Post Office self-sustaining.

When Barry became postmaster general in March 1829 he inherited not only McLean's postal deficit but also the responsibility for running the mails over those post roads that Congress had established in 1828 but that McLean had not yet serviced. With no choice in the matter, Barry did place postal service over those post roads; but this so increased the deficit that he had to warn Congress in 1830 that, because of the Post Office's finances, it was unlikely that more post routes could be established for three years unless Congress was willing to appropriate the money for them.

But the demands for new post roads were incessant, and in spite of the postmaster general's warning, Congress introduced a new post roads bill in 1831. When an attempt was made to amend it with a proviso that mail service over the new roads be put in operation only when sufficient funds became available, objections were loud enough to be heard all the way to the Post

Office Department. Richard Johnson, Kentucky congressman and future vice-president, felt he was under no imperious rule, as he called it, to ask the postmaster general whether the funds for new post routes were available. He was convinced, he said, "that the rapidly extending settlements, and still more rapidly multiplying population of the country, required the continuance of the rule, which had hitherto prevailed, of passing a bill of this kind every two years," and he for one was willing to appropriate the money from the Treasury for this if need be.

At this point Johnson came perilously close to overturning the principle of paying for postal service from postal revenues only, but in the end Congress rallied to the traditional policy. It refused either to appropriate money for new routes from the Treasury or to permit the postmaster general to establish service only when the funds became available. Yet the next year it saddled Postmaster General Barry with the job of establishing service over hundreds of new post roads that ran, like one in Tennessee, "from Newmarket, in Jefferson County, by Blaine's crossroads, Lea's springs, Powder Spring Gap, and Joseph Beelor's to Tazewell, in Claiborne County."

At the same time, Barry was under increasing pressure not only to extend the mails to the west but to improve the service to older, settled communities where the mails had long been sent. Those who had formerly been satisfied with weekly service now wanted a triweekly mail, and those with a triweekly, a daily. Instead of the horseback rider who had always brought the mail, the people wanted a two-horse stagecoach, and instead of a two-horse, a four-horse coach, the ultimate in transportation at the time.

Barry sympathized with these demands, and his arguments for increasing the service, learned in part from McLean, were reasonable enough to be used by his successors. Improved service, he believed, meant improved postal revenues, and upon this logic he provided numerous routes with stagecoach service and increased the frequency of the mail carriers' trips over many weekly and triweekly routes. By doing so, he enlarged the number of miles the mails were being carried annually from 13,610,039 in 1829 to over 20,000,000 in 1833. And as he had theorized, postal revenues increased dramatically—from $1,707,418 to $2,616,538 in the four-year period.

It was true that Barry moved too rapidly in improving the postal service and that mail contractors took advantage of him. It was also true that mail schedules were too often ignored under his management. But no postmaster general before him had so rapidly extended the mail service, and if the postal surplus had been used up in doing so, this was at least as much the fault of Congress as of Barry, and no doubt was what the people wanted anyway. "The surplus of the department," said one congressman, "went . . . to the entire people: it [the Post Office] might, in fact, be called the establishment of the people."

But Barry's enemies, some of whom had themselves been demanding better postal service in their districts, allowed him no rest. More enraged because he had replaced long-time employees of the Post Office Department with Jacksonian Democrats than because of his mismanagement of the postal service, they attacked him so vehemently that President Jackson at last mercifully appointed him ambassador to Spain in 1835, and put Amos Kendall in his place in the Post Office.

For six years before he became postmaster general, Amos Kendall had been a power in the Jackson administration. A New Englander by birth and rearing and a Kentuckian by chance, he had been in turn a lawyer, tutor to Henry Clay's children, editor of a Kentucky newspaper, and fourth auditor of the Treasury under Jackson. He was also a member of Jackson's "Kitchen Cabinet," and through the years his busy pen had turned out many a fine Jacksonian phrase for the president. For more than twenty years, Kendall had also been a friend of the man he replaced, and his only published comment on his predecessor was, in effect, that Barry was "too good a man" to be a successful postmaster general.

There was no need to say more. Barry died in England in August 1835, on his way to Spain, and the problem of the postal deficit was quickly forgotten in the rising postal revenues that developed that year. The improvements in the system Barry had inaugurated now began to pay for themselves, and in 1835 the curtailments in the service made by Postmaster General Kendall resulted in the Post Office's first surplus in four years. This was repeated the next year, and so confident was Kendall of continued surpluses that he suggested a reduction of postage in his annual report for 1836.

Kendall's 1836 report brought to a close what might be called the old regime in the Post Office Department. That year Kendall closed the department's old account books and opened new ones, Congress passed a new postal law providing for the reorganization of the department, and, as if to punctuate the beginning of the new era, the old Post Office building on E Street between Seventh and Eighth was destroyed by fire.

The fire had apparently begun in the building's basement, where ashes and fuel were stored through the winter months, and before help could arrive, flames had gutted the building. Postmaster General Kendall rushed to the scene from his house next door and directed operations to save as many valuable

papers as possible. Many were saved, but hundreds of others—
records of old post offices, for example—were burned. Ironically, years before, Postmaster General Meigs had bought a fire
engine for such an emergency and a volunteer company had
been formed to man it. But worn-out hoses had made the machinery ineffective, and Postmaster General Barry, possibly
because of the postal deficit, had refused, according to one
account, to spend the five hundred dollars for new equipment
that would have made the apparatus usable at the moment of
greatest need.

After the fire, Postmaster General Kendall found temporary
quarters for the department in Fuller's Hotel across the street
from the ruined building, and there he began the new account
books and reorganized the department in accordance with the
law Congress had passed earlier that year.

The Postal Act of 1836, written after the lengthy investigations into Postmaster General Barry's conduct of the department,
was forty-six sections long and attempted to correct every
administrative problem Congress had uncovered. Special rules
were made for making contracts with mail carriers, accounting
procedures were completely revamped, the postmaster general's
duties were more precisely defined, and postal employees were
forbidden to have financial connection with mail contractors.
By far the most important section, however, changed the method
of handling postal finances. From this time on, all postal revenues were to be turned in to the Treasury, postal budgets giving
estimated needs for the year ahead were to be submitted to Congress, and each Congress was to appropriate from the general
fund the money to operate the postal service.

All this had been done, but the postal policy itself remained
unchanged. As in the past, the postal service was still expected

to pay for itself even though the people's demands for mail service were greater than ever and mail routes were moving ever more expensively toward the setting sun. Since the people would not lessen their demands and Congress would not change the policy, trouble was bound to catch up with Postmaster General Kendall. And it did.

Although they had already enacted a post roads bill in 1835, members of Congress jumped eagerly at Kendall's optimistic report of postal finances in December 1835 and passed a new bill in 1836 creating hundreds of new post roads for their far-flung constituents. All that year and into the next Kendall, continuing as President Van Buren's postmaster general and basking in the euphoria created by a postal surplus, worked to install postal service over the new routes and, as Barry had done before him, to improve the service at the same time. The contract office, Kendall reported, was overwhelmed with business, and indeed it must have been. More than 28,000 miles were added to the nation's post roads between 1836 and 1837, and because of the improved service the number of miles the mails were being carried annually jumped from 25,869,486 in 1836 to 32,597,006 the next year.

That year, 1837, was the year of the great panic that swept over the nation leaving banks closed, states in debt, businesses ruined, and a deflated land boom through the west. But even this did not disturb Kendall's confidence. The postal revenues, he reported, had not been much diminished by the panic, and the Post Office had a surplus of $800,000. So Congress for the third time in four years enacted a new post roads bill in the spring of 1838 to take effect the following summer.

By the time this bill passed Congress, the great outlay of

money for postal extensions and service improvement, plus the panic, was threatening to annihilate the surplus. Actually it took two more years of large deficits to use up the $800,000, but by 1840—the year Postmaster General Kendall left to write editorials for Van Buren's presidential campaign—the surplus was gone, and the stage was set for the greatest crisis in the history of the Post Office.

On the winds of discontent that followed the panic, the Whigs whirled into office in 1841, and when Vice-President John Tyler succeeded to the presidency on the death of William Henry Harrison, Charles A. Wickliffe, former congressman, became postmaster general. The third Kentuckian to hold the office, Wickliffe served as chief of the Post Office four years and never once enjoyed a postal surplus. He spent his years in office eliminating nonproductive routes and useless post offices, reducing the frequency of the service where he dared, and reporting to Congress how pleased he was that the department's expenses were no greater than its revenues. But somehow, postal deficits showed up on the department's ledgers every year, and by 1844 the Post Office's popularity with the people, like its revenues, had seriously declined.

The reasons for the plight of the Post Office were legion. Looming above everything else were the high letter-postage rates, which had remained almost unchanged since 1792 even though the means of transportation had greatly improved and its cost had been reduced. In 1843, for example, it cost eighteen and one-half cents to send a letter from New York City to Troy, New York, but twelve and one-half cents to send a barrel of flour the same distance. Such exorbitant rates were an open invitation to Americans to avoid using the mail, and each year

61

more and more people sent their letters by friends and acquaintances rather than through the mails and so reduced the postal revenues.

Carrying letters outside the mails was against the law, of course, and the Americans' violation of this law would surely have shocked Alexis de Tocqueville, the observant Frenchman who traveled the nation in the 1830s marveling at how well Americans obeyed their laws. But Tocqueville was already back in France writing about law-abiding Americans when, perhaps for the first time since the Revolution, Americans began breaking a law en masse.

For years, in fact, the nation's citizens had evaded paying high postage rates by one device or another. Often they wrote messages on newspapers, which were sent more cheaply through the mails than letters. And when they feared that their writing might be detected, they underscored words in the newspapers to form a message, or better still, made tiny, hard-to-see pinholes in selected words. But where once the violation of the postal laws had been done surreptitiously, now in the 1840s it was being done openly and with gusto.

Those who ignored the postal laws lived almost exclusively in the densely settled portions of the East, and it was probably true, as some congressmen said, that their zest for breaking the law was the result of years of frustrated efforts to reduce the postage rates. "Having remonstrated in vain against what they deem to be exorbitant and oppressive rates of postage," ran a congressional report, "they have at last adopted the conclusion that it is right to oppose and evade laws which they consider unjust and oppressive."

They had some reason to feel aggrieved. Because they used the mails so often, their mail routes always produced surplus revenues; but instead of receiving the benefit of those surpluses in lower postage, they were compelled to pay the high rates to support the nonproductive routes in the sparsely populated districts of the South and West. And when they asked for reduced postage, their requests were always opposed by congressmen from the West and South who feared that such changes would diminish postal revenues and force the department to curtail service on their unremunerative routes in order to make the Post Office self-sustaining.

So the citizens of the East violated the law and brought the Post Office to its knees, and to end this crisis neither the congressmen from rural areas nor Postmaster General Wickliffe had workable solutions. The congressmen wanted harsher punishment for those who broke the laws, and Wickliffe refused to accept reduced postage rates if they meant that the Post Office could no longer pay its own way. Like all his predecessors, Wickliffe believed that the self-supporting principle was the only reliable guide for operating the Post Office. Abandon it and "throw the Post Office upon the Treasury," as the expression went, and the postmaster general would be bound by no limits in extending and improving the service. Waste and corruption would follow and the burden upon the Treasury would be enormous.

But this was the people's Post Office, and they, not the postmaster general, would decide what to do. And if the petitions and letters raining upon Congress in the early 1840s meant anything, it was clear many of them wanted a change in the postal establishment regardless of cost. Led by businessmen, always the most vocal patrons of the postal service, and supported by their state legislatures and by newspapers such as Horace Greeley's New York *Tribune*, by 1844 they had sent so many petitions to Washington demanding changes that low postage must have seemed more important to some congressmen than the "reannexation of Texas and the reoccupation of Oregon."

Lodged between this massive protest of their constituents against high postage rates and the reluctance of those from the South and West to reduce the rates, members of Congress from the populated areas tried to allay the fears of their colleagues from the hinterlands with the argument that a reduction of postage would not diminish postal revenues at all. On the contrary, cheap postage would induce more people to use the mails and in the end revenues would actually increase. This had happened in England, congressmen said, where only four years before, Rowland Hill, an imaginative postal official, had persuaded the British government to eliminate the distance factor in establishing postage rates and to set a flat rate of one cent on a letter traveling any distance within the realm.

Still, those senators and congressmen whose constituents lived in isolated regions were skeptical, and in the end, members of Congress could no longer avoid choosing, as they had for so long, between extending the service or balancing the budget. If the East was to have reduced postal rates, the South and West must be guaranteed their post roads even if the principle of a self-supporting Post Office had to be abandoned.

Once before, in the 1830s, when a few members of Congress had timidly suggested that the Post Office need not pay its way, their heresy was roundly condemned. But then it was still possible for members to stand upon principle and give their constituents the mail service they desired. In the 1840s this was no longer an option, and where congressmen had once defended the principle of self-support, they now boldly asserted there was no more reason for the Post Office to be self-supporting than for the army and navy to pay their own way. All performed public services; all were equally entitled to public money.

Whoever first made this deduction deserved the everlasting thanks of hundreds of congressmen, for it gave members of Congress a new way of looking at the Post Office, freed them from the worry of an unbalanced budget, and permitted them to do what their constituents wanted. Used with good effect between 1845 and 1851, it helped Congress enact a series of laws that launched the modernization of the Post Office and gradually reduced postage rates until by 1851 a half-ounce letter could be sent three thousand miles for three cents if prepaid and five cents if not.

But the price the urban areas had to pay the rural for this reduction of postage in 1851 was written into an amendment to the law which read:

That no post office now in existence shall be discontinued, nor shall the mail service on any mail routes in any of the States or Territories be discontinued or diminished in consequence of any diminution of the revenues that may result from this act; and it shall be the duty of the Postmaster General to establish new post offices and place the mail service on any new mail routes established, or that may hereafter be established, in the same manner as though this act had not passed.

So at last the old self-sustaining tradition was overthrown— not in so many words, of course, but in effect. By stipulating that the postmaster general could not discontinue, curtail, or refuse to establish mail service because of postal deficits, Congress obviously intended to appropriate money from the Treasury to bridge the difference between whatever the continuance of the service might cost and the postal revenues, and it did.

The People's Post Office

Only thirteen times from 1851 to 1968 did the Post Office take in more money than it spent; in all the other years, Congress made up the difference.

But the old policy was not forgotten. From then until 1970, congressmen continued to pay lip service to the doctrine of self-support, and the postmasters general almost always tried to manage the department as if there had been no policy change at all. Indeed, the new postal policy was less than two years old when President Pierce's postmaster general, James Campbell, began ignoring it.

In August 1852, Congress had passed a new post roads bill, and when Postmaster General Campbell took office in 1853 it became his duty to establish service over most of the new post roads. But the Post Office was running a huge deficit, partly because of the reduced postage rates but also because of the expense of carrying the mails to the Pacific. Campbell, pleading the lack of funds, refused to establish all the service provided by the act of 1852 in spite of both the new policy which required him to do so and the demands of rural congressmen that post offices be established in their districts.

By 1854, Campbell had antagonized a substantial number of congressmen, and his performance was a good illustration of the postmaster general's ability to thwart the will of Congress. But odd as it may seem, it was partly because of this estrangement between Congress and the postmaster general that Congress finally supported and adopted two reforms Campbell had recommended; the mandatory prepayment of postage and the mandatory use of stamps.

Both the prepayment of postage and the use of stamps had been authorized in the 1840s, and the long delay in making them mandatory suggested the wariness with which Congress approached changes in the people's Post Office. Prepayment of postage had to be dealt with gingerly because skeptical Americans, having observed their Post Office over the years, hesitated to pay for postal service before it was rendered. As for stamps, they had been used by a few local postmasters as early as 1840, but not until 1847, when five- and ten-cent stamps bearing the likenesses of Benjamin Franklin and George Washington had been struck off, was their use authorized on a nationwide basis. Five years later, Congress provided for the sale of stamped envelopes, but for a variety of reasons the people, particularly in rural areas, had been slow to use either stamps or the stamped envelopes.

Who first decided to make the prepayment of postage and the use of stamps mandatory—members of Congress or Postmaster General Campbell—is uncertain. However, by 1854 both had agreed on the necessity of doing so. Prepayment would reduce the number of unclaimed letters which were so costly to the department, and stamps would make possible an accurate check of letters mailed at any one post office and eliminate the clumsy waybills each postmaster had kept to record the number of letters passing through his office. Both would make the postal system more efficient, reduce the postal deficit, and make possible—so rural congressmen thought—the further extension of the mails.

In 1855, then, having arrived at its decision by this circuitous route, Congress made the prepayment of postage and use of stamps mandatory, the first to go into effect immediately and the latter on 1 January 1856; and if these two innovations did not provide the alchemy that could immediately change postal deficits to surpluses, they did at least increase the efficiency of the postal service.

The People's Post Office

Postmaster General Campbell's troubles, however, were not ended by this legislation. For his attempt to steer the postal bark by the self-sustaining principle had not only damaged his relationship with those members of Congress who wanted more post offices established in their districts but had led him into conflict with a number of southern congressmen whose constituents lived along the Mississippi River. A quarrel of long duration, the Mississippi River controversy began when Campbell became postmaster general, and it was still going on when he left office four years later.

In 1852 Congress had ordered a daily mail service upon the Mississippi River from Louisville to New Orleans, and before he left office in 1853, Sam Hubbard, President Fillmore's postmaster general, had contracted with a company to carry the mail over the new route. But Postmaster General Campbell had scarcely taken office before he canceled the contract, ostensibly because the company had not abided by its contract, but really because he thought it too expensive. To aggravate matters, as far as southern members of Congress were concerned, he put off month after month making a new contract to carry the mail because, as he said, all the bids he received were extravagant.

In his annual reports, Campbell tried to explain his position, which was uncomfortable to say the least, but Congress was in no mood to listen. The Mississippi mail, secured only after a long struggle and only after the change in postal policy, was important to the people in the little hamlets along the river, and congressmen meant to have the service regardless of cost. So Congress passed new legislation in 1854, once more ordering the postmaster general to install mail service on the river. But again Campbell hesitated, and when Congress met in 1855, those senators and congressmen from the Mississippi River region were beside themselves with anger. "Why, sir," said Senator James Jones of Tennessee, "the Crown itself would not dare do such a thing. . . . The law required him [the postmaster general] to execute these contracts. He has refused to do it. He has treated us with silence, with indifference, with contumacy, and with contempt. I, for one am not willing to bear it any longer."

Even this outburst did not immediately stir Campbell, who was still fighting postal deficits, and not until 1856, the last year of his administration, did he finally make a contract to carry the mail on the Mississippi. The contract itself was far from satisfactory to the interested members of Congress, and in March 1857, maintaining to the last that postal "laws should be so formed as to produce a sufficient amount of revenue to defray all proper expenses," Campbell retired leaving behind a group of disgruntled members of Congress.

The heir to Campbell's post and problems was Aaron Brown, President Buchanan's choice to run the great department. A wealthy man from Tennessee, Brown was anxious to soothe the ruffled feelings of senators and congressmen, and, unlike his predecessor, he had no rigid convictions about making the Post Office self-sustaining. His view, in fact, was that the Post Office performed so many services for the nation beyond simply carrying letters that Congress should neither expect it to pay its own way nor be unwilling to appropriate money from the Treasury for it. Freed therefore from the old restraint, Brown continued the Mississippi River service, inaugurated the expensive Butter-field stagecoach line to the Pacific, and extended the service liberally everywhere. In his first year in office he established more than 1,300 post offices and almost 28,000 miles of new post roads.

The People's Post Office

The postal deficits soared gloriously, of course, by nearly seven million dollars by 1859. Still Brown went his way, apparently unperturbed by the mounting expenses. But when he died very suddenly in March of 1859, his successor, Joseph Holt of Kentucky, was horrified by the deficit and the departure from the self-sustaining principle. With more valor than discretion, he began curtailing postal service as rapidly as possible to bring expenditures in line with revenues. Hard hit in the retrenchment was the Mississippi River service, which by the time the South seceded in 1861 had dwindled to almost nothing despite the anguished cries of those senators and congressmen to whom the Mississippi mail had become a symbol of federal injustice.

Southern secession and the subsequent suspension of hundreds of nonproductive mail routes throughout the South wiped out much of the postal deficit, and by 1863, for the first time in more than a decade, postal revenues promised to exceed expenditures. Now there was money for better postal facilities in the rural areas of the North, and that year cheaper postage came to the Far West when Congress eliminated distance as a factor in determining postage and made three cents the standard rate for carrying a letter from one end of the country to the other.

But urban America was the real winner when the South seceded. Largely for the convenience of businessmen who wished to send money safely through the mails, Congress had provided for registered letters in 1855. But now, in 1864, a money order system, established in England as far back as 1837, was also created, partly to accommodate the Union soldiers, but more for the sake of urbanites who were still looking for a safe way to send money through the mail. The clearest evidence of urban dominance of the postal system, however, was the establishment of city free delivery in 1863.

Although large cities had had a delivery system of sorts for years, it was neither free nor efficient, and the need for better service was great. But the cost of delivering the mail free to every city dweller's home threatened to be immense, and had the South remained in the Union, city free delivery would likely have had to wait until postal facilities in the South and West, such as those on the Mississippi River, had been provided. As it was, Congress met with only a minimum of opposition when it authorized the postmaster general to establish free delivery service wherever he thought necessary and raised the postage on drop letters—those mailed in the city for delivery within the city—to two cents to help pay for the new service. Two years later, after the postmaster general had suspended some of the free delivery services he had started, Congress took away his discretionary power and ordered him to establish free delivery in every city with more than 50,000 inhabitants.

By the close of the Civil War in 1865, then—thanks mostly to urban influence—the modern outlines of the postal service had been drawn. A flat-rate postage system had been adopted, stamps and envelopes and registered letters and money orders were in use, and city free delivery had been established. Moreover, on 1 July 1865 the department had a surplus of more than $800,000!

But the surplus was short-lived. With the war over and the South back in the Union, the suspended mail service was reopened over thousands of miles of unremunerative mail routes throughout the eleven states of the old Confederacy. Besides that, a great chain of humanity was on the move to the last

American frontier—to the mountains of Colorado, Nevada, and Montana, across the plains of Kansas, Nebraska, Texas, and the Dakotas—and after them came the mails. In just three years, Congress established more than 1,200 new post routes over almost 50,000 miles of post roads. So great was the demand for mail routes in these areas that Congress in some sessions was forced to pass two post roads bills—one at the beginning of the session and one at the end.

At this crucial point in postal history, the man in charge of the Post Office was Alexander Randall, pioneer Wisconsin lawyer, wartime governor of that state, ardent supporter of President Andrew Johnson, and one of the few postmasters general who believed the Post Office did not necessarily have to be self-supporting. "It has always been an erroneous theory in the history of the postal service of the United States," he wrote, "that it was established . . . on the principle that it should be self-supporting. It is a great public necessity to accommodate private citizens, and it will not do to say that no mail routes shall be opened, or post office established, until the business on the proposed routes or of the proposed office shall pay all expenses."

Between Randall, then, and the congressmen who demanded post roads there was no basic disagreement. The self-sustaining principle was out and postal deficits were in as such unlikely places as Weeping Water, Nebraska, Towanda, Kansas, and French Bar, Montana, began to appear on postal maps. By 1868 the deficit stood at more than six million dollars and Congress had once more taken to writing deficiency appropriation bills to cover the difference between postal revenues and expenditures.

The large postal deficits, however, in time brought a re-newal of the scramble for service and a reopening of the old quarrel between urban and rural America. And once again, pleas for a self-sustaining Post Office rang through Congress as first one side and then the other felt its interests threatened.

Urbanites wanted reduced postage rates and extensions of city free delivery to smaller cities, but in the early postwar years they made few gains. The adoption of penny postal cards in 1873 was as close as they could come to cheaper postage while continued postal deficits and the panic of 1873 made impossible an extension of city free delivery. True, Congress did authorize the postmaster general to extend city delivery to cities with 20,000 inhabitants in 1873, but the very next year it was forced to raise the population minimum to 30,000.

In the late 1870s, however, postal revenues rose, deficits declined, and the movements for reduced postage and city delivery extensions gathered strength. By 1882, for the first time in sixteen years, the Post Office had a surplus, and the next year, on the recommendation of President Arthur and Postmaster General Timothy Otis Howe, Congress reduced the postage to two cents on a letter weighing half an ounce; two years later two cents would mail a letter weighing a full ounce. That same year Congress also authorized the postmaster general to begin a special delivery service in free delivery towns and cities and in towns with a population of 4,000 persons.

City delivery extensions were also possible now. In 1879, the postmaster general was once more permitted to extend free delivery to cities with 20,000 persons, and by the end of the next year, 104 cities had the service. But the more city delivery systems were established the more they were coveted by those who did not have them. In the early 1880s, congressmen from the nation's smaller towns, who once might have been on the side of rural America in opposing city delivery extensions, now found themselves forced by their constituents to demand the service for their towns. So they leagued themselves with those from the cities who already had free delivery and could not with good grace refuse it to smaller places, and fought for the establishment of city delivery in towns of 10,000.

Congressmen from rural areas pleaded for a return to a self-supporting Post Office, but in vain. Alluding often to the army and navy to prove that the postal service did not have to be self-supporting and arguing that service came first, members of Congress from small towns and urban areas swept the opposition before them, and in 1887 authorized the postmaster general to establish free delivery in towns of 10,000 where postal revenues were at least $10,000 a year. Better still, the postmaster general could, at his own discretion, extend the service to even smaller towns, and through the years, as towns agreed to build and maintain good streets and sidewalks and number their houses, the service was extended until at the end of World War I more than two thousand towns and cities had free delivery systems.

The extension of free delivery to towns of 10,000 and less virtually ended the city free delivery movement, but postal services in the cities continued to be improved in one way or another at considerable cost. In city after city, particularly in the early part of the new century, new post offices were built—usually conveniently close to the railroads, where many remain today—expensive machinery to cancel stamps and conveyor belts to move the mails about the post offices were introduced, and in the largest cities, pneumatic tubes were run beneath the streets to speed the mails from branch post offices to the central office. But the urban drive for one-cent postage in the late 1880s and 1890s failed, principally because the nation's farmers at last forced Congress to appropriate large sums of money for mail service in rural America.

Not that Congress had not always spent money for the rural mail service. Indeed it had. But compared to the city's, the rural mail service was a poor country cousin. No letter carrier in uniform brought the mail to the farmer's gate each day. Instead, rural America's mail service was composed principally of what was called star route service. To save money by eliminating the expensive stagecoach mail service wherever possible, Congress had, as far back as 1845, provided that on certain mail routes the postmaster general might contract to have the mail carried without specifying the means of carrying it. The only requirement was that the mails must be carried with "celerity, certainty, and security." Mail routes to which this arrangement applied were designated in the Post Office Department records with asterisks and therefore came to be called star routes.

By 1891, rural America was filled with 16,410 star routes, running over more than 230,000 miles of post roads, and over these roads, loping along on their ponies or riding in carts or buckboard wagons, mail carriers hauled the mail from some town or railroad depot to more than 60,000 little fourth-class post offices scattered across the countryside. And to these post offices, once or possibly twice a week, the farmers went for their mail.

The system, though poor and time-consuming, was all the farmers had ever known and, until the 1890s, probably all they ever expected to have. Then suddenly in the nineties, plans were being made to deliver the mail to the farmers. Who the father of this idea was has become a matter of dispute, but the first postmaster general to recommend it was President Harrison's John

Wanamaker, a Philadelphia merchant who worried much more about postal service than deficits.

Wanamaker could scarcely have proposed such a scheme at a more propitious moment. Times on the farm were hard in the 1890s, and farmers in some areas were outraged because the government appeared to be helping businessmen instead of them. The difference in mail service between the city and country was one good example of discrimination, and the farmers made the most of it. Through their organizations—the Grange, Farmers' Alliances, and similar groups—they filled the mails with petitions for rural free delivery mail, and so forced Congress to do something.

Congress boggled at the probable expense of sending thousands of rural mail carriers through the countryside to bring "every man's mail to every man's door" and in 1896 tried to find a way out by establishing a rural free delivery experiment in the hope, no doubt, that it would prove unsuccessful. But the experimental routes indicated that the farmers' mail could be delivered, and when, in one rash moment, the postmaster general invited farmers who wanted the service to petition for rural mail routes in their communities, an avalanche of petitions all but buried congressmen from rural districts.

These petitions congressmen sent to the Post Office Department with their endorsement, and postal officials, without waiting for Congress to enact post-roads bills as had always been done, established mail routes through the countryside in accordance with the petitions received. Within two years, more than 150 such routes were established, and some members of Congress who could see what this would do to postal revenues tried to kill the experiment in 1898. But it was already too late. Congressmen from rural districts, arguing as their urban colleagues had that the Post Office did not need to pay its way, voted down all moves to abandon the service.

Unable to kill the experiment, yet unwilling to keep it on an experimental basis, Congress made it a permanent part of the postal service in 1902. Within a decade, more than 40,000 rural mail routes wound their way over the roads and byroads of rural America, and where they went they displaced the little fourth-class post offices where farmers had always received their mail. In 1901, there were 76,945 post offices in the nation, the largest number ever reached, and of these more than 70,000 were fourth class. By 1920, only 41,102 such post offices remained, and many a little community, having lost its identity when it lost its post office, disappeared from the face of the land.

Excluding the cost of carrying magazines and newspapers, no other postal service was as costly as rural free delivery. As mail routes were being established by the thousands and rural mail carriers' salaries grew with the service, Postmaster General Albert Burleson, serving in President Wilson's cabinet, estimated that the loss on rural delivery alone in 1914 was $40,000,000.

Burleson, a congressman from Texas before he entered the cabinet, was a staunch defender of a self-supporting postal policy, and the costly rural free delivery service was like a festering sore to him. For eight years he tried in one way or another to curtail it. At first he proposed letting the rural routes out to the lowest bidder, but Congress refused to do this because rural members of Congress would not have one kind of service for the cities and another for the country. Failing this, he tried to reduce the number of rural mail routes by doubling their length and forcing mail carriers to use automobiles to cover them. The disruption of the service that followed this premature venture into the auto age so antagonized farmers and subsequently their representatives in Congress that Congress, in an unprecedented move, removed the postmaster general's power to reorganize the rural service. All that was left to the postmaster general, then, was to put off the establishment of new rural routes, and this he did, returning to the Treasury year after year large sums of money that Congress had appropriated to establish new rural mail service.

By World War I, the Post Office Department was being operated on the old theory that it must pay its way, and Postmaster General Burleson had at the war's end actually achieved a postal surplus. But it had been done for a price. The rural mail service had been curtailed and disrupted, and the city service, where unhappily uncertain motor transportation had been substituted for the pneumatic tubes, was no better off. Demoralization gripped both the city and rural letter carrier force, and the Republicans were promising a return to good mail service if they won the election in 1920. When they did win, the Post Office drifted back to the customary postal deficits. The service, however, was somewhat better and the people apparently were satisfied, which was proof enough, if proof were needed, that Congress had not misread the will of the people through the years. For whatever administrators might think, experience proved that the people first wanted service from their Post Office and afterward a balanced postal budget if possible.

III

Bond of Union

The United States was born in the shadow of a theory that a republican form of government could never successfully govern so vast a territory as that possessed by the Union. It was an old idea, advanced by philosophers and apparently supported by history, and it seemed particularly applicable to the United States. "Independent of the opinions of many great authors," wrote Virginia's Richard Henry Lee in 1787,

that a free elective government cannot be extended over large territories, a few reflections must evince, that one government and general legislation alone never can extend equal benefits to all parts of the United States: Different laws, customs, and opinions exist in all different states, which by a uniform system of laws would be unreasonably invaded. The United States contain about a million square miles, and in half a century will, probably, contain ten millions of people; and from the center to the extremes is about 800 miles.

Seven years of experience under the Constitution had not convinced all Americans that the theory Lee had discussed was wrong, and President Washington felt compelled to refer to it in his farewell address in 1796, urging his countrymen to reserve judgment on the fate of the Union. "Is there a doubt whether a common government can embrace so large a sphere?" he asked. "Let experience solve it. To listen to mere speculation in such case were criminal. . . . It is well worth a fair and full experiment."

Perhaps thinking Americans would have been less apprehensive about the future of their Union if communication among its diverse people had been better. But in a land stretching eight hundred miles from its center to its extremes and with room enough for its descendants "to the thousandth and thousandth generation," as Jefferson described it, where information could travel no faster than a ship sailing, a man walking, or a horse galloping, the nation's great treasure of unoccupied land was as much hindrance as help in strengthening the ties among the various parts of the Union.

A few timetables suggest the problem. In 1798, when John Adams was president, it took forty days to send and receive a letter from Portland, Maine, to Savannah, Georgia. Between Philadelphia and Lexington, Kentucky, thirty-two days were required for the same service, and from Philadelphia to Nashville, forty-four. So slow, indeed, was land transportation in this period that important American towns were as close, in point of time, to London as to one another. Portsmouth, New Hampshire, was as near to Liverpool as it was to Augusta, Georgia, and Philadelphia as near to London as to Pittsburgh.

Such poor communication scarcely inspired confidence in the permanence of the Union. It made doubly difficult the task of overcoming the nation's distances, of weaning Americans from loyalties to their local and state governments to the national government, and even of impressing them with the reality of the central government about which they rarely heard and evidences of which they rarely saw.

But if the wretched communication system did little to weaken the theory that the Republic could not endure, it did much to help the Post Office. For the Post Office then was the nation's only regular system of communication and assumed an importance far beyond the mere carrying of letters and newspapers. Only through the postal system could members of Congress correspond with their constituents, and their constituents with their congressmen. And only by mail could a Yankee exchange ideas and sentiments with a Southerner, and the Westerner with the Easterner. So in an age when men looked for whatever bonds might hold the Union together, they turned to the Post Office.

In the warm afterglow of patriotism that suffused the nation after the War of 1812, the word "Union" took on an almost mystical quality that stirred men's emotions and memories and made arguments in its name especially cogent. Then, when the "era of good feeling" faded and the strains upon the Union increased, the argument that the Post Office was uniting all sections of the nation was all the more appealing. In 1830, for example, at the close of the decade of growing sectionalism, a congressional committee described the Post Office as "an establishment . . . entirely national in its character . . . affording to friends, residing in different portions of the Union, the sweets of frequent friendly interchanges of sentiment and good feeling so desirable; and thus, by free and familiar intercourse, drawing still closer the bond of union."

Again and again in the thirty years before the Civil War, members of Congress alluded to the Post Office as a bond of union as they argued for the new post roads their constituents were demanding, and the postal system spread rapidly across the country on the strength of the argument that it was such a bond. And in many ways it was.

By 1830, the nation was bound together by the great southern, northern, and western mails that penetrated the various sections along main post roads. From the principal post roads, like nerves from the spinal column, more than 100,000 miles of smaller post roads ran into the countryside taking the mails to over 8,000 post offices and making it possible for Yankees at Sharon, Vermont, to correspond with Southerners at Britton's Mill, North Carolina, and residents of Hyde Park, New York, with pioneers at Borodino, Michigan.

So rapidly had the postal network spread, in fact, that Michigan Territory had not only the post office at Borodino but thirty-six others as well, which amounted to one for every 855 of its inhabitants. It also had at least three post roads, two of which had a weekly and one a fortnightly mail service, and if the people in the territory did not see the larger significance of their mail service, the much-traveled Alexis de Tocqueville, who was in Michigan about that time, did. "In Michigan forests there is not a cabin so isolated," he wrote, "not a valley so wild, that it does not receive letters and newspapers at least once a week; we saw it ourselves." And the effects of this phenomenon, he thought, were worth recording. "Of all the countries in the world," he noted, "America is the one where the movement of thought and human industry is the most continuous and swift. Not an American but knows the resources of all the parts of the vast country he inhabits; all the men of intelligence know each other by reputation, many by sight. . . . I believe that I have never happened to speak to an American

Bond of Union

about one of his fellow-countrymen without finding him aware of the latter's present position and life history."

In this effort to bind the nation together with post roads and post offices, special consideration had been given to the new governments that were rising as rapidly as log cabins on the frontier. Attempting to tie them to the state and national governments as rapidly as possible, Congress had authorized the postmaster general in 1825 to establish a post road to the courthouse of any newly established county seat in the land without waiting for Congress to create such a road by law.

Remarkably, considering the growing fear of the power of the national government in some areas, the new postal service had been planted within the various states, even those most jealous of their rights, without objection to this operation of the national government within their borders. Far from objecting, states clamored for the service. South Carolina, the leader of the fight to nullify laws of Congress, had apparently been even more vigorous in obtaining post offices than Massachusetts. In 1831, South Carolina had a post office for approximately every 1,000 of her free inhabitants, including the one at Calhoun's Mills, whereas the ratio in Massachusetts was about one post office for every 1,400 persons.

To secure these post offices and post roads, Americans had to appeal to the central government in Washington, to address petitions to their congressmen, and to complain to the same source when the mails were late. This helped to teach rough-handed settlers as well as more literate townspeople to look to the national government for help and to regard the Union as a source of their prosperity. At the same time, they learned to live with their postal service without fear that the central government was using it to encroach upon their rights, so that later, when rampant sectionalism threatened to snap the cords of union, the mail service, unlike the churches and political parties, continued to operate unmolested and to help hold the Union together. And finally, because precedents had been set for the establishment of the mail service in calmer times, it was the one government service that could be enlarged in all the states during the turbulent 1850s without rousing the suspicions of the South.

Beyond this, the postal service made the national government visible to every man, woman, and child in the nation and so helped solve the problem Alexander Hamilton had had in mind in 1788 when he wrote that "a government continually at a distance and out of sight" could hardly "be expected to interest the sensations of the people." For it was true, as congressmen never tired of repeating, that no branch of the national government touched the lives of so many Americans so often, so intimately, and so favorably as the Post Office.

Especially was this the case in the early nineteenth century when Americans were likely to go from year to year with scarcely any evidence, aside from the mails, that the national government existed. Even on the eve of the Civil War, a southern congressman could still point out that, but for the collection of taxes, the postal service was the only way the national government was known in the South. "We know nothing of the Government but to feel its power of taxation," he said, "except through the post office. We feel its taxing power, and if your revenue officers did not demand tribute from us, we should not know you unless the post-boy brought his mail."

True, the Post Office did not always present a favorable image of the government, but this did not necessarily diminish its value as a bond of union. For even when the mails were late and complaints were made, citizens were forced to think of the national government, if only to shake their heads in despair at its operations. And if the rickety stagecoach that carried the mail, the forlorn building that served as a post office, and the slovenly postrider who plodded along country roads with the mail were unimpressive, still they were representatives of the national government and reminders to the people of its presence in their midst.

Besides providing Americans with these symbols of their government, the Post Office was the first agency of the central government to teach them the difficult lesson that money raised in one part of the Union must be used to help those in another part: that surplus postal money taken from the busy, productive mail routes must be used to extend mail service over sparsely populated and nonpaying mail routes.

This was a proposition not easily grasped by a people more used to thinking of their states than of the Union, and as early as 1810 a Pennsylvania congressman was grumbling about it. The mail routes in his state, he claimed, had been credited with a $30,000 surplus, and he demanded to know which states had postal deficiencies. "I do not think," he said, "one State should be saddled with expense, too much, for the benefit of others."

Despite such complaints, which lasted far into the nineteenth century and occasionally threatened to disrupt the service, the Post Office Department continued to take money from paying states and use it in those whose mail services did not pay their way. And when at last the surpluses from wealthy states failed to cover the cost of extending the mails into sparsely populated areas, Congress appropriated money from the national Treasury for that purpose on the grounds that the mail routes were needed to strengthen the Union.

While the Post Office was strengthening the ties of union by its presence within the states, it was also fostering the building of roads connecting remote settlements with centers of population throughout the nation and so helping in yet another way to bind the Union together. Before post routes could be established, roads, or at least trails, over which the routes would go had to be built, and this was one of the first community projects the pioneers undertook in any settlement. The road the settlers in Indiana had built between Indianapolis and Elizabethtown, Kentucky, in 1827, for example, was no boulevard, but it was made a post road, as were thousands of others just like it in the course of years. But once a road became a post road, the settlers were bound by the postal law of 1825 to free it of all obstructions—fences, gates, bars—and keep it in good repair or run the risk of seeing the mail service moved to another road. Moreover, if they wanted better mail service, they had to improve their post road. The Indianapolis-Elizabethtown road was a case in point. Only three years after it had been made a post road, Postmaster General Barry, explaining that "the roads at the present moment would scarcely admit of stage transportation," rejected a request for a stagecoach mail service there.

The postal service not only spurred settlers to build and improve their local roads, it was also used to advance the cause of those who advocated national aid for the building of roads within the states.

The movement to obtain the national government's support for making internal improvements within the states began in earnest as soon as the War of 1812 was over, and one of the greatest proponents of the idea was John C. Calhoun. On fire with the nationalistic spirit the war had engendered and perhaps seriously worried lest the extent of the country prove too great to govern, he made a ringing appeal in 1817 in favor of his bill to use money from the national Treasury to build roads and canals throughout the states.

"We are under the most imperious obligation," Calhoun had said, "to counteract every tendency to disunion."

Whatever . . . impedes the intercourse of the extremes with this, the centre of the Republic [Washington, D.C.] weakens the Union. Let us then . . . bind the Republic together with a perfect system of roads and canals. Let us conquer space. It is thus the most distant parts of the Republic will be brought within a few days travel of the centre; it is thus that a citizen of the West will read the news of Boston still moist from the press. The mail and the press . . . are the nerves of the body politic. By them the slightest impression made on the most remote parts is communicated to the whole system.

Of course it was true that the Constitution had not expressly given Congress the power to do what Calhoun wanted it to do, but this objection was brushed aside with the assertion that Congress could build the roads under its power to establish post offices and post roads. Although the logic of this was lost upon President Madison, who vetoed Calhoun's bill when it reached him in 1817, still the point had been made; and nearly a hundred years later, when another postal extension made it seem reasonable, the point was argued with more success.

But the government's failure to build a network of roads and canals throughout the Union had little effect on the growth of the mails, and if an ever increasing volume of letters meant greater unity among Americans, the Post Office was indeed fulfilling its role as a bond of union. According to the best statistics available, and these are none too reliable, a population of nearly 4,000,000 persons in 1790 sent only 265,545 letters through the mails. Thirty years later, the number of letters in the mail for one year was still less than one for each American. But from 1830 to 1850, while the nation's population was not quite doubling itself, the number of letters mailed increased five times. In 1850, nearly three letters were mailed for every man, woman, and child—both free and slave—in the nation, and just four years later the number of letters mailed jumped from 69,426,452 to 119,634,418, or from about three to seven for every man, woman, and child.

The increase in the flow of letters stemmed in part from the postage reductions made at mid-century, but more especially it arose from the growth in the nation's business. Indeed, it is possible the average American received only a few more letters in 1850 than his father had in 1800, and that the increase in the number of letters mailed was largely the result of businessmen's increasing reliance upon the postal service to handle business affairs that were continually spreading beyond their local communities. In any case, the Post Office had become the good right arm of business in antebellum America when sentiments of union were being formed, and in this capacity may have made its greatest contribution to uniting Americans.

Up and down the country and across its broad expanse, year by year, the great mails carried not only the commercial correspondence that bound business to business and customers to businesses, but money as well. "In the course of every year," wrote Postmaster General McLean in 1828, "no inconsiderable amount of the active capital of the country, in some form or other, passes through the mail." This exchange of money, often in the form of drafts on banks in various parts of the nation, as well as correspondence, did much to acquaint Americans with one another and may have been among the most vital reminders of the dependence of one section upon another.

But valuable as all its services were to the cause of union, the postal service was, in the years before the Civil War, almost as likely to be an agent of disunity as unity. Even in the early 1800s the Post Office was not entirely free from the curse of sectionalism, and once at least in the Jeffersonian years, southern congressmen vigorously complained that the North had obtained better mail facilities than the South. Such disputes, however, could be easily settled in those days if only by increasing the post routes in the dissatisfied section. But in the 1820s, mounting sectional interests, following the furrow plowed by the panic of 1819 and the quarrel over slavery in Missouri, tainted all they touched, even things like the postal service which were desired by all.

Perhaps it surprised no one in the pre–Civil War period that the postal service, desirable as it was, did not itself escape the fires of sectionalism but even fed the flames it was supposed to quench. A creature of Congress, active in all states and territories, it was too intimately associated with members of Congress and their constituents to avoid the great sectional quarrels that rent the nation. The possible extension of the postal power of the Constitution itself, so boldly urged in "the era of good feeling" to permit the national government to build roads and canals, became in the late 1820s and remained for years a threat to southern interests particularly. But this was a small dispute compared with the Post Office's involvement in the slavery question.

Communication was the Post Office's business, of course, and communication, eagerly sought by both North and South, was a bond between them so long as both sections had no violent disagreements. But the mail, bearing new and radical ideas, could be dangerous to established institutions, especially if those institutions needed walls for protection. Such an institution was slavery, and as early as 1802 the possibility that the American mail might breach the wall was suggested by Gideon Granger, the Yankee postmaster general. Taking note of the insurrection of slaves in Santo Domingo and the fears this revolt had raised in the South, Granger wrote sympathetically of southern objections to the use of Negro mail carriers. "Everything which tends to increase their [the slaves] knowledge of natural rights," he wrote to a southern senator, "of men and things, or that affords them an opportunity of associating, acquiring, and communicating sentiments, and of establishing a chain or line of intelligence, must increase your hazard, because it increases their means of effecting their object."

Granger pointed out that slave mail carriers tended to be above suspicion and would be able, since they communicated with other postriders, to carry out an insurrection. It was important, too, in Granger's view, to remember that postriders were the most intelligent slaves.

They are the most *ready to learn* and the *most able to execute*. By traveling from day to day, and hourly mixing with the people, they must, they will acquire information. They will learn that a man's rights do not depend on his color. They will, in time, become teachers to their brethren. They become acquainted with each other on the line. Whenever the body, or a portion of them wish to act, they are an organized corps, circulating our intelligence *openly*, and their own privately.

The postmaster general's letter, which he admitted was "of a nature too delicate to engraft into a report which may become public," and the law that followed it forbidding slaves to carry the mail revealed much about the nature of slavery and made it easier to understand why Southerners reacted as they did a generation later, when northern abolitionists began to load the great southern mail with abolitionist literature.

By the 1830s people north of the Mason-Dixon line had adopted various attitudes toward slavery: some were unconcerned, others wanted to send the slaves back to Africa, and a few were demanding the immediate abolition of slavery. In 1832, the abolitionists had founded the New England Anti-Slavery Society, and the next year the American Anti-Slavery Society. Led by zealots like William Lloyd Garrison, they sought to promote abolition by educating the populace on the evils of slavery, and for that purpose prepared and sent through the mails thousands upon thousands of antislavery tracts. Perhaps as many as one million pieces of such literature were published in 1835 alone, and much of this was sent south in the mail, apparently not as President Jackson supposed, to cause a Negro rebellion, but simply to educate the whites.

But the arrival of this great pile of abolition literature, coming as it did while memories of two Negro insurrections—Nat Turner's in Virginia and Denmark Vesey's in South Carolina —were still fresh, frightened and enraged southern whites, some of whom resorted to mob action to prevent the spread of this incendiary material. In Charleston, South Carolina, a mob led by former senator Robert Hayne, the man who had a short time before tilted with Daniel Webster in a famous debate over the nature of the Union, invaded the post office, gathered up the offending literature, and burned it.

In other times and under other circumstances, this flagrant violation of the sanctity of the United States mails might have resulted in the immediate arrest and punishment of the leaders of the mob. But now the administration was reluctant to act. Postmaster General Kendall, possibly fearing that his recent appointment as postmaster general would not be confirmed if he took strong steps, wrote the postmaster at Charleston that there was a "higher law" communities might obey than the postal law and seemed content to let postmasters use their own judgment about whether or not to deliver incendiary literature. Nor did President Jackson, who only three years earlier had threatened to invade South Carolina to enforce the federal law, move to punish the offenders. While insisting, unlike his postmaster general, that the law must be obeyed, he urged upon Congress another law to prevent the Post Office, designed, as he wrote, "to foster amicable intercourse and correspondence between all members of the Confederacy, from being used as an instrument of an opposite character."

Disregarding in his blunt, direct way the pertinent parts of the First Amendment, President Jackson advocated a law forbidding postmasters to mail incendiary literature. But John C. Calhoun, for reasons as complex as the man himself—his hatred of Jackson, his unwillingness to give the national government the right to decide what was inflammatory material, and his desire to frighten and unite the South behind him— called the president's proposal "censorship." He proposed a bill to allow postmasters to send antislavery literature through the mails except to states with laws forbidding the distribution of such material. Censorship, in other words, might be practiced by the states but not by the national government.

The postal law of 1836 rejected both the president's and Calhoun's recommendations. Declaring that any postmaster who detained the mail with the intention of preventing its delivery could be fined, imprisoned, and removed, this law seemed to uphold the freedom of the press. But not so. In the South the law was simply ignored, both by those states that had laws preventing the spread of antislavery literature and by those that did not, and in the North few people protested. So from the 1830s to the Civil War, a cotton curtain, the price of union perhaps, was drawn at the Mason-Dixon line, and if upon occasion inflammatory literature made its way south, it rarely reached its addressee.

While slavery was tearing the nation apart in the 1830s, so too were other national issues. The protective tariff, the national bank, the building of roads and canals, the distribution to the states of the money taken from the sale of public land —issues so irrelevant today that modern Americans can only wonder at the bitterness they kindled in the antebellum years— were rarely debated without raising sectional animosities.

Of all these, the most controversial was the protective tariff. Because it was primarily an agricultural region with goods to sell abroad and with few manufactured goods to protect, the South vigorously opposed protective tariffs and, always suspicious of the North, saw in most issues of the day northern conspiracies to raise the tariff. The building of roads and canals with money from the federal Treasury and the distribution of money from the sale of the public lands, many Southerners believed, were schemes to reduce the money in the national Treasury. When this happened, Congress would be forced to raise the tariff simply to have money enough in the Treasury to pay for ordinary operations of the government.

Inevitably the Post Office too was drawn into this cauldron of conflicting interests and made an instrument of sectional controversy. Beginning in the 1840s, Southerners interpreted both the large appropriations Congress made for the Post Office and the first serious efforts to reduce the postage as northern schemes to decrease the money in the Treasury.

Congressman William Payne of Alabama, for example, revealed what was on the southern mind in 1841 when he objected to Postmaster General Granger's request for a large appropriation to cover the postal deficit. He called the proposal "one of a series of measures, intended to aid in exhausting the public Treasury," and linked it with the tariff. "A tariff, for protection," he said, "is the ultimate object of the dominant party in this Hall; and this bill, like every other act of this Congress; [*sic*] tends to the accomplishment of this all pervading, but iniquitous scheme."

The same reasoning explained the South's opposition to the great postal reform bills of 1845 and 1851, which reduced the postage rates. Nine of the twelve senators and sixty of the seventy-four congressmen who opposed the reform bill of 1845 were southern, and the reason for the South's opposition was neatly summarized in the attempt of Mississippi congressman Jacob Thompson to amend the title of the act to read: "A bill to make the Post Office a nuisance and to guarantee the Tariff Law [a high tariff] of 1842."

But neither incendiary literature in the mails nor differences of opinion on postal laws weakened the contention that the postal service was uniting the country. "It may be questioned," wrote Postmaster General Cave Johnson as he referred to an old theory in 1848, "whether a free government over such extensive territories as those of the United States could be maintained without it." Indeed, this view of the Post Office was particularly appealing at mid-century, and the debates on the postal reform bill of 1851 rang as never before with words about the postal service's role in binding the nation together. "The passage of a single good law," cried one northern congressman as he pleaded for reduced postage, "may diffuse an amount of good, increasing in each successive year to an incalculable amount. It will do more to confirm the attachment of the people of every section to our beloved Union, than all the Union meetings that have or can be held either North or South."

Never before had the argument been so relevant. Only the year before, the nation had been shaken to its foundations by the debate over the question of slavery in the territories newly acquired from Mexico. So far had relations between the North and South deteriorated that Southerners talked openly of disunion if slavery were forbidden in California and New Mexico, and John C. Calhoun, who had once spoken so eloquently of binding the Union together now, with death on his face, was carried into the Senate to argue against compromise. There, too ill to give his own speech, he listened intently, with what thoughts no one can say, as his friend from Virginia read it for him. "The cry of Union, Union, the glorious Union,'" ran his speech, "can no more prevent disunion than the cry of 'Health, health, glorious health!' on the part of the physician can save a patient lying dangerously ill."

And so the nation teetered on the edge of disaster. When at last the Union was saved by compromise, it was only natural that men who looked for a way to support their desire for cheap postage should argue that this legislation would tie the Union together as nothing else could. It did appear in the 1850s that real efforts were being made to use the mails in this way.

In the autumn of 1850, while the great compromise was being completed, Congress passed a bill establishing almost 800 post roads, hundreds of them in the South, and year after year during the decade continued to plant new post roads in the aggrieved section as if this alone might save the Union. Between 1850 and 1861, more than 2,000 post offices and some 25,000 miles of post roads were established in the states that were to form the Southern Confederacy.

At the same time that the Post Office was scattering post offices and post roads broadside across the South for the sake of union, it was busily transporting mail to the Pacific coast for the same reason. By 1857, costly semimonthly mails were running with regularity by steamer from the Atlantic coast to the Isthmus of Panama, across the Isthmus by rail, and up the California coast by steamer again to San Francisco and Oregon. Besides this route, two overland post roads had been established. One ran from Independence, Missouri, to Salt Lake City and on to Placerville, California, and the other ran from Independence to Santa Fe and Albuquerque and on to Stockton, California.

But all this was not enough to satisfy Californians. The overland mails, they complained, were uncertain and totally inadequate to meet their needs, and the land and sea route was unsafe and unsatisfactory. It ran through a foreign country where the mails were always in danger of being robbed by bandits or rebels or both, and the transportation was controlled by a heartless monopoly.

All this was true, but the Californians who complained about their postal service and demanded changes had more in mind than a mail service. What they really wanted was a transcontinental railroad to bring them their mails. Failing this, they wanted the next best thing: the establishment of a stagecoach line across the continent to bring them both passengers and mail.

Members of Congress who supported the proposition to establish a stagecoach line to the Pacific cited the need for a bond between East and West and solemnly assured their colleagues that failure to act might mean the loss of California. "Historians have informed us," said Pennsylvania senator Richard Brodhead, "that mountains make enemies of people who would otherwise be friends. We have a vast range of mountains and a great desert between our Pacific possessions and the Atlantic States. . . . Hence, the great question will be presented before long, whether it would not be as well, if it could be done, to have separate governments. I do not suggest it; but if we are to live in peace together, we must have rapid communication."

That men took seriously the bond of union argument had already been proved in the early 1850s by the fight between the North and South in Congress over the location of a projected transcontinental railroad. Both sections understood that California and the Far West would be tied economically and perhaps politically to that section through which a railroad from the Pacific coast ran, and because neither section would yield to the other, no railroad could be built. For the same reason it seemed unlikely that even a stagecoach line, which men saw as a forerunner of a railroad line, could be established. But in 1857, Congress did at last appropriate $600,000 for a semi-weekly stagecoach mail service to run from the Mississippi River to the Pacific. This was finally accomplished, however, only by permitting the man who received the mail contract to choose the route over which he would run his stagecoaches.

Unhappily, the rapid extension of the mails into the South and out to the Pacific served only to widen, not to heal, the breach between the North and South. By 1859, the expanded mail service had swelled the postal deficit enormously, and in the lame-duck session of Congress that year, members of Congress wrangled endlessly over the deficit and the postal appropriation for the following year. Angrier still was the debate over the location of the overland stagecoach route to the Pacific. For instead of permitting the mail contractor to select the route over which his stage line was to run as the law specified, Postmaster General Brown and President Buchanan's southern-dominated cabinet had, two years before, more or less coerced the contractor, John Butterfield, to accept a southern route that ran from Saint Louis and Memphis to Fort Smith, Arkansas, then to El Paso and on to the Pacific. This route was an estimated 900 miles longer than it needed to be, and since it ran through the South and was not selected according to the law, northern legislators tried to amend the Post Office appropriation bill to force the postmaster general to allow the contractor to change the route if he wished.

So bitter was the debate over this bill that the northern-dominated House of Representatives and the southern-controlled Senate could come to no agreement. For the first time in history Congress adjourned without providing an appropriation for the Post Office. To make matters worse, it was at this critical moment that Joseph Holt succeeded to the postmaster generalship upon Aaron Brown's death and began to cut back on the postal service. Holt not only reduced the Mississippi River mail service but laid a heavy hand on the nonproductive post roads and post offices in the South, and so aroused southern anger at the federal system that this, according to one historian, was "to become one of the less tangible factors leading to secession."

Perhaps the crowning irony of all this was that the vast extension of the mails into the South made in the 1850s to weld the Union together probably did more to strengthen the union within the Southern states than the union between the North and South. Largely because of its enlarged postal facilities in that period, the South's newspaper circulation increased by more than 100 percent, and, excluding the Negro population, the per capita circulation in certain southern states compared favorably with that in the free states. But unfortunately for the cause of union, the South's censorship of southern mails meant that southern opinion alone circulated more widely in the region. This of course, tended to unify rather than diversify southern thought. Moreover, the decade of rapid postal extension coincided with the rising spirit of southern nationalism, and through southern mails, in an ever widening arc, went the fiery pamphlets of such organizations as the Southern Rights Association, which aimed at rousing national sentiment throughout the Cotton Kingdom. And finally, to compound the irony, the solidifying of southern opinion, achieved through a mail service that never paid its way, was done largely at northern expense.

At the same time in the North, where the mails were not censored, cheaper postage and additional postal facilities made the postal system an increasingly useful vehicle for spreading abolitionist literature—*Uncle Tom's Cabin*, published in 1852, for example—and helped foment northern opposition to the South's peculiar institution as John C. Calhoun had foreseen and feared.

On the other hand, the mails to the Pacific did eventually prove to be a bond, not between California and the South as Southerners had hoped, but between California and the North. In the North in the spring of 1860, a freighting firm headed by William H. Russell, Alexander Majors, and William B. Waddell had privately established a Pony Express to speed the mails from the Missouri to the Pacific coast. Their purpose was to prove the feasibility of a northern mail route and to obtain a substantial mail contract from the government.

Bond of Union

The Pony Express's method of operation was as old as the Persian postal system and not without precedent even in the United States. Its route stretched from the Missouri River across the plains of Nebraska and Wyoming to the Great Salt Lake and Nevada, over the Sierras, and on to Sacramento. Along this course at ten- to fifteen-mile intervals way stations had been built. Here the postriders paused only to change horses before continuing on to the next station. When each rider had ridden some seventy-five miles, he turned his mailbag over to the next rider and waited at one of the home stations until it was time for him to carry the mail back over the route he had just traveled. In this fashion and with a speed that thrilled Americans, the mail was carried across half a continent in about ten days.

Although the Pony Express was outmoded by the telegraph in less than eighteen months, it came in time to provide the swiftest possible means for carrying President Lincoln's dispatches to California as the nation plunged into war, and it also proved the feasibility of the route. But the mail contract Russell, Majors, and Waddell hoped for never came. Instead, as the Civil War threatened, the Butterfield stage line was moved from the South to the North and placed upon the Pony Express route. And here in 1861, with an appropriation of $1,000,000, Butterfield's old company, now the Overland Mail Company, began carrying a daily mail which one congressman assured the nation would "bind the Pacific States more closely to the Union" with ties more powerful "than any bands of either iron or gold."

Throughout that desperate winter of 1860 and 1861, while the Pony Express riders steadily galloped the mails to the Pacific coast with scarcely a pause for snow or hostile Indians and the Overland Mail Company's stagecoaches made their daily runs, the Union rapidly disintegrated. By early March when President-elect Lincoln had stolen into Washington, D.C. for his inaugural, the Confederate States of America had already been shaped from the loins of the old Union. Yet President Lincoln held onto the mail service as if this last tie with the seceding section might somehow still preserve the Union. "The mails, unless repelled," he said in the inaugural address, "will continue to be furnished in all parts of the Union"; and his postmaster general, Montgomery Blair, realizing, as he said, that the mail routes were the only way of diffusing correct information among the people of the South, stubbornly refused to close the mail routes in that area and even tried to reopen some that had been discontinued by his predecessor.

But then came Fort Sumter, and Southerners, unable to tolerate in their midst what was to them a foreign postal service, refused to reopen closed services and began taking over all United States post offices within their region. Recognizing at last that the mails could not do what men would not have done, Postmaster General Blair announced sadly to Congress in 1862 that he had suspended all service in the rebellious states. After this, except for occasional censored mail exchanged under a flag of truce, communications between the people of the North and South could pass only through clandestine channels. Well over 100,000 letters sent south during the war ended up in the Post Office's dead letter office, suggesting not only what the flow of mail would have been had the mails continued to operate but also perhaps why the South was so quick to take over mail facilities in the Confederacy.

Whatever effect the continuation of the mails to the South might have had upon the relations between the two sections, the closing of the mail made clear in the North how very expensive the southern mail system had been and how much Congress had invested there, partly for the sake of union. After the South's secession, it was but a short time before the United States Post Office was enjoying surplus revenues, which were used to extend the mails throughout the North and to the Pacific coast to bind the free states ever more closely together.

The Post Office in the Southern Confederacy, however, never really brought unity there. With the help of United States postal forms and regulations taken from the Post Office in Washington, D.C. by southern clerks who worked there, and by conducting a night school to train his postal employees, Postmaster General John Reagan quickly organized the Confederacy's postal system. Unfortunately, the Confederation's constitution provided that the Post Office must pay its way, and in order to accomplish this objective, Reagan had to eliminate hundreds of miles of post roads and dozens of post offices. The postmaster general was commended for his skill in making the postal service self-supporting, but months before the end of the war, with the deliberate curtailment of the system to save money and loss of service in areas occupied by northern troops, the Confederation's mail routes, still paying their way, had all but disappeared.

With the collapse of the Confederacy in the spring of 1865 came the efforts "to bind up the nation's wounds," as Lincoln put it, and in this process the postal service played a part. William Dennison, postmaster general in 1865, sent postal agents into the South as soon as hostilities had ended with instructions to offer their services to the provisional governors in the defeated states and to reestablish immediately the essential post roads and post offices providing postal service to county seats. The rest of the suspended post roads and post offices were to be reopened as rapidly as possible.

Bond of Union

Some small part of the tragedy of the South, its economic demoralization and its stagnation after the war, could be seen in what followed. After more than a year's work, the postal agents had been able to reopen only 2,778 of the nearly 9,000 post offices the proud Confederacy had once had and only 60,000 of its more than 70,000 miles of post roads. The next year, the South still had less than half its old mail service, and as late as 1877 some southern congressmen complained that their districts even then had less than half the mail service they had had in 1861. This may well have been true, for not until 1878 did the South finally have as many post offices as it had had in 1860.

This slow rebuilding of the southern mail service was partly due to the extension of new mail service to the Great Plains and Rocky Mountain region, where Americans were also clamoring for mail. A large appropriation made for star route service in 1877, for example, proposed and supported by southerners specifically for extending the mail service in the South, was used almost entirely to take the mails to the Black Hills of South Dakota, where gold had just been discovered.

It may have been true, too, as was sometimes implied, that the Republicans, who dominated Congress from the close of the war to 1876, paid less attention than they might have to the mail service in the South. In any case, after 1876, when the Democrats periodically controlled the House of Representatives and a southerner was frequently chairman of the House Committee on Post Office and Post Roads, the southern mail service was rapidly extended. In fact in just one year, 1879–80, when David M. Key from Tennessee was postmaster general and the Democrats controlled the House of Representatives, the star route mileage in the states of the old Confederacy was increased by almost 13,000 miles, for a total of more than 87,000 miles.

Bond of Union

After this the South had almost all the star route service it could profitably use, and from 1880 on expansion of the postal system in that region consisted mainly of adding post offices and increasing the railroad mail service. And these, too, came hurriedly in the 1880s. Between 1880 and 1891, the number of miles the mails were carried by rail in the Confederacy grew from 15,412 to 35,105, and the number of post offices from 11,209 to more than 19,000, which was almost as many post offices as all the free states together had in 1860. This increase of more than 7,000 post offices represented more than 40 percent of all post offices established in the decade, a figure suggesting the increasing power of the South in the nation's councils.

All this postal service in the South cost almost three and a half million dollars more than it produced in postal revenues in 1891, but no monetary value could possibly be set upon its contribution to the strengthening of the union between the South and the rest of the nation. In 1891, at their 19,000 post offices, where Postmaster General Wanamaker had urged the postmasters to fly the Americn flag to inspire loyal sentiment, Southerners spent more than $7,000,000 for stamps, stamped envelopes, and postcards. This was nearly as much as the entire revenue of the Post Office Department in 1860, and represents a surprisingly large amount of correspondence. More than 53,000,000 pieces of mail passed through the seven free-delivery post offices in Georgia alone in 1891. Of this amount, more than 9,000,000 pieces were newspapers filled with national advertisements proclaiming the value of products as diversified as Lydia Pinkham's Compound and Swift's meat. As Southerners were thus drawn into the national economy, economic, if not spiritual, bonds were strengthened.

While all the mail passing through the South's extensive postal system helped smooth the road to reunion, postal legislation itself, like the serpent in the garden, was luring southern legislators from old obstructionist ways, softening their suspicions of the North, and weakening their traditional opposition to a strong central government. In the 1870s and 1880s, southern members of Congress, like their antebellum fathers, were still defending states' rights and branding new legislative proposals unconstitutional as if the Civil War had never taken place. One could hear, for example, in the Southerners' opposition to the bill to reduce the postage to two cents in 1883, almost every argument their kinfolk had made against a similar bill in 1851. But in the 1890s, the southern attitude in Congress toward postal legislation began to change.

Rarely had southern members of Congress, even from the early days of the Republic, supported postal innovations. Even less had they been among the leaders who promoted such changes. In the early 1890s, however, after Postmaster General Wanamaker officially blessed the idea of delivering mail to farmers, southern congressmen quickly took the lead in support of this novelty, and one, Tom Watson from Georgia, ever after claimed to be the "father of the R.F.D." In a sudden shift of opinion, Southerners, now arguing that the Post Office, like the army and navy, need not pay its way, cast aside the old principle of a self-supporting Post Office. They, as much as any group, were responsible for pushing rural free delivery of mails from an experiment in 1896 to a permanent part of the postal system in 1902.

Rural free delivery of mail quickly became the most expensive of all postal services, but perhaps nothing the national government had done through the long years following Appomattox did as much to unite the North and South, heal old wounds, and strengthen the bond of union between the two sections. Rural mailboxes along country roads and rural mail carriers, salaried by the government and making their rounds past isolated farm homes, became the new presence of the Union within the South and, unlike the post offices, were daily reminders of the beneficence of the national government. And the remarkable increase in the number of letters, uncensored periodicals, circulars, and daily newspapers that went to southern homes because of the daily mail service could only serve in the long run to shatter barriers between the North and South, soften old prejudices, and remove rural isolation.

Besides all this, rural free delivery of mail helped entice Southerners from their cherished principle of states' rights by encouraging them to appeal to the national government for aid in building their roads. For by threatening farmers with the loss of their mail service if they failed to keep their roads in good repair, the Post Office made southern farmers road conscious and helped force them into a national good-roads movement. At first, the good-roads movement merely aimed at teaching farmers how to improve their roads enough to prevent the loss of their rural mail routes; but when good road building and repair seemed beyond the capability of local governments, national aid for local road building became the movement's principal goal.

Years before, John C. Calhoun and Henry Clay had tried to bind the nation together with a system of roads and canals financed by the national government only to be rebuffed by the argument that this was unconstitutional, and from then until the twentieth century Southerners had consistently maintained this position. But now, threatened by the loss of their rural mail routes and, more important, impoverished by poor roads they seemed helpless to improve, they leaped over the constitutional barricade with the following logic: all roads over which rural mail routes ran were post roads; the national government had the power to establish post roads; "establish" meant build or repair, and so the national government had the power to help the states build or repair local roads. Even more, the government had not only the power but also a duty to help build local roads. It used the local roads to deliver the mail to farmers and therefore should help maintain them. Besides this, if rural free delivery could operate only where roads were good, then the national government must help build roads in backward areas so that the daily mail service could be brought to all farms in the nation.

Only a few years before, such ideas would have been heresy in the South, but now an Alabama senator, John H. Bankhead, could lead the movement to secure government aid for local road building and a congressman from South Carolina could suggest the change that had overtaken the South. "But coming here from the South," said Congressman J. Willard Ragsdale, "with our loyalty to this Government unquestioned, the people of the South want to stand behind this Government and occupy a place in it, and we ask but a small share of the appropriations." And so in 1916, exactly a hundred years after President Madison vetoed Calhoun's bonus bill, Congress enacted legislation "to provide that the United States shall aid the States in the construction of rural post roads."

The mail service, of course, was only one of many bonds tying the North and South together in the years following the Civil War, just as it was only one of many factors drawing the South from its states' rights position. But its role had been an important one, and how far it had helped lead southern representatives from the South's old principle was indicated by the fact that only two congressmen from the states of the old Confederacy—both from Texas—voted against the good-roads measure.

IV

Diffusion of Knowledge

The expression "diffusion of knowledge," like Daniel Webster's celebrated "liberty and union," had a special meaning for nineteenth-century Americans. It implied "mass communication," as the jargon of contemporary America would have it, but it meant more precisely the dissemination of political information among the mass of Americans for the special purpose of making self-government possible. The phrase was used at least as early as the 1790s and suggested the earnest conviction of Americans in those years that the success of their "government of opinion," as they called it, rested upon an informed public. "Wherever information is freely circulated, there slavery cannot exist," remarked Connecticut's Elbridge Gerry in 1791; "or if it does, it will vanish as soon as information has been generally diffused."

The American belief that knowledge, coupled with morality and religion, was essential to good government was not new, of course, in 1790. But the unanimity with which the nation's early legislators, conservatives and liberals alike, apparently

accepted the necessity for the diffusion of knowledge was remarkable. Since they were shrewd, perceptive, and even skeptical men, fully aware that what they called "error of opinion"
must circulate side by side with "sound doctrine" in an open
society, one might have expected them to have serious reservations about the wisdom of scattering information broadside
throughout the Republic. In fact, some of them did, as the Sedi-
tion Act of 1798 indicated. But this act was an aberration, and
the nation's postal history offers considerable proof that most
American lawmakers believed that, whatever the risks, the
people must be informed, especially on those matters relating to
the government.

As members of Congress saw it in the 1790s, political knowledge could be immediately diffused among the people in two
ways: first through newspapers and second by the free distribution of public information through the congressional franking privilege. Since these depended for success upon the postal
service, most of the great debates on the Post Office in Congress
from the 1790s to World War I touched in one way or another
on the need to retain the franking privilege and reduce the
postage on printed matter in order to develop an enlightened
public opinion.

Both objectives figured prominently in the nation's first important postal debate in 1791 and 1792. While President Washington was instructing Congress in the value of the Post Office
as an "instrumentality in diffusing a knowledge of the laws and
proceedings of the Government," members of Congress were
voting to give the franking privilege to themselves, postmasters,
and their constituents who wrote to them, on the ground that
the people must be informed. At the same time, and using the

same argument, they opened the mails to the country's newspapers.

Until 1792, newspapers had not been allowed in the mails, although ever since the Revolution postriders had carried them outside the mail by private arrangement with publishers. But now, convinced that the "circulation of political intelligence," as a committee in the House reported, was ". . . justly reckoned among the surest means of preventing the degeneracy of a free government," members of Congress not only permitted newspapers to be sent through the mails but to be sent at incredibly low postage rates. The same act that set the postage rate on a one-page letter going no farther than 60 miles at six cents, allowed a bulky newspaper to go 100 miles for one cent. One and a half cents was required for a newspaper going any distance, while the postage on a one-page letter going more than 450 miles was twenty-five cents. In addition, all newspaper editors in the nation could exchange newspapers with one another through the mails free of charge, and postriders could, if they wished, still carry newspapers outside the mails under their own arrangements with publishers.

Three years later, even this law was liberalized still further, so that every newspaper circulating within the state of publication paid only one cent postage no matter how far it went within the state. In that year, too, periodicals were first admitted to the mails, but at a considerably higher postage rate than newspapers. To mail their pamphlets or magazines, publishers had to pay one cent a page for the first 50 miles, one and a half cents between 50 and 100 miles, and two cents for every sheet going beyond 100 miles.

This generous postal policy, particularly with respect to newspapers, was perhaps the most important single element in the development of the nation's press. It meant that almost any ambitious young American with an old Franklin hand press, a printer's stone, some type, paper, roller, inking pan, and a bit of faith, hope, and the Post Office's charity thrown in, could set up shop in some prospective metropolis in the wilderness and begin printing a newspaper. And it made possible the greatest proliferation of newspapers the world had ever seen. In 1801, approximately two hundred newspapers were being published in the nation; some thirty years later, there were twelve hundred, the great majority of which were small, local papers whose editors scarcely knew from issue to issue whether another would follow. Located in widely scattered communities throughout the nation, fed in 1830 by 8,401 post offices and more than 115,000 miles of post roads, most of these newspapers were kept alive by the frank, cheap newspaper postage rates, and the free exchange.

The free exchange was really the foundation of the little newspaper in America. Without telegraph, television, or radio, with no Associated or United Press or money to have purchased such things had they been available, village editors had to rely for news upon the free papers they exchanged among themselves. When the mail came, they hurriedly scanned their exchanges, took whatever they wanted from what they read, and reprinted it in their newspapers, apparently without fear of plagiarism or copyrights. Like air and water, editorials as well as news seemed to belong to everybody, and one editor's thoughts were copy for another's press. But if the mails were late, as frequently they were, editors informed their readers of that fact and filled their newspapers with material on hand, such as letters someone in the community had received or George Washington's will, which once appeared in the *Palladium* at Frankfort, Kentucky.

Some of the items editors used as fillers when the exchanges were late or of little value were taken from the franked material sent them by their senators and congressmen and again cost them nothing. As the years went by, the amount of this franked matter—the speeches of members of Congress and volumes of documents containing reports from congressional committees and the various branches of government—became enormous. Some of these speeches and reports were sent directly to interested citizens, but many more went to the editors of small papers. There, in the little newspaper offices around the country, the volumes piled up to become, as one congressman noted, a kind of library which hot-headed citizens could use at election time to prove a point.

The little newspapers in rural America, whose offices so often bulged with government documents, were the special darlings of Congress, whose policies were deliberately designed to foster them and make them competitive with city newspapers. It was to protect them against the encroachments of the urban press that Congress set the postage rate a half-cent higher on interstate newspapers going more than 100 miles. And in 1851, when even this advantage seemed inadequate, Congress improved the position of the country press by providing that all weekly newspapers published within any given county might be mailed free to subscribers within that county.

Behind this move to protect the small country newspapers, besides the hope of informing the public, were many motives—the fear that the growing use of steam power by the city press would so reduce its cost that it would drive rural newspapers out of business, southern fears that urban newspapers were likely to be filled with northern ideas, and most of all, rural America's fear, as old as the nation itself, of urban America. "The poisoned sentiments of the city," said a North Carolina congressman as he argued to protect the rural press in 1850, "concentrated in their papers, with all the aggravation of such a moral and political cesspool, will invade the simple, pure, conservative atmosphere of the country, and meeting with no antidote in the rural press, will contaminate and ultimately destroy that purity of sentiment and of purpose, which is the only true conservatism."

Along with the fear that urban immorality would penetrate the countryside through urban newspapers went the belief that a monopoly of the city-controlled press, whose political atmosphere was "not always congenial to a spirit of independence," as a Senate report suggested in 1832, might undo democracy. "A concentration of political power," continued the report, "in the hands of a few individuals is of all things, most to be dreaded in a republic. It is, of itself, an aristocracy more potent and dangerous than any other; and nothing will tend so effectually to prevent it as the sustaining of the newspaper establishments in the different towns and villages throughout the country."

Time and again throughout the early nineteenth century, urban legislators demanded lower postage on interstate newspapers going more than 100 miles and tried in various ways to eliminate the discriminations in favor of the rural press. They argued that the government's policy bred a sectional press, nurtured sectional opinions, prevented citizens of one state from understanding those of another, and, in effect, limited the spread of intelligence. And this, in fact, was true, or partly true; but nothing could change the mind of Congress on this subject. County newspapers continued to go free through the mails, and the rural press was defended by paeans of praise from congessmen who regarded it as wholesome and virtuous and essential to democracy.

Notwithstanding all the arguments advanced to protect the country newspapers, Congress's solicitude for them was largely a tribute to their political power. Partly because the material brought to country editors by their cheap news service was mostly political in nature, their newspapers were far more politically oriented than the press is today. Virtually every newspaper supported a political party with passion; and almost every editor dipped his pen in vitriol and, to the delight of his partisan readers, flayed the opposition in such picturesque language that members of Congress became wary of supporting increased postage rates on newspapers lest they find themselves the object of some irate editor's attack. Happily, in the case of newspaper postage, the members could support the demands of newspaper editors for cheap rates. They knew that in doing so they were encouraging the spread of newspapers and the diffusion of knowledge as far as the farthest post road ran.

The political nature of American newspapers was an American phenomenon. It was noticed by Tocqueville, who marveled that the press was "the power which impels the circulation of political life through all the districts of that vast territory." And although he apparently did not see how Congress's postal policy was responsible for it, the keen Frenchman did observe that the vast number of newspapers reduced the political power of any one of them, prevented the control of American political thought by two or three large newspapers, and presented Americans with almost as many shades of political opinion as there were newspapers.

But the postal policy that helped make American newspapers

both political and cheap also contributed to their raffish tone. For it must be conceded that the cheap newspapers Congress nurtured catered, like modern television, to Mr. Everyman's tastes. This had something to do with their vulgarities, as one Englishman pointed out to his peers in the House of Lords in the 1830s. "Newspapers are so cheap in the United States," he said as he argued against cheap newspapers in England, "that the generality even of the lowest order can afford to purchase them. They therefore depend for support on the most ignorant class of people. Everything they contain must be accommodated to the taste and apprehension of men who labour daily for their bread, and are of course indifferent to refinement of language or reasoning."

The British lord indicated the limitations of Congress's policy of fostering cheap newspapers, but in suggesting, at least by implication, that the mass of the people had newspapers, he also revealed its success. So successful, in fact, had been the policy of putting newspapers in the hands of Americans that it had made them a "newspaper people," as one congressman said. Their appetite for news was insatiable, and the circulation of newspapers, from the members of Congress—who for years at the beginning of each congressional session voted to give themselves two or three newspapers at government expense—to the loneliest pioneer, was so widespread as to elicit surprised comment from many of America's foreign visitors.

Like Alexis de Tocqueville, Alexander Mackay, an English traveler in America in the 1840s, observed the great outpouring from the nation's press. "In connexion with American news-papers," he wrote, "the first thing that strikes the stranger is their extraordinary number. They meet him at every turn, of all sizes, shapes, characters, prices, and appellations. On board the steamer and on the rail, in the counting-house and the hotel, in the street and in the private dwelling, in the crowded thoroughfare and in the remotest rural district he is ever sure of finding the newspaper." Mackay also testified indirectly to the success of Congress's policy of supporting the rural press. "With us," he wrote, "it is chiefly the inhabitants of the towns that read the journals; in America the vast body of the rural population peruse them with the same avidity and universality as do their brethren in the towns."

The quantity of reading material that poured through the mail as a result of Congress's determination to inform the public grew from year to year like the postal deficit and created an enormous burden for the Post Office Department. In 1794, just two years after the passage of the act that started it all, the postmaster general complained that newspapers made up seven-tenths of all mail matter, and the number of newspapers mailed in relation to the number of letters only increased through the years. Visiting the Washington post office in 1832, one member of Congress noted that the southern mail for one day was composed of twenty bags filled with printed matter, and one bag, not quite full, of letters. That same year, it was estimated that the weight of the printed matter was fifteen times greater than that of the letters.

The department did its best to move all this mail about the country as rapidly as possible. Fortunately, as the mails grew larger the methods of transportation improved, and the department used them all, from the horseback rider to the fast train service, to speed the mails along. But even with better means of transportation, the tons of newspapers, periodicals, and government documents emptied into the postal service's circulatory system clogged the arteries, particularly in the antebellum days, and inspired a never ending stream of slow mails and poor service.

The loudest critics of this mail service were the newspaper editors, and a postal official's instructions in 1832 to a new mail contractor not to leave behind any newspapers addressed to an editor illustrated the Post Office Department's sensitivity to the power of the press. "If a newspaper to an editor should be detained," the official warned, "it would make more noise than to leave a hundred letters on commercial business."

The editors had their problems, of course. If their newspapers failed to reach their customers because of a breakdown in the mail service, the customers complained; or, if their own exchanges were late, or, as sometimes happened, never came at all, there was no news to print. But the irony of all this, which must have infuriated postal authorities, was that the poor mail service of which the editors complained was mostly caused by their own newspapers, which crowded the mails, multiplied the cost of the service, and never paid their way.

Newspapers, of course, were not expected to pay the cost of their transportattion. Their postage rates were far too low for that. In order to enlighten the public, Congress had, in effect, voted to subsidize newspapers and obviously expected the letter postage to make the postal service self-sustaining. But in the 1790s, when the policy had been formed, they had no notion of how successful it would be, of how many newspapers it would spawn, and of how quickly the cost of transporting newspapers would outrun the ability of the letter postage to pay for that transportation. In 1832, for example, as nearly as could be determined, when the weight of newspapers and pamphlets was said to be fifteen times greater than the weight of letters, it cost an estimated eight times more to carry the former than the latter.

This was bad enough from the viewpoint of the postmasters general, who had to balance the books, but those harassed public servants were as exercised by their inability to collect the postage due on newspapers as they were by the low rates of postage. According to the postal law of 1825, local postmasters were supposed to collect the postage due on newspapers three months in advance of delivery, and editors were supposed to secure their newspapers in open-end wrappers and certify the number they sent to other printers as well as the number of their subscribers.

The law was impossible to enforce. Editors refused to pay the postage on their newspapers in advance, and the postmasters, who were allowed to keep half of what they collected, found it virtually impossible to collect the money in advance from those who received the papers. And even when they were successful in their collections, a significant number of those free enterprising agents of the Post Office in the nation's little villages were as likely as not to pocket all instead of half the postage.

In the face of all these problems, the postmasters general, a conservative group on the whole, did the best they could to answer complaints, provide better service, keep the local postmasters honest, collect all the postage due on newspapers, and make the postal service self-sustaining. One postmaster general, Return J. Meigs, even went so far in 1814 as to forbid the mailing of books, because, as he later said, "the mails were . . . overcrowded with novels and the lighter kind of books for amusement," which he apparently felt scarcely diffused knowledge. Besides these things, the postmasters general worked hard to enforce the laws Congress passed as the service developed—laws to prevent the theft of newspapers from the mail, delay of the mails, and the mailing of wet newspapers, which were such a burden to stagecoach contractors.

None of this prevented postal deficits, and every attempt to strike at the heart of the fundamental problem by raising the postage rate on newspapers, periodicals, and pamphlets or by abolishing the frank accomplished nothing. Once, in the late 1790s or early 1800s, a change in Congress's policy of supporting the press might have been possible. After the War of 1812 it was not. By that time the press had become too powerful and the people too anxious to have their newspapers for the government to alter the policy. In 1822, for example, when the postmaster general suggested the elimination of the newspaper exchanges, the reverberations from the press were so great that Congress would not even accept a substitute measure providing for a limit of fifty free exchanges for every editor. The result was that by 1838 some editors were exchanging between five and six hundred newspapers, according to one report.

As the postal deficits climbed, especially in the 1840s, so did the pleas from the Post Office Department to raise newspaper postage rates, abolish the frank, and so eliminate the postal deficit. In 1846, Postmaster General Cave Johnson even attacked, obliquely if not boldly, the policy of spreading information by way of cheap postage on newspapers. Noting that there were already enough newspapers to disseminate knowledge to almost every community in the nation, he argued that there was no reason "why those who buy and sell newspapers should have the cost of transportation paid out of the revenues collected from the great body of the people." And like all postmasters general, at least from the 1820s on, he blasted the franking privilege that filled the mails year after year with tons of bulky government documents and increased the cost of transporting mail until it seemed impossible to make postage reductions.

There was no turning back. Postmasters general like Johnson, who inveighed against the franking privilege and the low postage rate on printed material, not only made no progress but lost ground. At mid-century the nation was growing fantastically. Texas, California, and the Mexican cession had just been added to the Union. The nation hummed with new enterprises—new factories, new railroads, shipping, farming, pioneering—and Congress, too, had more business to conduct. Consequently, printing presses were busier than ever. Now there were more newspapers—an estimated 55,000,000 were mailed in 1847— more speeches, and of course more government documents to mail, and the great postal acts, enacted between 1845 and 1852, only made their distribution easier.

The franking privilege, for example, was virtually untouched by these famous postal acts in spite of the great opposition to it. By 1844, petitions with some 15,000 signatures and resolutions from eight state legislatures had piled up in Congress pleading for an end to the frank, but still members of Congress refused to give up their cherished privilege. Hotly denying the charge that the pages of the documents were used only to line old trunks, they asserted that out in the villages and hamlets and on the farms of the nation, by candlelight and firelight, their constituents did read the government documents they received, and it was unthinkable to rob them of their right to know what their government was doing.

Local postmasters, it was true, had their franking privilege temporarily taken from them in 1845, and Congress agreed in 1847 to appropriate a certain sum of money to cover the cost of transporting franked mail. But the postmasters' privilege was restored in 1847, and the money Congress appropriated to pay for mailing their franked material probably never did so, particularly after 1852, when Congress provided that the *Congressional Globe,* which contained all the laws and debates of Congress, was to go free to all their interested constituents. How much this attempt to enlighten the public cost the Post Office Department no one will ever know, but from 1852 to 1873, when it gave way to the *Congressional Record,* the *Globe,* along with other government documents, did pass through the mails free of charge.

As for other printed material, it was to go cheaper than ever after mid-century, so that diffusion of knowledge could keep pace with the growing nation. In 1852, only one year after Congress had decided that weekly newspapers were to go free within the county of publication, it set the postal rate for newspapers mailed within the state of publication and weighing no more than an ounce and a half at a half cent apiece. Even more breathtaking in its generosity was the stipulation that newspapers weighing as much as three ounces could be sent to any place in the nation for only one cent. The rate was higher on newspapers weighing more than three ounces, but the postage on all newspapers was to be reduced by one half if it were paid in advance either quarterly or yearly at the post office of mailing or delivery. An added bonus for newspaper publishers was a provision allowing them to enclose within their mailed newspapers subscribers' bills and receipts which normally would have had to go under letter postage.

The vigor with which newspaper interests were defended in Congress in those years was disclosed by a New York congressman when, in 1852, a mild attempt was made to restrict the one-cent privilege to newspapers weighing two ounces or less. Denouncing this proposal, the congressman declared that the two- and even two-and-a-half-ounce limitation would force news- papers to print on light, flimsy paper which would in turn make them more difficult to read, ruin the eyes of countless Ameri- cans, and greatly impair the art of printing in America. That the two-ounce limitation might also adversely affect the distribution of two large New York newspapers—the New York *Courier and Inquirer* and the *Herald Tribune*—was presumably of much less significance to the congressman than what it would do to the eyesight of Americans.

By the time this act was passed, Congress was forced to do something about the mailing of books and periodicals. In 1825 the postage on periodicals had been reduced somewhat from the extraordinarily high rates established in 1794, but compared to the newspaper rates, those on magazines were still high. More- over, periodicals were allowed into the mails only at the discre- tion of the postmaster general. Nevertheless, after the War of 1812 the practice had been to permit magazines in the mails, and so lenient had been the policy that by the 1830s printed matter of all kinds passed over the nation's post roads as periodical material.

The benevolent attitude of the postmasters general plus the reduction in postage rates had much to do with the rapid rise of the periodicals in the quarter-century between 1825 and 1850. In that period, which became a kind of seedtime of the American magazine, the number of periodicals rose from something less than a hundred to about six hundred, ranging all the way from sophisticated publications like the *North American Review,* which weighed a pound in 1837 and cost twenty-five cents pos- tage, to the three-quarter-ounce *Missionary Advocate* that went through the mail for five cents.

Diffusion of Knowledge

Books, on the other hand, had no legal status in the mails. They were referred to in no postal law throughout the first half of the nineteenth century, and Postmaster General Meigs's policy of excluding them from the mails had apparently for the most part been followed. Consequently, in the late 1830s and early 1840s a mongrel publication—part periodical, part book, and part newspaper—developed. Adopting a format like that of a newspaper in order to obtain the cheap newspaper postage rates, but containing reprints of complete novels, two publications—*Brother Jonathan* and the *New World*—each weighing about a pound, found their way into the mails and brought literary masterpieces to a mass audience for the first time in history.

In his first annual report in 1841, Postmaster General Wickliffe complained of the injustice of transporting these huge newspaper-magazines all the way from New York to Louisville, Kentucky, for a cent and a half when it cost twenty-five cents to send a one-page letter that far. He asked Congress for postage rates that would discriminate between bona fide newspapers and mammoth periodicals. But Congress did nothing until 1845, when at last it raised the rates on such publications, thereby ruining the cheap reprint business. But *Brother Jonathan* and the *New World* left their mark on the book business. In their short existence they had set a precedent for the publication of the cheap novel that would be followed in years to come, and they had taught Americans to expect the cheap book. Never again would book publishers be able to charge as high a price for their books as they had before the appearance of these two newspaper-periodicals.

With the collapse of the cheap reprints in 1845, book publishers were relieved of an irritating source of competition, and their business improved amazingly. Some indication of the growth of their businesses was suggested by the census figures that showed that the value of their products had risen from an estimated $5,500,000 in 1840 to approximately $12,500,000 in 1850. This made it appear that Americans were well on their way toward "making a market for books which the old world has never dreamed of," as the editor of *Harper's Monthly Magazine* was to say a short time later.

Before Americans could reap the full harvest of all the newly published books and periodicals, the postage laws had to be changed. Books had to be admitted to the mails so that the average American could order and receive them directly from the publisher. And the postage on magazines had to be reduced so that the "sound sentiments" of those publications could be widely disseminated. For, as one congressman noted, the content of newspapers was changing, and Americans now had to "look to the magazines for much of the literary, scientific, and moral matters," which formerly reached them in their newspapers.

So in the summer of 1852, at the same time as they drastically reduced newspaper postage rates, members of Congress also eliminated the sixty-year-old postage discrimination between newspapers and periodicals and allowed magazines to go through the mails at the newspaper rate—one cent for every three-ounce magazine going any distance within the nation, and one cent for each additional ounce or fraction thereof; and, as with newspapers, these rates were to be reduced by one-half if they were prepaid.

Book publishers too found comfort in the mid-century postal laws. By 1851, books were admitted to the mails for the first time, and the next year they were given special postage rates. After September 1852 a book weighing as much as four pounds might be admitted to the mails at the rate of one cent per ounce for those going less than three thousand miles and two for those going a greater distance.

Under these laws, books, newspapers, periodicals, government documents, and the *Congressional Globe* poured through the mails in one mighty torrent, diffusing information, certainly, if not knowledge or wisdom, as the nation drifted into civil war. According to the census returns, the circulation of newspapers alone increased by 166 percent in the decade. At the same time, circulars and advertisements of all kinds were dumped into the mails. Many of these were printed to look like newspapers or periodicals in order to secure the cheap postage rates but were not, nor intended to be, bona fide newspapers or magazines.

The havoc this rush of mail created in the nation's post offices was exceeded only by that resulting from the booming postal deficit of the late 1850s. Not only was the bulk of mail considerably increased by the postal acts of 1851 and 1852, but those laws had also provided some three hundred different postage rates for the various kinds of mailed matter. These slowed down, if they did not paralyze, the postmasters' ability to determine the correct rate for any given piece of mail.

Furthermore, the reductions offered for the prepayment of postage merely added to the confusion and apparently made the process of collection little more effective than it had been. By 1862 some $200,000, according to the postmaster general, was being lost each year because of the department's inability to collect the postage due on newspapers.

To end this confusion over the rates, and hopefully to collect the postage due on newspapers and magazines, Congress took time in 1863, in the middle of the Civil War, to enact legislation demanding the prepayment of postage on newspapers and periodicals at the post office of either mailing or delivery and to group, for the first time, the mail into various classes. Letters composed the first class, and newspapers, periodicals, magazines, pamphlets, and even book-length manuscripts mailed between author and publisher, the second. All other printed material, except the franked items, of course, was placed in the third class and forced to go at a higher rate.

Still bent on disseminating information among the people, Congress, as always, favored newspapers and periodicals in the new law. Postage rates on these agents of enlightenment were graduated upward according to the frequency of their publication—daily, weekly, monthly, or whatever—but the average cost figured out at about a half-cent per copy. However, except for specimen copies of a publication some editor might wish to send to a prospective subscriber, only those newspapers and periodicals having a known list of subscribers and a known place of publication could obtain these cheap rates.

This law saw the nation through the Civil War, but the nagging old problems—the franking privilege and the inability to collect postage on second-class mail matter—remained. And when the war was over and new mail routes had to be built in the South and West and the volume of mail continued to swell, the postal deficit rose once more, rousing the anxiety of John Angel James Creswell, President Grant's postmaster general.

Before his elevation to the postmaster generalship, Creswell had never given any indication that he would be the kind of man to attempt to reform the postal service. But scarcely had he taken office before he began to complain about the postal deficit. He lamented the department's inability to collect the postage due on second-class matter and railed against publishers and businessmen who filled the mail with specimen newspapers and advertisements dressed up like newspapers in violation of the law.

It was against the franking system, however, that Creswell, a recent member of Congress who himself had enjoyed the privilege, aimed his heaviest blows. "It reduces the Department to a state of hopeless dependence," he wrote in 1869, "and destroys to a great extent its usefulness." According to a count made at the Washington post office for twenty days in January 1869, more than 32,000 pounds of franked letters were received and mailed, and over 200,000 pounds of documents were sent. Projected over a year, these figures suggested, he said, that the postal service had carried over 4,000,000 pounds of franked matter at a total cost closer to $5,000,000 than to the $700,000 Congress appropriated for the purpose.

Nor would Creswell accept the argument that the government must disseminate information through the use of the frank. "An unburdened press, managed and directed by private enterprise, can do more than Congress to enlighten the masses," he wrote. "Better by far that the franking privilege should be abolished, and that all newspapers sent to regular and *bona fide* subscribers . . . should be carried free without regard to weight, throughout the United States."

In his war on the frank, Postmaster General Creswell was helped by the undeniable fact that the privilege had become a national scandal. An estimated 31,000 government officials had the right to frank their mail, and many of them did so by using a stamp, or facsimile as it was called, bearing their names. But so often had these facsimiles been copied, loaned, or simply stolen, that hundreds, possibly even thousands, of unauthorized people were using them to frank their mail.

In the backwash of outraged protests against this practice,

Congress did abolish the facsimile stamp in 1869. But this partial victory over the franking evil was not enough. Postmaster General Creswell allegedly sent postal agents around the country to gather antifrank petitions at the rate of one cent a signature, and he and President Grant, supported by the nation's press, which was doubtless anxious to reduce the weight of the mails to protect its own mail subsidy, pushed Congress to eliminate the franking privilege altogether.

Matters came to a head in 1873. That year, in spite of old arguments like that of the Nebraska congressman who said his constituents rode twenty miles to get their government documents at the post office, Congress wiped out the franking privilege. In the winter when Congress reassembled and franked matter would normally have piled up at the Washington post office, the mails, for the first time in decades, departed with almost no government documents aboard.

If the loss of their franking privilege was a serious financial blow to the members of Congress, it at least gave them a good excuse for raising their pay, which they did at the same time they forsook the frank. Under the circumstances this was a reasonable adjustment which their constituents might have understood had the legislators been content with the raise alone. Unfortunately they also voted themselves a bonus by making their salary increase retroactive for two years, thereby turning their pay raise into an infamous "salary grab" that roused the anger of the nation and forced the chastened members to reduce their salaries to the old level the next year.

The salary reduction augured ill for Postmaster General Creswell's conquest over the franking privilege. Having lost their raise in pay, senators and representatives were naturally more inclined to regret the loss of the frank and to find arguments for restoring it. Actually this was not hard to do. For one thing, government documents continued to be printed, and now, mailable only at great cost, they were stacked in huge piles in the Capitol's document room, where they served as an argument for the restoration of the frank. It was wasteful, congressmen said, to print the documents only to have them gather dirt in the document room. Furthermore, the government was failing in its duty to diffuse knowledge. The free mailing of public documents, said one congressman in 1874, was "one of the many ways under our form of government in which we educate our people."

Fortunately for the lawmakers, some proof that government documents were educational came at this moment from members of a new organization of farmers called the Grange, who had set themselves to study better methods of farming and counted heavily on the annual reports of the commissioner of agriculture to help them. Their petitions demanding copies of these reports began reaching their congressmen in 1875, just in time to reinforce the case for the restoration of the frank.

Perhaps the most convincing argument members of Congress used to regain their franking privilege was that the frank's elimination had neither reduced the postal deficit nor saved the government much money, since more than a million dollars had to be appropriated annually to provide for the postal needs of various government departments whose officials could no longer use the frank.

So members of Congress timidly backed their way into a restoration of their franking privilege. In 1875, they gave themselves the right to frank the reports of the commissioner of agriculture as well as the seeds the commissioner had always distributed, and when the reaction to this proved to be tolerable, between 1877 and 1879 they restored their right to frank all government documents including the *Congressional Record*. Finally, in 1895, they gave themselves the right to send all their letters weighing no more than an ounce through the mails free, thus regaining virtually all the privileges they once had. The only losers in all these changes turned out to be the postmasters and those who wanted to write to their congressmen. Their franking privileges were never restored except for the postmasters' official business.

Postmaster General Creswell did not remain in office to see the undoing of his victory over the franking privilege, but before he left office in 1874 he had helped initiate a series of remarkable laws aimed at correcting the old and troublesome problem of collecting the postage on second-class mail matter.

Although the postal law of 1863 had attempted to stop evasion of the postal laws by providing for prepayment of postage on newspapers and periodicals at the post office of either mailing or delivery, postal officials discovered that collecting postage on these publications was still much like dipping water with a sieve. Somehow the postage due on second-class mail matter never found its way back to the department. An estimate made in 1874, for example, showed that more than 500,000,000 copies of the 5,871 newspapers and periodicals published in the nation in 1870 passed through the mails from 1869 to 1870. The total postage on these publications, even taking into account the papers that went free, should have been something over $2,000,000. Instead the department had collected just slightly more than $800,000.

The trouble was that newspaper and periodical postage was still usually collected at the post office of delivery rather than at the office of mailing. The problems this caused were explained to Congressman James Garfield by a village postmaster in the early 1870s. "I collect a hundred accounts every quarter for postage on newspapers," he told the Congressman, "or four hundred accounts a year, at nine cents each. . . . In doing so I have an infinite amount of trouble. A man comes in for his newspaper; he has not the money to pay the quarter's postage, or he cannot make the change, or I cannot make it, and I violate the law and let him have the paper for several weeks without paying the postage. He is a friend of mine; I do not want to make him angry, and finally I pay the postage out of my own pocket." Or, as frequently happened, the postage was not paid at all.

The solution, as anyone could see, was to collect the postage at the office of mailing, but the obvious was not the easiest. Reduced to its lowest terms the problem was, as it had always been, how to collect postage on second-class mail at the office of mailing and still not alienate the nation's publishers, who would, of course, have to pay the postage when they mailed their publications.

One possible way out of this dilemma, hit upon in the early 1870s when Creswell was still postmaster general, was to combine the collection of postage on second-class mail at the office of mailing with a drastic reduction of the postage rate. In this way publishers would be appeased by the reduced postage, and the Post Office Department, enabled at last to collect the postage due at the time of mailing, would perhaps receive more money than it had when the rates were higher but uncollectable.

This happy solution was accepted on all sides, so that between 1874 and 1885 postal authorities and members of Congress, assisted at times by publishers and representatives of chambers of commerce and boards of trade, ironed out a series of laws that revolutionized the way of mailing second-class matter. Taken together, these laws not only forced publishers to register

Diffusion of Knowledge

their newspapers and magazines with their local postmaster, who decided which publications might be sent at the reduced rate, but also instituted a novel collection system. No longer would postage on second-class mail be assessed by the piece and frequency of publication; instead, newspapers and periodicals would be weighed in bulk and charged so much per pound.

Reflecting both the government's old policy of diffusing knowledge and the power of the press, Congress established an astonishingly low tariff for this bulk mail. At first the postage was set at two cents a pound, and when even this seemed too high, it was changed in 1885 to one cent. This made it possible to send approximately eight papers for what it had previously cost to mail two. To obtain these rates, however, a publication had to be published at stated intervals—four times a year at least—to issue from a known office of publication, possess a legitimate subscription list, and have no bindings of board or cloth. It was also to be published for the dissemination of information of a public character or to be "devoted to literature, the sciences, arts, or some special industry."

Two other provisions of these laws, though passed with little debate, turned out to be important. One made it possible for publishers to mail *daily* as well as weekly newspapers throughout the county of publication postage free and to send sample copies of their publications to those not on their subscription lists at the second-class rate. The other put books in the third class and fixed their postage rate at a half cent an ounce.

So, at last, one hole in the Post Office's leaky collection system appeared to have been plugged. By forcing publishers to prepay the postage on their publications, Congress made the collection of postage on second-class mail not only possible but also more systematic. For collections were now made largely by those postmasters whose post offices were located in the larger cities where most of the second-class matter was mailed. In fact, about half of all postage received from second-class mail in 1877 was collected at New York, Chicago, Boston, Philadelphia, Saint Louis, and Cincinnati.

All this legislation, as revolutionary in its way as the new American industry taking shape in the period, was pushed through Congress with a battery of arguments slightly, but significantly, changed from those used in the antebellum period. Diffusion of knowledge had become dissemination of information, and although the spread of political information had, in the eyes of Congress, even increased in importance because of the vast number of immigrants who had to be Americanized, still the information to be disseminated had become much more encompassing. The postal service was now referred to again and again as the great educator of the nation, and as the terms of the legislation suggested, an educator not only of political affairs but of science, literature, art, and industry as well.

By making the postal service the great American educator, however, Congress opened Pandora's box in the middle of the Post Office Department. Practical Americans, always quick to discover the discoverable where profit was possible, found innumerable ways to use the new postal laws to their own advantage, and their ingenuity was truly remarkable. Hardly had the new second-class postal laws been written before businessmen began adding a bit of news to the house journals that advertised their businesses, publishing them periodically, drumming up subscription lists, and sending them through the mails as periodicals at the cheap postage rate.

More than this, the new postal laws begat an entirely new kind of magazine whose plain purpose was to advertise the products of assorted businesses. Beginning with a subscription list barely large enough to qualify for second-class postage, and sometimes with no bona fide list at all, the publishers of these magazines flooded the mails with sample copies of their publications, as the law allowed them to do, and urged their readers to "send a postage stamp and you will learn something to your advantage." What they learned was that whether they wished it or not, they had become subscribers to the advertising magazine.

In this way the publishers of the new magazines multiplied the names on their subscription lists, thereby increasing the circulation of their journals. This, in turn, attracted more and more advertising accounts to their magazines from businessmen who were impressed by magazines with large circulation lists.

But not content with their exaggerated subscription lists, the editors of the new magazines mailed literally thousands of sample copies, often as many as four or five to the same person, simply to build a greater circulation than their padded lists showed. One such magazine called *Comfort*, for example, circulating in the 1890s, claimed to have a subscription list of 750,000 but boasted of a guaranteed circulation of 1,250,000, perhaps the largest circulation of any journal in the country. Indeed, so great was the flow of sample copies, not only from the *Comfort* but from *Prices Current* and other similar journals, that one weary businessman who had the misfortune to be a "subscriber" to several, received nearly one hundred pounds of them weekly in spite of his repeated pleas that they cease.

As alarming as the development of the advertising magazines was to postal officials, however, it was no more so than the rise of the paperback books which the new postal laws fostered.

The origin of the paperback books in nineteenth-century America could be traced back at least to the early 1840s when

Diffusion of Knowledge

Brother Jonathan and the *New World* and their imitators were being published. But the cheap dime-novel paperback Americans knew in the post–Civil War years was developed by the Beadle brothers, Erastus and Irwin, who presented an unsuspecting public in 1860 with *Malaeska, Wife of an Indian Hunter*, a dime novel enclosed in orange paper covers.

Malaeska was number one of a promised series of such publications, and if the Beadles had not deliberately put their novels in paper backs and published them serially to secure the cheap postage rates accorded periodicals, they did, like all their competitors, take advantage of the low rates to send their dime novels from one end of the country to the other. Particularly was this true after the passage of the bulk mailing law of 1874, which, perhaps not accidentally, played into the hands of the Beadles and their many imitators and competitors. For having already begun in the 1860s to publish their novels periodically from a known place of publication, after 1874 they had only to show that their publications had literary merit and to swear that they possessed subscription lists to fulfill the requirements for second-class mail matter. This they were always able to do, and their books by the thousands entered the mail at the cheap second-class postage rate.

Sent to a sprinkling of subscribers but principally to book dealers in towns and villages not reached by the express companies, the paperback "libraries" and "serials" so familiar to Americans of the period poured through the mails like water over Niagara Falls until in 1891 Postmaster General Wanamaker reckoned their annual weight at more than 50,000 tons. One publisher alone, he noted, sent 1,600 tons of paperbacks through the mail annually, and at certain seasons of the year some publishers mailed as many as 2 tons of books a day!

Diffusion of Knowledge

Added to the bona fide magazines and newspapers that had always been mailed cheaply, this great flow of paperback books, advertising magazines, sample copies, and trade journals produced by the new postal laws increased the weight of second-class mail matter from 69,952,432 pounds in 1881 to a staggering 315,000,000 pounds in 1895. The postmasters general were forced to divide their time between worrying about the rising cost of handling the growing mountain of mail and trying to eliminate the abuses of the second-class mailing privilege. Needless to say, neither activity was particularly profitable.

Postmasters had the right, of course, to refuse the cheap postage rate to periodicals that did not meet the law's definition of second-class mail. But this right was not easily exercised. In the first place, postmasters were reluctant to exclude magazines from the cheap rate lest they be accused of censorship, a charge they were particularly sensitive to. But more than that, they could not always tell under the new rules which magazine should be sent at the cheap rate and which should not. Was the *Iron Age*, for example, a legitimate magazine or merely an advertising journal? Considerably more than half of its pages were used to advertise the products of various companies, but it also contained industrial information, specialized material to be sure, but valuable to those interested in such things and clearly within Congress's new definition of knowledge that could be sent cheaply through the mails. Besides all this, a postmaster's exclusion of some periodical from the second-class privilege was likely to lead to a lawsuit which the Post Office Department seemed predestined to lose.

This was true of the paperback books at least. In 1877, when the postmaster at Chicago refused to give Donnelley, Lloyd and Company's *Lakeside Library* the cheap postage rate, the company took the matter all the way to President Hayes's attorney general, Charles Devens, who reversed the postmaster's decision. Because of this landmark decision, for more than two decades it was impossible to exclude the paperback books from second-class mail.

But the decision was obviously in line with Congress's intention, for two years later, with the paperback publishers looking over their shoulders, members of Congress deliberately, albeit indirectly and a bit hastily, gave paperback publishers the cheap postage rate. They defined second-class mail as "printed paper sheets, without board, cloth, leather, or other substantial binding, such as distinguish printed books for preservation from periodical publication."

After that the postmasters general were helpless to dam the flow of reading material that streamed through the mail and included everything from the daily paper and *Century Magazine* to the *Old Sleuth Series*, the *New York Ledger*, *A Tale of Two Cities*, and *Prices Current*. Apparently only a law could stop it, but Congress, either still determined to diffuse knowledge or fearful of the publishers' wrath, or both, refused to interfere. Not even in the 1890s when Congressman Eugene Loud, chairman of the Post Office and Post Roads Committee in the House of Representatives, told his colleagues that the literature they were sending through the mail was trash, that the Post Office was losing more than $10,000,000 a year hauling second-class matter, and that they should support his proposal to deprive paperbacks and advertising magazines of the second-class rates, would Congress change the law. In fact, the Post Office Department even lost ground in 1894 when Congress forced it to give the second-class privilege to fraternal and professional journals.

Not until 1901, when the postmaster general, without waiting for a change in the law, challenged the old 1877 ruling and began removing the second-class privilege from publishers whose publications had no bona fide subscription lists, did the paperback and advertising magazine mail begin to diminish. This was not easily accomplished. In that very year, Congress decreed that the postmaster general could not suspend a publication's second-class privilege until its publisher had been given a hearing. These hearings came so rapidly—more than fifty cases in ten years—that special appropriations had to be made to hire a lawyer to defend the postmaster general's rulings.

Meanwhile, Congress had become occupied with the development of the rural free delivery of mail, which, as it turned out, proved to be another great boon to the nation's press and the policy of disseminating information.

Newspaper publishers had been among the first people in the nation to see the advantages of rural free delivery, and aside from the farmers themselves they were its greatest advocates. And why not? They knew as well as they knew anything that farmers would subscribe to daily newspapers if they had a daily mail service. And they also knew that since 1879 daily as well as weekly newspapers could be sent free in the mails throughout the county in which they were published. No wonder, then, that in 1891, when Postmaster General Wanamaker first began to drum up support for rural free delivery, he was able to enlist the editorial support of more than one hundred newspapers.

Pushed by such powerful friends and catapulted through Congress on the old diffusion of knowledge argument, the RFD spread like a prairie fire through the countryside in the early 1900s. As the editors had expected, the newspaper business boomed so spectacularly that a writer in the *Editor and Publisher* was convinced that daily newspapers had "never had such a boom in circulation as they have since the rural free delivery was established." In 1911, more than a billion newspapers and magazines reached farm homes over rural mail routes, and the RFD was being called the "great university in which 36,000,000 of our people receive their daily lessons from the newspapers and magazines of the country."

What proportion of all this second-class mail that reached farm homes over rural mail routes in 1911 was composed of magazines is not recorded, but it must have been large. For great changes had been taking place in the publication of magazines since the early 1880s, and by 1911 magazines were nearly as omnipresent in middle-class American homes, both urban and rural, as newspapers.

Between 1885 and 1905, the number of magazines in the nation had almost doubled—from about 3,300 to some 6,000. Besides those in existence in 1905, many had died along the way, so that possibly as many as 11,000 magazines had been published in the period. At the same time, the magazines themselves and the publishing business generally had changed dramatically.

Before 1885, the old standard magazines like *Harper's Monthly*, *Atlantic Monthly*, and *Century Magazine* had carried very little advertising. This was partly because most advertising in that period was done by local stores in local newspapers for a local clientele, and partly because advertising on a national scale, such as it was, had been largely taken over by the trade journals and advertising magazines.

But the production of goods for a national market that developed so rapidly in the post–Civil War years and the cheap second-class postage rates revolutionized the methods of advertising and the publication of magazines as well. Increasingly the nation's larger businesses who sought a national market took over their own publicity and began advertising in the old standard magazines. This, of course, was a bonanza for publishers, and not only inspired a rash of new magazines but also led the newcomers in the field to reduce the prices of their publications from a half dollar or so to fifteen cents.

At the same time that publishers were developing their cheap magazines, they also began filling them with articles that exposed the seamy side of American life. These periodicals demanded a purification of American society, offered blueprints for reform, and in the early years of the twentieth century, aroused the interest of the people both in reform and in the magazines. Coincidentally, all these changes in the publications of magazines occurred about the same time that rural free delivery of mail was rapidly being extended. This helped create a responsive market for the new magazines in rural America.

The result of this timely combination of circumstances was to increase the number of magazines sold, swell publishers' profits, augment the Post Office's burdens of transporting magazines pregnant with advertisements, and send the postal deficit soaring to such heights that both President Theodore Roosevelt and President Taft were forced to seek ways to reduce expenses. They had two choices: they could delay the development of rural delivery or they could raise postage rates on second-class mail. Neither approach was painless. One would rouse the farmers and their friends in Congress; the other was certain to antagonize the publishers.

President Roosevelt approached the question gingerly. He neither attacked the RFD nor called for higher second-class postage rates. Instead, in 1901 he directed Congress's attention to the abuses of the second-class privilege and noted that although second-class mail composed three-fifths of the weight of the mail, it paid in postage only $4,294,445 of the $111,631,193 it cost to operate the postal service. This was Roosevelt's final statement on the problem, but in the succeeding years, his postmasters general continued to dwell on the great loss the Post Office Department was sustaining by transporting second-class mail.

How great this loss was no one knew for sure, and beginning in 1905, Congress appointed one postal commission after another to find out, only to end up with a mass of uncertain statistics. So disorganized was the department's bookkeeping system, it was said, that it was all but impossible to determine the cost of any one service. But not all the effort was in vain. The first of these investigations led the Post Office in 1906 and 1907 to conduct the most systematic weighing of the mails ever made, demonstrating beyond much doubt that the old policy of diffusing knowledge was costing the government a pretty penny.

Fortunately for President Roosevelt, the commission's most significant report showing a loss on second-class mail, together with a bill to overhaul the entire Post Office Department, was not completed until 1909, too late for him to consider it before leaving office. And so it was left for the hapless Taft, as unlucky a president as his predecessor was lucky, to take action on the report. And, in fact, by the end of 1909 President Taft could scarcely ignore the report even had he desired to do so. For the postal deficit stood at $17,500,000 and a deficit in the national Treasury was imminent. Taft sent word to all departments to "cut to the quick," and in his State of the Union message pounced upon the problem of carrying second-class mail. Going beyond the commission's report, which had not specified the Post Office's exact loss in carrying newspapers and magazines, Taft reported that it cost nine cents a pound to handle this kind of mail and that the government was losing $63,000,000 a year on it.

Because magazines were usually carried a much greater distance than newspapers, authorities believed more money was lost on their transportation than on newspapers. For this reason, Taft's solution to the second-class postage problem, worked out by his postmaster general, Frank H. Hitchcock, was to charge magazines with two postage rates—one cent a pound for that portion of the magazine devoted to educational material and four cents a pound on that given to advertising. But periodicals whose mailings weighed less than four thousand pounds and those which the postmaster general might consider newspapers if he chose—weeklies, for example—were not to come under this regulation.

In the long history of diffusing knowledge through the postal system, Taft was the first president to make such a direct assault on the nation's publishers; and the publishers, long accustomed to postal subsidies, struck back at the president's proposition through their organization, the Periodical Publishers of America, and in the pages of their magazines with a myriad of arguments that cast some interesting reflections upon the complicated problem of postal-rate-making, the publishers, and the Progressive period itself.

Most of what the publishers wrote in opposition to the president's recommendations for second-class mail appeared first in a statement made by the Periodical Publishers of America. Charging that the president's figures were incorrect, they pointed out that no one, not even the postal commission, knew exactly what it cost to handle second-class mail matter, and that the Post Office was so badly managed it was impossible to tell. Indeed, they argued, if a proper accounting had been made, it would have shown that periodicals brought more money into postal coffers than they took out because their advertisements stimulated much of the lucrative first-class mail.

Where then, did the postal deficit come from? It came, according to the publishers, from the costly establishment of the RFD, from overpaying the railroads, from subsidizing steamship companies for carrying the mail, and possibly from the inefficiency of the department. After all, they noted, the Canadian Post Office carried second-class mail matter more cheaply than it was done in the United States, and profitably, too.

Moreover, the publishers pretended not to understand why President Taft had singled out magazines and not newspapers for higher postal rates if second-class mail matter were carried at a loss. Could it be that the president was more sympathetic toward newspapers than periodicals? With Kansas senator Joseph Bristow many of them believed that the drive to raise the postage was political and not financial and that the president was attacking the periodicals because they had not supported his conservative administration. "I believe that behind this there is a desire to suppress some of the magazines," said Senator Bristow, "instead of encouraging the dissemination of literature."

This suspicion was sharpened by the suggestion that the postmaster general could decide which papers were periodicals and which were really newspapers that could qualify for the cheap postage rate. This power gave the postmaster general, in effect, they said, the right to decide which periodicals would live and which would die, and the implication was that those that had been outspoken against Taft would be periodicals; the others would be newspapers. "This bill," wrote one irate lawyer,

Diffusion of Knowledge

"would make splendid legislation in Russia, but it is diabolical in free America."

This charge was never proved, of course, and its veracity was questionable. In any case, Postmaster General Hitchcock answered every objection the publishers made point by point, showing exactly how the Post Office Department had arrived at its statistics on the cost of carrying second-class mail, disclosing a communication from the Canadian postmaster general showing that the Canadian Post Office too had lost money carrying second-class mail, denying that he sought autocratic power over the mail, and suggesting that the proposed new postage rates would not destroy the magazines.

A number of newspapers too, relieved no doubt that they were to be spared the increased rates, sided with the postmaster general and chided the magazines for their many exposés of the selfishness of others when they themselves were standing at the public trough. "The magazines," said the Boston *Herald* in 1911, "have been having a glorious time in the past decade running amuck among the men and combinations leading the finance, industry, commerce, and politics of the country; they have spared neither age nor sect; they have been shriekingly virtuous and passionately denunciatory; they have unveiled graft; they have impugned motives; they have lambasted leaders and derided dynasties; and they have set up a spartan standard of honesty and a heroic code of patriotic ethics. . . . Now the shoe is on the other foot; and the common man is grinning at the preachers, patriots, and purists who appear to be much the same predatory patriots the 'interests' and the 'trusts' were alleged to be. . . . The magazines are getting for a penny something that costs the Government nine pennies."

Diffusion of Knowledge

But none of the arguments used by Postmaster General Hitchcock and his supporters were strong enough to defeat the magazines. The president's proposals were turned down in 1911, and not until 1918, when President Wilson's postmaster general, Albert Burleson, was in charge of the department, did Congress advance the postal rates on magazines. At that time a new scheme was proposed providing that the postage charged for the educational material in second-class mail matter be raised to one and a half cents a pound and that the postage on the advertising portion therein be increased from zone to zone according to the distance such matter was carried from the place of mailing.

Once again the publishers protested. Arguing that the contemplated zone system would prevent magazines from circulating far from their places of publication because of the increased costs, they maintained that such a system would create a sectional press at the very time there was need of promoting national unity. But this was a wartime measure, and Congress was less inclined to listen to the publishers when so many sacrifices were being made than it might otherwise have been. In any event, the zone act was passed about as Burleson had proposed, and second-class postage rates were at last increased.

Except for the temporary wartime increases during the War of 1812, this raise in postage on printed material was the first since postal rates had been established in the 1790s. For well over a century, Congress had steadily reduced the postage on reading material to push its policy of diffusing knowledge. Like many such policies of the national government this one was nobly conceived, selfishly used, and defended with specious arguments. But in its primary purpose it was successful beyond all expectation. It contributed immeasurably to the democratic

process and made Americans as a whole perhaps the best informed people in the world in the nineteenth century.

How this had been done was summarized in a speech given to
a New York audience by Postmaster T. L. James in the 1880s.
"The constant tendency of our postal system has been toward
the extension of the privileges of the mails in every branch of
correspondence and every form of literary production," he
said. "Its facilities first made possible the cheap publication of
newspapers, and later on standard works of literature by placing
upon all periodical popular reading matter the lowest rate of
postage ever known in a civilized land. In no other country have
the masses ever before enjoyed such an inestimable intellectual
privilege, and no money expended by the Government in any
of its multiform agencies has ever conferred such enormous
advantages."

But the old policy of diffusing knowledge did not end with
the increase in postage rates in 1918. From that time to 1970, during which information became so abundant that the bad threatened to drive out the good, newspapers and magazines were
still carried through the mails at a fraction of their cost. Newspapers still circulated cheaply through the county of publication, and members of Congress clung stubbornly to their franking privilege. And perhaps it is still true that most of the useful
knowledge that enters American homes comes not through the
airwaves but through the mails.

V

Government Business versus
Private Business

The American Post Office, unlike those of Europe and England, was never allowed to develop its full potential as a business. Government owned and operated and spread through a nation almost fanatically devoted to free enterprise, the American postal service was much like a stranger in the land, whose possible contributions to society were restricted by the political and economic presuppositions of those whose country he inhabited.

Most nineteenth-century Americans believed, theoretically at least, that monopoly, which the Post Office surely was, was bad; that competition was the unexcelled regulator of the economy; that Congress had no right to coerce private property; that any extension of the postal power the Constitution had given Congress was dangerous; that free political institutions could not exist without free enterprise; and that the government should never do what private enterprise could. All these ideas and their corollaries were used, at one time or another, to limit the growth of the Post Office.

Nevertheless, there were some Americans—cranks and reformers mostly, but joined in the early 1900s by a large segment of middle-class people—who thought otherwise; and because of their attempts to extend the postal service and the traditionalists' efforts to restrict it, the Post Office became a kind of testing ground for the economic theories Americans cherished. In the inadequacies of the postal service, champions of free enterprise found an argument against socialistic experiments. On the other hand, those who saw the abuses of unbridled capitalism as the nineteenth century wore on pointed with pride to the Post Office as an example of the benefits a government-owned business might bring to the people.

The arguments over the Post Office's proper place in the economy were long and heated, but in the end Congress, in purely practical fashion, almost always opted for the proposition that the postal service must not compete with, but must support, private business. The result of this twist in the doctrine of free enterprise was that the Post Office was given numerous unprofitable assignments to help the private sector of the economy at the same time as it was forbidden to engage in business ventures from which it might have profited.

In the nation's early years, the dogmas of free enterprise did not much trouble the architects of the postal service. Probably because of the colonial experience, the men who wrote the Constitution had few qualms about giving Congress the right to establish post offices and post roads. And few there were in those days who thought this power could be used to augment the power of the central government. "The power to establish post roads," wrote James Madison in the *Federalist Papers* in

1788, "must in every view be a harmless power, and may perhaps by judicious management, become productive of great public conveniency."

Nor did Congress or the early postmasters general hesitate to use strong measures to secure efficient postal service in their first brush with private enterprise. In 1794, following a precedent established in the colonial period, Congress authorized the postmaster general to have the mails carried on private stagecoach lines. This was done because the mails had already become too heavy for horseback riders to manage alone and because it was thought that the letters and newspapers would be better protected from robbery and weather in stagecoaches than on the backs of packhorses. But it was also done—and this was typical of Congress's double use of the Post Office—to encourage stagecoaches, subsidized by postal money, to go where they otherwise would not have gone and thus establish a transportation system throughout the young Republic.

Because competition was assumed to be the surest road to the lowest price, Congress directed the postmaster general to secure bids from stagecoach lines for carrying the mail over the post routes. For six weeks, later twelve, he was to advertise throughout the areas where the post roads ran. His advertisements were to note both the manner and frequency with which the mail was to be carried—daily, weekly, or whatever. When the bids were in, he was expected to make a contract with the lowest bidder, but he was allowed to consider such other factors as the reliability and sureties of the bidder before awarding a contract.

Armed with this authority, the postmaster general immediately contracted with stagecoach lines to carry the mail, and so began the Post Office's long association with the nation's private transportation companies.

Government Business versus Private Business

Not everything that went wrong in this early relationship between private enterprise and the government was the fault of the private businesses. Snowdrifts and bottomless roads, broken wheels and broken axles, runaways and irascible ferrymen were all beyond the control of these early captains of the nation's transportation companies. Nor was it true that all private contractors were scoundrels who gave the least amount of service for the money or that good mail service was never obtained. For the most part, the mails did get through, if late, even in the most trying times.

But postal officials learned very quickly, as Postmaster General Gideon Granger noted, that the first concern of the stagecoach operators was not the mail but passengers; and the history of the relations between the Post Office and stagecoach lines is filled with violated contracts, broken promises, and poor service. Too frequently, stage drivers passed the post offices at which they were supposed to pick up the mail without stopping, arrogantly refused to keep their time schedules, waited for passengers at inns beyond the time alloted by the Post Office Department, and missed connections with the stages with which they were supposed to exchange mails.

Then, too, they frequently failed to put the mail in the stagecoach boot where it would be protected and often dumped it off at post offices along the way in such haste that papers and letters were mangled beyond legibility. Even worse, if the coaches were filled with passengers and space was at a premium, they abandoned the mail altogether, particularly the newspapers, leaving them to come by the next stage if possible. "The newspaper mail is now conveyed in canvas bags," wrote one early traveler on the mail stagecoach, "and a portion of these are thrown off at the stage office whenever the conveyance of passengers requires. In a journey from New York and back again last fall I witnessed this in many cases. Since then I have understood why the newspaper mail miscarries when the letter arrives."

In the first decade of the nineteenth century, the Post Office officials met this poor service with a bold experiment which few questioned at the time. So bad had the stagecoach service between Baltimore and Philadelphia become by 1799 that Postmaster General Habersham established a government-owned stage line there, prescribing along with schedules and other regulations even the specifications for the United States mail coach. "The body painted green," he wrote, "colors formed of Prussian blue and yellow ochre; carriage and wheels red lead mixed to approach vermillion as near as may be; octagon panel in the back, black; octagon blinds, green; elbow pieces or rail, front rail and back rail, red as above; on the doors Roman capitols [*sic*] in patent yellow 'United States Mail Stage,' and over those words a spread eagle of a size and color to suit."

Upon this line government stages operated successfully for more than a decade in spite of the harassment of the private coaches that attempted to drive them from the road. After three years, the government's equipment on the line was valued at $16,000 and had shown an estimated profit of more than $11,000. "For the last year and a half," wrote Postmaster General Granger, who had succeeded Habersham in 1801, "the fare of the travellers has defrayed the expenses of the establishment, and the actual profit has been for that time equal to the whole expense of transporting the mail." Furthermore, the mail had been carried with speed, regularity, and safety, thus proving that it could be done.

This experiment was successful enough that Congress, still

apparently unworried about the philosophical implications involved, considered extending the government stages from Portland, Maine, to Louisville, Georgia, and had this been done the history of transportation in the nation might have been altogether different. But for one reason or another—probably because of the large initial cost of such a project—the line was never established.

That it was not the fear of government ownership that prevented Congress from undertaking this venture was suggested by Postmaster General Granger's establishment in 1810 of another government line from Philadelphia to New York, where the private lines had given unbelievably bad service. This government line, although not as financially successful as the other had been, did nonetheless carry the mail with such regularity that it seemed worth the expense. At least this was the opinion of Postmaster General Meigs, who followed Granger.

Early in his administration, Meigs had attempted to turn this line over to private stagecoach operators, but the only bid he received had been so exorbitant that he had continued the government line, which operated, as he wrote, "as a check upon contractors, both in repressing, and stimulating contractors to a faithful discharge of their duty." It was, in fact, a kind of nineteenth-century yardstick by which to measure the performance of private enterprise.

After the War of 1812, however, the mood of the nation changed, and if this period did not mark the "end of Arcadia," to use one historian's description of the era, it did at least signal the beginning of a new and vigorous business activity. Manufacturing had grown during the war until it was more than the handmaiden of agriculture, and the country teemed with new industrial enterprise and hopes of profit. In the new era, Congress imposed the nation's first out-and-out tariff to protect American manufacturers and established the second national bank. Reflecting the new enthusiasm for private business and free enterprise in this period, General Meigs ended the government-owned stagecoach lines shortly after the end of the war, and the government ceased to compete with private businesses in carrying mails and passengers.

With the disappearance of the government-owned stage lines, the Post Office lost the yardstick it had used to gauge the cost and service of the private companies and had to resort to two devices to keep them in line: detailed contracts which specified the contractor's exact obligations in carrying the mail and, of course, the competitive bid.

The detailed contracts did help as long as the postmaster general was unafraid to penalize contractors who failed to fulfill their duties. Postmaster General John McLean, for example, vigorously imposed fines on mail contractors for contract violations in the early 1820s, and unlike his predecessor, would accept no excuses for failure to perform the service. But the competitive bid, through which Congress tried to take advantage of the great regulator of the economy, very early showed those flaws which, like recurring epidemics, were to trouble the Post Office throughout the nineteenth century.

Private contractors, shrewd businessmen that they were, had not been slow to learn all there was to know about how to make competitive bidding ineffective. In order to hold their routes when contracts were renewed, they hired straw bidders, irresponsible men who offered ridiculously low bids for mail routes, received their contracts, then failed to perform the service, thereby virtually forcing the Post Office to do business with the old contractor, often on his terms. Or contractors would offer one bid for a large number of routes, so that postal officials, unable to determine the low bid for each route, often gave all the routes to the large contractor as an easy way out. But their most effective trick was the improved service routine.

Apparently this began innocently enough. A contractor would make a low bid and discover upon receiving the contract that he really could not carry the mail for the contract price. So he would ask the postmaster general for additional money, pleading that he could not continue to carry the mail if more money were not forthcoming. And postal officials, always under pressure to get the mails through and hesitant to take the time to advertise for new bids, frequently increased the contractor's stipend even if it meant going above the prices other contractors had offered in their bids.

So common had this practice become by 1825 that Congress attempted to restrict it with a law declaring that no money above the contract price was to be given a contractor unless additional service on that route was required. But most contractors, if they thought long enough, could find a reason for improved service, and what began in innocence ended as a deliberate method for squeezing more money from the Post Office. By the 1830s, routes were being changed from weekly to triweekly, from triweekly to daily, and from horse to coach, all with improved service, to be sure, but not always necessary.

In 1831, for example, a contract for carrying a weekly mail by horseback over two routes in Pennsylvania was let for $275 a year. The next year the service on the routes was improved to a triweekly mail carried by a four-horse coach at a cost of $4,500 a year, and the contract was given to James Reeside, one of the nation's largest mail contractors in those years. In 1833, the routes were again improved, and a daily mail service was installed at a cost of $7,411 a year. So in less than three years these routes had been improved from a weekly mail service served by horseback to a daily service transported by a four-horse stage; but when Congress began an investigation of the Post Office, the routes were reduced to a weekly horseback service at a cost of $605 a year. No one seemed to know why the improved service had been made in the first place, although it was probable that the postmaster general had made the changes either because some congressman or local businessman had demanded them or because he wished to extend the passenger service of the Reeside lines.

Contractors also knew—particularly those who were growing rich at the game—that to retain their contracts it helped to have a friend at the Post Office, and many did. When their contracts were being let, they descended on Washington like so many guests at a barbecue and could be seen day and night trooping about the city, talking to their friends in the Post Office and presenting their sureties to postal officials. They were, in fact, important politically, so much so that President John Q. Adams, probably at Henry Clay's suggestion, once took more than a hundred of them on a tour of the White House, even showing them the upstairs rooms. And when President Jackson succeeded Adams in the White House, two hundred contractors called to pay their respects to the new president.

In their efforts to evade the purposes of the competitive bids and defraud the Post Office the contractors were, of course, aided by postal officials, as investigations through the years indicated. This collusion, for which postal officials were more roundly censured than the businessmen who perpetrated the act, raised the cost of mail transportation considerably and in time became an argument for transferring the Post Office to private hands.

Government Business versus Private Business

But given the same handicaps postal officials had, it is doubtful that private businessmen could have negotiated contracts much more successfully. Unable to own its transportation system, which might have helped, the Post Office Department was at the mercy of powerful contractors who wanted more money for their services, businessmen and citizens who wanted better mail service, and congressmen who represented all these interests and pounded incessantly on the doors of the department, demanding action. What private businessmen might have done under these circumstances no one knows, but it seems logical to suppose that they would either have curtailed the postal service or raised postage rates. Probably they would have done both.

In any event, the postmasters general did the best they could, and in the 1830s stagecoach lines were carrying the mail over more than 17,000,000 miles of roads annually, not with regularity one could set his watch by, to be sure, but with reasonable satisfaction. Almost as important as this, however, was the fact that the Post Office had so organized the stagecoach lines, sending them where they would never have gone under the profit motive and forcing them to coordinate schedules with other lines, that one could travel by stage throughout most of the settled portions of the Union by 1830. The price came high, however. By postrider and sulky the cost of carrying the mail in 1829 was five cents a mile and by stagecoach, thirteen cents.

By that time, however, the afternoon of stagecoaching in America had already come, for its existence was even then being threatened by steam power. In 1807, when Robert Fulton first experimented with a steamboat on the Hudson River, that threat was scarcely observable. But sooner than anyone had reason to expect, a new era in transportation had begun. In 1811, a steamship named the *New Orleans* made its way down the

Mississippi River to the city of its own name. Five years later, the *Enterprise* steamed from New Orleans to Louisville, and the age of the steamboat on the Mississippi had begun.

In the meantime, 1813 to be exact, Congress had authorized the Post Office to transport the mail by steamboat, and soon wherever steamboat and stagecoach lines paralleled one another along the seacoast and the rivers of the nation, steamboats won both passengers and mail contracts from the stages. Early in 1829, when Andrew Jackson made his way by steamboat from Louisville to Pittsburgh on his way to his inauguration, the mails were being carried about 300,000 miles annually by steamboats.

The principal importance of the steamboats to the mail service, however, was not so much their competition with the stagecoach as their inauguration of the age of steam transportation in America. For they were the harbingers of steam engines that came riding upon iron rails to crisscross the nation and doom the stagecoach business.

The railroad era really began at Baltimore on 4 July 1828, when Charles Carroll, last surviving signer of the Declaration of Independence, turned a spadeful of earth to mark the beginning of the building of the Baltimore and Ohio Railroad. The directors of the railroad, who gathered to watch the ceremony, had planned the development of their road carefully. Not content with the $10,000 or so the government had already spent to survey the railroad for them, they were soon demanding that Congress invest funds in the enterprise, reduce the cost of iron by lowering the protective tariff on iron imports, and grant them permission to build a lateral line through the District of Columbia.

And why should the government do all this? Partly because,

so members of Congress argued, of the great help the railroad would be in carrying the mails. It was a good argument and bore fruit in time. True, Congress never invested government funds in the early railroads as it did in the building of canals, but it did give the Baltimore and Ohio the right to build through the District of Columbia, and it did reduce duties on iron imports, so that throughout the 1830s the government gave perhaps as much as $5,000,000 in reduced tariffs for the building of railroads.

Since this had been done for the railroads so that they might be used to improve the carrying of the mails, it came as a shock to postal authorities to learn that the railroad managers, like the stagecoach operators, were determined to squeeze every penny they could from the Post Office.

The first intimation of what the relations between the Post Office and the privately owned railroads would be came in President Jackson's administration while Amos Kendall was postmaster general. In 1835, it became possible to travel from Washington, D.C., to Boston by steam power. One could go from Washington to Baltimore on the Baltimore and Ohio Railroad, and with the help of steamboats, from there to Philadelphia via the New Castle and Frenchtown Railroad. Again combining steamboat travel with the Camden-Amboy Railroad, it was possible to go from Philadelphia to New York and from New York to Providence by steamboat, and from Providence to Boston on the Boston-Providence Railroad. And all this could be done in just thirty-seven hours! Such speed caused one writer to wonder if it were real or a dream and inspired Kendall to try a bold experiment.

With visions of sending the mail from Washington, D.C., to Boston in thirty-nine hours, allowing for half-hour stopovers at

Government Business versus Private Business

Baltimore, Philadelphia, New York, and Providence, Kendall sent his agent that year to negotiate contracts with the railroad managers by which they would agree to carry the mails and coordinate their train schedules so that the mails could go through without interruption.

It was an exciting prospect, but the reception Kendall's agent received made it clear that railroad managers felt they were under no obligation to carry the mails cheaply. The Baltimore and Ohio Railroad demanded $250 a mile per year to carry the mail from Washington to Baltimore and even refused to carry just one box of daily mail over the route for $100 per mile annually.

The other lines were no more cooperative. To carry the mail from Baltimore to Philadelphia, the railroad owners wanted $320 per mile; the Camden-Amboy Railroad asked $300 for its cooperation; and one of the companies outside New York demanded $250. And all this came at a time when the House Committee on Post Office and Post Roads had unanimously agreed that the postmaster general might go as high as $75 a mile per year for carrying the mail by rail! Under the circumstances no contracts could be written with the railroads, and what mail was carried by rail in the early 1830s was carried by private arrangements between the mail contractors and the railroads.

It was a discouraging beginning for the managers of the Post Office, but only a foretaste of what was to come. The railroads had a firm monopoly, and the old contract procedures worked out with stagecoaches to take advantage of competition broke down completely with the railroads. Without competition, bids for the railroads' services were as meaningless as appeals to the railroad managers' patriotism, and for the first time the postmaster general was without a lever with which to pry better rates from the transportation companies the Post Office had to do business with.

In the late 1830s, as the railroads fastened their rails upon more and more miles of the countryside, thereby making themselves all the more indispensable to the mail service, they continued to treat the Post Office like a cast-off beggar. Not only was the Post Office forced to pay most of what the railroads demanded, but it also had to accept the poor service they gave.

Unlike the stagecoach operators, the railroad managers would not rearrange their schedules to make connection with other trains or stagecoaches. Indeed, such contracts as were made between the Post Office and the railroads left scheduling completely in the hands of the latter. Nor would the trains at first travel at night to hurry their mails to their destinations. When at length they did do this, they demanded enormous sums of money.

To reach some kind of understanding with the railroads, Congress made all railroads post roads in 1838 and authorized the postmaster general to pay as much as 25 percent more for railroad transportation than was paid for similar service in the stagecoaches. The postmaster general scarcely knew how to interpret "similar service," but the next year Congress permitted him to pay as much as $300 per mile per year to some railroads for carrying the mail. But even this was not enough. The service remained poor, and the railroads' demands for more money were incessant. Before he left office, Andrew Jackson, raging at the railroad monopoly, suggested the possibility that the United States might "without transcending their constitutional powers, secure to the Post Office Department, the use of those roads by an act of Congress which shall provide within itself some equitable mode of adjusting the amount of compensation."

Government Business versus Private Business

In short, what President Jackson was suggesting was the possibility that Congress force the railroads to take the mail on whatever terms it chose to make. But neither the president nor Congress really wanted to force the railroads to do their bidding, and certainly most members of Congress did not believe it could be done. Congress was convinced that the railroads' state charters protected them from the national government. More important, railroads were private property and few people in that day believed the government could coerce private property, as the expression went.

High prices, poor service, and the inability to control a private monopoly were not, however, the only problems the railroads presented the Post Office in these years. Inadvertently, they also plunged the postal system into the greatest crisis of its history. By cheapening and improving transportation, the railroads made possible a private business in carrying letters outside the mails that so depleted postal revenues by 1844 that people were talking about the imminent collapse of the Post Office.

Given the American's penchant for finding ways to make money, some citizen sooner or later was bound to see in the developing railroads the possibility of carrying packages, money, and messages from city to city by rail for a price. Sooner rather than later, by 1839 as it happened, William F. Harnden, a Massachusetts Yankee, began traveling the rails and steamboats carrying packages in his carpetbags and his customers' messages in his head. Very quickly he was followed by Alvin Adams, another Yankee, and within two years by more than fifteen others whose companies in 1843 were transporting large numbers of letters outside the mails every day.

Until then the express companies had handled letters more or less covertly, since it was an unlawful practice. But that year the Post Office Department brought suit against the Adams Express Company for violating the postal monopoly and lost. After that, the express companies openly established what amounted to an opposition post office, advertised their services, and boasted of their superiority over the regular mails.

And in some ways they were superior. Not only could they take letters from town to town faster than the Post Office could, but because of the Post Office's high postage rates they could do it more cheaply. Besides this, they often delivered the letters they carried directly to the homes of the addressees.

But the express companies carried only the profitable mail. They took the letters and left the large, unmanageable mail—the newspapers, franked matter, periodicals—sent at the cheap and unprofitable postage rate for the Post Office to handle. Nor did they even attempt to carry all the letters, but took only those entering the busy trade between cities. The occasional letters sent over the long and expensive routes of the South and West were still carried by the Post Office.

So the express companies took the cream of the business and left the rest to the Post Office. But even so, a number of literate men of that free-enterprising age, convinced that the government should play no overt role in the economy, used the example of the Post Office as proof of their conviction that a private business was superior to a public one. And through press and periodical they began an assault upon the postal monopoly and its competition with private business. According to one journalist writing in 1840, the Post Office was "wholly at war with our free institutions"; and William Leggett, the caustic critic of monopoly and editor of the *New York Post*, wrote: "We are ourselves, inclined to the belief, that if the clause in the federal charter which gives Congress the control of the Post Office had never been inserted, a better system would have grown up under the mere laws of trade."

Not even the Post Office's struggle to carry the mail to the far reaches of the nation impressed the advocates of a privately owned Post Office. If a private business owned the Post Office, "the solitary squatter in the wilderness might not," admitted a writer in *Hunt's Magazine* in 1840, "it is true, hear the forest echoes daily awakened by the postman's horn, and his annual letter might reach him charged with a greater expense than he is now required to pay. But there is no place on the map which could not be supplied with mail facilities by paying a just equivalent; and if they are now supplied for less, it is because the burden of post office taxation is imposed with disproportional weight on the populous sections of the land."

Near mid-century, then, the nation was troubled by two great monopolies—one public, one private. On the one hand stood the railroads, arrogant and powerful and apparently determined to exact the last penny for carrying the mails; on the other, the Post Office, rapidly being crushed by what seemed to be excessive railroad charges for mail transportation and by private business's invasion of the postal monopoly. In this crisis, Congress had several choices: it could turn the Post Office over to private enterprise, force the railroads to reduce their rates for transporting the mails, or find another solution.

Unwilling to make a drastic move, Congress picked the third possibility and in 1845 attempted to solve the situation with three provisions. That year it passed a law providing stiffer penalties for those who violated the postal monopoly; at the same time it reduced the postage rate in the hopes of luring letters back to the regular mails. And it also tried to appease the railroads with a law classifying all railroads according to the size and importance of the mails they carried and the speed with which they were conveyed. Those in the first class could be paid as much as $300 per mile per year, those in the second, $100, and those in the third, $50.

This law did save the postal monopoly and the Post Office. In time, the business of carrying letters outside the mails between cities dried up and moved to the cities themselves, where private concerns established city delivery systems. But here, too, Congress came to the rescue of the Post Office. It first made all the streets post roads, then established city free delivery, which gradually took away most of the private companies' business. In 1860 when the successor to D. O. Blood and Company's delivery system in Philadelphia was ended by court action, the Post Office's struggle with competing mail companies was won.

But the law of 1845 did little to curb the railroad monopoly so that the mails could be carried more cheaply and efficiently. The railroad management continued to ignore the pleas of the Post Office Department to rearrange schedules and provide faster service. Nor would they consent under any circumstances to the postmaster general's partial control of their schedules. They had, of course, their own reasons, and good ones too, for sending their trains at the speed they desired and at the times they wished, but they sometimes seemed to go out of their way to give poor mail service. Some railroads, like the New York and Philadelphia Railroad, even refused to carry free of charge the department's mail agents who accompanied the mails from town to town.

Worse still, the railroad managers made a mockery of the classification scheme by simply refusing to sign contracts to carry the mails. Instead, they carried the mail on a day-to-day basis, always threatening to throw it off without a moment's notice, so that the postmaster general was never quite sure whether the railroads would carry the mail or not. By 1859, fourteen years after the classification system had begun, the mails on 137 of the 318 railroad routes were being carried without contracts. These were among the most important routes in the nation, according to the postmaster general, and yet they refused to "enter into engagements with the department which the law and the highest interests of the postal service demand."

By the time of the Civil War, then, the struggle between the two great monopolies was still going on, and though it was true that the cost per mile for carrying the mail by rail had decreased slightly, the cost was still enormous when compared with that in other nations. While the Canadian Post Office, for example, paid $30 a mile for moving its mail by rail in the daytime and $40 for nighttime service, the American department paid between $50 and $300 per mile, and its total cost of railroad transportation had increased in just twenty years from $432,568 to $3,349,662. These were grim figures to those in the Post Office Department who contemplated the future. For it was already obvious that as the railroads penetrated the more sparsely settled areas of the land carrying smaller and smaller amounts of mail yet demanding increasing sums of money for their services, the costs would be tremendous and the returns small. Moreover, there seemed to be no escape from this, for the railroads had become indispensable to the postal service and were to become even more so in the 1860s, when a new method of distributing the mails through railroad post offices was developed.

The idea of a railroad post office in the United States developed on the Hannibal and Saint Joseph Railroad in the early 1860s. In July 1861 this railroad began to carry the mail from the East to Saint Joseph, Missouri, where it connected with the great overland stagecoach mail to the Far West. From the start of this route there had been trouble. Before the incoming mail could be transferred to the stagecoach line, it had to be sorted at the Saint Joseph post office. Since the train was sometimes late anyway, the additional time it took to sort the mails often made it impossible to make connections with the departing stagecoaches. To prevent this, the assistant postmaster at Saint Joseph, William A. Davis, got permission from the Post Office Department to board a railroad car long before it reached Saint Joseph and there begin to sort the mail so that when it reached Saint Joseph it could be transferred immediately to the stage-coach.

From this beginning, the idea of a railroad post office was pushed along by George B. Armstrong, postmaster at Chicago in the 1860s, who was authorized by Postmaster General Montgomery Blair to begin a railroad post office experiment on the road between Chicago and Clinton, Iowa. The superiority of this method of handling the mails was so readily apparent that it was only a short time before the railway post offices in specially constructed mail cars were placed on all the important railroad mail routes and a division of the railway mail service was established under Armstrong's superintendency.

The railroad post office was regarded as one of the wonders of the age. Before their establishment, distributing post offices had been located here and there across the country where the mail was sorted out and sent to other destinations. Before the Civil War, for example, all letters for New England that passed through Galena, Illinois, were sent to Boston to be distributed, and all those for Wisconsin and Michigan were sent to the distributing office at Chicago and there rerouted to the proper post offices in those states. With the new railroad post office, however, much of this sorting and distributing of the mail could be done on the train as it sped along at thirty or forty miles an hour, and many of the old distributing offices gradually disappeared.

But the new postal cars cost money to build and operate. For one thing they had to have heat and light. And so the railroad managers argued that their compensation under the old classification system established in 1845 was no longer just or adequate. Of course they had been saying this before the postal cars had been invented, but now they had a new string to their bow, and the results of the first real weighing of the mails they carried, ordered by Postmaster Alexander Randall in 1867, supported their claims.

The weighing of the mails in 1867 was conducted by the railroads themselves and thus was open to some suspicion, but whether it proved they were underpaid or not, it did show that scores of injustices had crept into the old classification system. On four routes receiving $300 per mile, for example, the weight of the daily mails ranged all the way from 22,581 pounds on a route between Baltimore and Washington to 7,668 pounds on a route between Baltimore and Cumberland. In another classification, a route between Xenia, Ohio, and Cincinnati carrying 9,385 pounds of daily mail received $225 per mile, while the same amount was paid a route between Cincinnati and Hamilton carrying only 2,518 pounds. True, the weighings did not take into account such things as the importance or the speed of the mails, but even so the inequities in the system were too apparent to be ignored.

So in the late 1860s the railroads apparently had some legitimate complaints against the Post Office. At least both Postmaster General Randall and his successor, John Creswell, believed they did, and both urged Congress to make changes. Added to these recommendations in the early 1870s was a threat from a group of railroad directors that they would withdraw postal cars from service unless their compensation was adjusted upward.

In 1872, in the face of this pressure, Congress rewrote the old law of 1845 and tried to shift the burden of decision to the postmaster general by allowing him to increase the pay of the railroads by as much as 50 percent if need be, knowing full well he could not do this without bankrupting the Post Office. Of course he did nothing, and the whole question was thrown back into Congress's lap in 1873.

That year a bill was drawn up proposing to pay the railroads largely on the basis of the weight of the mails they carried over the entire length of their routes. A sliding scale ranging from $50 per mile per year for carrying 200 pounds of mail a day to $200 for carrying 5,000 pounds per day was established and to this was added extra money for the use of railway post office cars—$25 per mile a year for cars forty feet in length, and $30, $40, and $60 for cars forty-five, fifty-five, and sixty feet long. All together, according to the bill's sponsors, the new law would add some $500,000 to the cost of mail transportation on the railroads.

The bill came before the Senate at the same time midwestern farmers were forming Granges across the land to attack the railroad monopoly, and no doubt this had something to do with the hostility with which it was greeted in the Senate. In any case, Senator John Sherman of Ohio, not always given to criticizing the railroads, jumped upon their directors, denouncing as unfounded their contention that the railroads made more hauling pig iron than they did the mails and suggesting that this bill would cost more like $1,500,000 than $500,000. Yet what could be done? A number of senators believed they had no choice but to vote for the measure, for unless they did, the railroad directors would remove the postal cars from the service.

It was the old dilemma Congress had faced many times already—the powerful monopoly pitting its strength against a Congress that could not coerce private property. "What, then, is the poor predicament of the Congress of the United States?" asked Senator Justin Morrill of Vermont. "Do we have to yield to their demands?" Congress, said another senator, was going to have to act strongly. Commerce and the Post Office were linked, he said, and the question must be decided whether Congress had a right to regulate this commerce between the states.

Words, words, words—but Congress was not yet ready to defy the railroads. The day after he had criticized the railroad directors, Senator Sherman found that he must support the bill because it was necessary to replace that clause in the law of 1872 authorizing the postmaster general to raise the rates by as much as 50 percent.

So the bill passed and became law. Immediately new mail weighings were made and the new compensation set, and the cost of mail transportation on the railroads rose the next year, not by $500,000 as the advocates of the bill had anticipated, but by almost $1,500,000, as Senator Sherman had predicted. And of course the postal deficit, for which inefficiency, politics, and mismanagement were often blamed, increased accordingly.

But unfortunately for the railroads, this law was passed in the year of the great panic, and the slack economy that followed this catastrophe forced Congress to reduce the railroad compensation by 10 percent across the board in 1876 and by another 5 percent two years later. The 1876 law also provided that all railroads to whom Congress had given land on the explicit understanding that the mails were to be carried on such railroads "under the direction of the Post Office Department, at a reasonable price" were to receive only 80 percent of what others received for carrying the mails.

The reaction of the railroads to these unprecedented reductions was swift and predictable. The four great railroad lines in the East passed their reductions along to their employees in 1877 by cutting their wages 10 percent, an act which led, incidentally, to the great railroad strike that paralyzed the nation that year. Besides that, some of the most important railroads withdrew special mail trains from the service, refused to maintain the regular postal car service, and ignored requests to improve train schedules. Only by favoring certain lines with special mail weighings, by the generous use of a special fund Congress had appropriated "to obtain proper facilities," and by remitting fines charged for the failure to perform service were the postmasters general able to induce the large roads to give respectable mail service throughout the next decade. Not until the mails had grown heavier and the ordinary railroad compensation had become larger was the department able to discontinue these more or less irregular methods of securing adequate rail transportation for the mails.

The great power of private businesses in conjunction with the economic and political ideas of the period that made it impossible for Congress to coerce the railroads also prevented the Post Office from encroaching on private telegraph and banking enterprises, both of which might properly have come within the jurisdiction of the Post Office as they had in other nations.

By the first years of the 1870s, when Congress changed the method of compensating the railroads, the debate over a postal telegraph had been going on for nearly three decades. It had begun as far back as 1838, when Samuel F. B. Morse had come to Congress asking for money to help him test the electromagnetic machine he claimed could send messages by wire from one place to another. Indeed, he had already proved this much. What he needed was equipment to string wires for a hundred miles or so to show the feasibility of sending messages over long distances. Unable to obtain private capital to back him, he begged Congress for an appropriation for five years, and finally, in 1843, $30,000 was appropriated for that purpose.

To some congressmen, Morse's experiment seemed foolish in the extreme, and Cave Johnson, congressman from Tennessee, had contemptuously submitted an amendment to Morse's appropriation proposing that half the fund be given to experiments in mesmerism. But Johnson was ignored and the experiment went ahead. A telegraph line was stretched from Washington to Baltimore, and when the Democrats met in the latter city in May 1844 for their nominating convention, everyone heard that Morse's machine had just sent the message "what hath God wrought" from Baltimore to Washington.

By the next year, the Post Office Department had charge of the experiment, and, ironically, Cave Johnson, now President Polk's postmaster general, earnestly recommended that the government assume ownership of the telegraph.

Congress had every reason to follow Postmaster General Johnson's recommendation. It had always been a rule of the Post Office that intelligence, as they called it, should never travel faster than the mails. The reason for this was simple. In the slow-moving world Americans inhabited in the early nineteenth century, news was golden to anyone who could get it ahead of the mails that gave it to everyone. Word of trouble in Europe

Government Business versus Private Business

obtained before it became common knowledge, or even the weather in Alabama, might be enough to give a cotton speculator all he needed to know to make a fortune in the cotton market. To prevent such speculation, and to give everyone the same information at the same time, the mails had to travel as fast as man, and the Post Office Department through the years had gone to great expense to see that private messengers did not outrun the mails.

Postmaster General McLean had become sensitive to this problem in the 1820s when the importance of rapid communication between the great cotton market at New Orleans and the money market in New York became apparent. From that time and for years afterward, at least until the Civil War, maintaining a speedy mail service between the two cities became one of the important preoccupations of the Post Office Department. But this was not the only route in the nation that concerned the department, and so great was the need for speed on certain routes around the country that Congress authorized the postmaster general to use pony expresses in 1836, years before the famous Pony Express from Saint Joseph, Missouri, to Sacramento had been thought of.

Having learned from this experience that the mails should be delivered ahead of, or at least at the same time as, private messages, postal officials were determined that the Post Office should control the telegraph. For here was an innovation capable of flashing news about the country as fast as sound. In the hands of the government, the telegraph could be used to give news to all the people at the same time. In the hands of private ownership, it could become a monopoly to be used for private gain. "In the hands of individuals or associations," wrote Postmaster General Johnson, "the telegraph may become the most

Government Business versus Private Business

potent instrument the world ever knew to effect sudden and large speculations—to rob the many of their just advantages, and concentrate them upon the few. If permitted by the government to be thus held, the public can have no security that it will not be wielded for their injury rather than their benefit."

Besides the urgent recommendations of the postmaster general—made in two successive reports—the House Ways and Means Committee wrote a report in 1845 favoring government ownership of the telegraph, and that same year a bill was submitted to Congress providing for the building of a telegraph line from Washington to New York. Meanwhile, Samuel Morse himself continued to operate his telegraph line under the direction of the Post Office and professed to be willing to sell the machine to the government for $100,000 in order to prevent its falling into private hands.

But suddenly there was a lack of interest in government ownership of the telegraph. The editor of the New York *Post* wrote in late 1846 that if the telegraph "were to become the property of the government, it would suffer as all enterprizes [sic] suffer, which are taken out of the hands of individuals. It would cost more; it would be less punctual; there would be less anxiety to obtain custom[ers] by efforts to accommodate the public."

Apparently this was what Congress thought too. In any event, the telegraph bill was never acted upon, and even Postmaster General Johnson seemed to have had a change of heart. "The operation of the telegraph between Washington and Baltimore," he wrote in 1847, "had not satisfied him that under any rate of postage that could be adopted its revenues could be made equal to its expenditures."

So Congress let the telegraph slip from its grasp, and soon Morse's invention found its way into private hands. Dozens of private telegraph companies were born overnight. Telegraph poles suddenly sprouted along the nation's roads and railroads as mile after mile of message-bearing wires were hauled aloft and strung from pole to pole, while down on the ground such confusion spread that a telegram from New York to the frontier town of Chicago would have to pass through as many as four companies.

Not all companies could make money, however, and gradually the larger swallowed the smaller until by the 1870s, scarcely twenty-five years after Morse's great success, the Western Union Telegraph Company operated some 93 percent of the miles of wire and stations in the country, transmitted 90 percent of all messages, and had, in fact, become, as a committee in the House of Representatives noted, a "receptacle for failed and insolvent telegraph companies."

Shortly after the Civil War, then, Postmaster General Johnson's worst fears about a private business's control of the telegraph had been realized. A congressional committee reported in 1870 that the directors of Western Union had made such exorbitant charges, doubling and quadrupling their rates in the West and South as compared with those in the East, that they had built up colossal fortunes for themselves and had even been able to pay dividends and extend their company's lines from their profits rather than from their capital. Even more disturbing was the company's control of the news through the New York Associated Press.

The origins of this association went back to the early days of the private telegraph companies, when, as had been expected, speculators began using the telegraph for their own purposes. In the late 1840s, steamships sailing from England to America habitually touched first at Halifax, then sailed on to the United

States. But before they reached Boston and New York the European news they had left in Halifax had already reached the hands of speculators through the telegraph that ran from New Brunswick to Boston. A public outcry against this misuse of the telegraph led in 1848 to the formation of the New York Associated Press, a group of seven New York newspapers that began to collect and make public the market reports as they poured into New York by telegraph. At the same time, they also began gathering and distributing the general as well as commercial news.

In time, as Western Union came to dominate the telegraph business, the New York Associated Press sold its commercial reports to Western Union's commercial department, and the rest of its news it sold to various press associations around the country. Then, by a mutually beneficial agreement made in 1865, Western Union agreed to work with no other than the New York Associated Press, and the New York Associated Press in turn agreed that all its news items sold to other associations would be sent over Western Union wires.

In this way the privately owned telegraph had spawned another great monopoly, one that struck at the freedom of the press itself. For the New York Associated Press could deny its facilities to any newspaper and so limit that newspaper's effectiveness and possibly even destroy it. "No newspaper has obtained a position as a first-class newspaper," reported a congressional committee in 1870, "without the Associated news."

Alarmed by this monopoly, some members of Congress made an attempt in 1866 to wrest the telegraph from private hands and turn it over to the Post Office as England was about to do and as had already been done in European countries. But Europe was not America, and Europeans, perhaps less troubled by economic dogmas, could do what Americans could not. Postmaster General William Dennison, who had been appointed by Lincoln and was still serving when this issue arose, thought a postal telegraph unwise partly because of "its questionable feasibility under our political system," and most members of Congress, boasting of the businessmen who had built the largest telegraph system in the world, agreed. If there was a problem here, the remedy, they believed, was more competition.

Accordingly, Congress enacted legislation in 1866 giving all companies then formed or to be formed equal rights in developing telegraph lines in the hope that somehow this would promote more competition in the field. But apparently there were nagging doubts that this would break the monopoly or lower the cost of sending telegrams. For the law also provided that private companies must send government messages at certain specified rates and that all companies then in existence must agree to sell out to the government within five years if it was believed this would serve the public interest.

This law was only a paper tiger as far as the control of Western Union was concerned, but the debate over it provoked a controversy between advocates of public and private business that disturbed the peace of Congress for seven years. During this time, petitions supporting a postal telegraph cascaded upon Congress, speeches were made, bills were drawn up, and so many hearings were held on the subject that the president of Western Union complained he could not get his work done because he was spending so much time in Washington testifying before congressional committees.

By coincidence, the struggle over a postal telegraph was brought to a head in the early 1870s at the same time Congress was haggling over the compensation to be paid the railroads for carrying the mail; and, surprisingly, the man who led the fight for the government-owned telegraph was President Grant's postmaster general, John A. J. Creswell.

Before becoming postmaster general, Creswell had been a Maryland politician with no apparent predilection for attacking private business interests. But Creswell was a nationalist who gloried in the strength of the government and its institutions. Galled by Western Union's attempt to renege on its responsibility to send government messages at prices fixed by the postmaster general, as it was supposed to do under the law of 1866, he began to fear the day when Western Union, as its president had already prophesied, "would soon be without competition"; and with more courage than caution, he jumped into the fight for public ownership in 1871 with a recommendation that Congress establish a postal telegraph.

The next year he not only repeated this recommendation, but to the despair of nineteenth-century advocates of free enterprise he renewed, with emphasis, an earlier recommendation that Congress establish postal savings banks and use the deposits from these banks to build the Post Office's telegraph system.

Although postal savings banks had been used successfully in England since 1861, they had scarcely been mentioned in America until Creswell made his recommendation, possibly because they seemed unessential to an agrarian people. By the time the recommendation was made, however, more and more Americans were accumulating a little spare money, and it was obvious that postal savings banks would be a great boon to those who had been accustomed to hiding their money under a mattress or behind a loose stone in the chimney.

Such banks, so the argument ran, would be as near to all

Government Business versus Private Business

Americans as their post offices and as safe as the government itself. They would pay an interest rate of perhaps 2 percent, encourage habits of thrift among the working class, draw money —so desperately needed in the nation at the time—from its hiding places to stimulate the country's business, and make it possible for migratory Americans who deposited their savings at the post office in Dubuque, Iowa, to draw them out in San Francisco.

Because there would be no runs against postal savings banks, they would promote economic stability and prevent financial panics. Then, too, deposits in these banks could be used to absorb a portion of the national debt and so prevent the outward flow of dollars that went to pay the interest on government bonds held by foreigners. And, finally, postal savings banks would protect those least able to protect themselves against swindlers, unsafe deposits, and unwise investments, and at the same time increase the investors' loyalty to the government by giving them a stake in a stable economy.

Postal savings banks and the postal telegraph too, both successfully tried elsewhere, seemed logical and useful extensions of the postal service. But both encroached upon the vast domain of private enterprise, and both found a dozen articulate enemies for every outspoken supporter. In Congress, the opponents of these measures saw them as dangerous to the nation's institutions. The political party in power, they said, would control the telegraph for its own purposes, and postal savings banks would drive private banks to the wall. Hordes of office seekers would fill government jobs in both businesses, and both would be mismanaged, inefficient, and costly, and serve the public less well than privately managed businesses.

On the whole, however, the advocates of government ownership had the longer, if not the sounder, list of arguments. The privately owned telegraph was, they said, a monopoly much more dangerous to the nation's free institutions than a government monopoly would be. Already it controlled the press and hindered the development of new publications. It did not extend to all places in the nation as a postal telegraph would and so served the public badly; and because of its high monopolistic rates, the telegraph was too expensive for common people to use even when it was located where people had access to it. "In this wide field of operation no money-making privilege should be tolerated," wrote Postmaster General Creswell in 1873. "As well might a charter be granted for the exclusive use of air, light, or water . . . as to restrict for the sake of profit the use of electricity, that most subtle and universal of God's mysterious agents."

As for postal savings banks, supporters brushed aside the arguments that they would compete with private banks. Those, they said, who would deposit their money in postal savings banks would not, in any case, put it in private banks. This was surely the lesson to be drawn from the fact that in the 1870s scarcely more than 2,000,000 of the nation's people had bank accounts. Postal savings banks, their proponents argued, were for those millions who either did not trust private banks or found it inconvenient to use them.

Good as these arguments appeared to be, they were not good enough to counter the opposition of private business and the main current of the day's political and economic ideas. Postmaster General Creswell resigned his post in June 1874, almost surely because of the pressure of businessmen, and his replacement, Marshall Jewell, a Connecticut businessman, returned to the old ideas concerning the government's relationship to private enterprise. "There must be a limit to government interference with private enterprise," he wrote in 1874, "and happily it better suits the genius of the American people to help themselves than to depend upon the state."

Probably most members of Congress received this message with a sigh of relief. In any case, proposals for a postal savings bank and a postal telegraph were quickly buried in congressional committees where many legislators, no doubt, hoped they would be forgotten. But somehow they were not. True, President Cleveland's two postmasters general in the 1880s had no interest in them, but postmasters general who served the Republican presidents in the period gave ringing endorsements to either the postal telegraph or the postal savings bank and sometimes to both. Postmaster General John Wanamaker not only supported a postal telegraph in the 1890s and attacked the overpayment of compensation to the railroads, but also urged upon Congress the establishment of a parcel post system and so threatened the existence of the private express companies.

Since the 1840s, when they had caused the Post Office so much trouble, the express companies had grown enormously wealthy. By 1890 a handful of them, including Wells-Fargo, the American Express, and the Adams' Express, had carved up the nation among themselves. Each had a virtual monopoly in its section, and there, protected by their arrangements with the railroads, who profited as the express companies profited, they charged what the traffic would bear and so became another odious monopoly. Like the United States postal cars, express cars were attached to passenger trains and moved their customers' merchandise at least twice as fast as freight. In this way they carried everything that had to be moved in a hurry—from money to oysters.

Such service was much superior to anything the Post Office

had to offer. In 1879, over the protests of the express companies, Congress had provided that packages of merchandise no larger than four pounds might be sent through the mails at the flat rate of one cent an ounce. A four-pound package, in other words, cost sixty-four cents to mail whether it was going two miles or two thousand, and as it turned out this provided no real competition to the express companies. Americans sent their small packages going long distances by mail to take advantage of the flat rate and sent their other packages, large and small, by express. Of course, the Post Office lost money transporting packages over long distances for a flat rate, and it was mainly to capture the short-distance package business and so offset the losses on the long-distance trade that Wanamaker proposed a parcel post system similar to those in European countries.

Wanamaker's administration of the Post Office stretched from 1889 to 1893, the very years his proposals were more likely to get a hearing in the nation than at any previous time. For the mood of the country was changing. The rapid growth of industry had thrown the country out of balance and created great cities, monopolies, and a budding proletariat; in addition, it had disturbed old notions about individual opportunities and raised new problems that could be settled only by the national government. In these times, the old ideas concerning the proper relationship between the government and private enterprise began to come unglued as more and more Americans began to believe the government ought to own and operate some businesses for the benefit of the people.

Now, at last, the Post Office was no longer a stranger in the land, and just as it had once been used to illustrate the ineffectiveness of a government-operated business, so now it became the example par excellence of efficiency for all those who wanted to put the government in business. In what was surely one of the greatest tributes ever given it, it was described by one observer in the 1890s as a "model of efficiency after which the corporate managed railways might well pattern."

Traditionally the Post Office had been especially popular among rural people, who associated it with the flag, freedom, and all things American, and having learned the value of a government-owned business from their observation of the Post Office, they found it altogether reasonable that the government could carry their corn to market as easily as it brought the mail to their post offices. It was only natural, therefore, that the Populist party, which sprang from their midst in response to the hard times of the 1890s and the rapidly changing economic conditions, should have advocated the government ownership and operation of the railroads and the telegraph and telephone lines and the establishment of a postal savings bank at the same time Postmaster General Wanamaker was recommending these things to President Harrison.

Defeat came to the Populist party in the 1890s, as it did to all third parties of the period, but Populist ideas lingered on to be endorsed by middle-class Progressives of the early 1900s. Soon many of the old economic assumptions were under attack everywhere, and one by one the Progressives pushed through reforms that had been unthinkable in an older America. And in the wake of the new attitudes the Post Office was finally allowed to perform some of those services the British and European post offices had long been offering.

In 1910, after the nation's bankers had been assured that they would be able to dump their low-interest-bearing bonds on the new postal savings banks and thus free themselves to acquire new government bonds at a higher interest rate, the postal savings system was established. Two years later the express companies had to accept the creation of a parcel post business managed by the Post Office. Following this, the Post Office was even allowed to promote a farm-to-table movement for the purpose of transporting food from the farm directly to customers in the cities through parcel post, and this in turn led to an ill-fated and short-lived motor transport service owned and operated by the government.

From the postal savings bank and parcel post, Congress turned, in its reform-minded mood, to the railroads and the perennial problem of how much to pay them for carrying the mail. From the late 1870s to 1912, no Congress had failed to discuss the matter, and in that time five major investigations had been made to determine what it really cost the railroads to haul the mail. Masses of black statistics were compiled, and the commissions reported learnedly on the costs of rail transportation per linear foot, wrote knowingly of the differences in carrying passengers, express, and the mail, and made recommendations which were never acted upon. For the mass of figures, like the sphinx at Thebes, posed a difficult riddle, and after all the investigations, Congress never seemed to know any more about the cost of transporting the mail by rail than it had before.

Admittedly the subject was complex, and the truth seemed to be that neither the Post Office nor the railroads had more than a shadowy notion of how much it cost the railroads to move the mail. Because the railroads lumped together the expense of carrying passengers, express, and the mail, there was no way of determining just how much it cost to carry the mail alone. But it did appear—not strangely perhaps—that the Post Office was helping the railroads defray the cost of carrying passengers just as it had helped the stagecoaches in an earlier day. This seemed particularly apparent throughout the West and South, where passenger traffic was light.

Whatever the fact, railroad managers would never say, though repeatedly asked, what it actually cost to carry the mails. Instead, they resisted every effort to reduce their compensation and complained bitterly that they were underpaid for their services. They objected vigorously to the expense of moving the mails from the depot to the post offices, which, in some cases, they had to do. They also argued, with some justice, that because the department weighed the mails only once every four years, they had to carry increasing amounts of mail through a three-year period without corresponding increases in compensation. The effect of this was particularly noticeable when parcel post began in 1913, and the railroads had at first to carry the huge piles of packages without additional pay.

On the other hand, those who demanded reductions in railroad compensation noted that the weighings were made over a thirty-five day period which included Sundays and that to find the average number of pounds a railroad carried daily, the department habitually divided the total weight by six rather than seven. This obviously increased the average daily weight of the mails beyond the actual amount, and forced the department to pay for the transportation of mail that was not, in fact, being transported.

Whatever the justice of their position, it was a fact that except for one slight modification in 1907 the railroads had been able to stymie every attempt to reduce their compensation for more than three decades, even though the freight and express rates had considerably diminished over that period. Year in and year out, the Post Office Department had to pay the railroads at the old rate fixed in the 1870s and based largely on the weight of the mails carried, no matter how much the railroads' actual costs for carrying the mail might have declined. The result was that in 1910, according to one congressman's figures, it cost $15 to carry a ton of merchandise from New York to Chicago by freight, and $25 by express; but to transport a ton of mail the same distance cost $71.39, and it seemed reasonable to assume that, however little the railroads had made carrying the mails in the past, they were well-paid in 1910.

In any event, the spiraling costs of mail transportation, which had risen from slightly more than $5,000,000 in 1870 to over $49,000,000 in 1910, alarmed the Progressives. Indeed, so often had Congress attempted and the railroads resisted modification of the law that the compensation for carrying the mails had become a symbol of monopolistic extortion to many Progressives, and they were prepared to break a lance against it. Early in the century they began their efforts to reduce the railroads' compensation. Finally, over the violent objections of the railroads, amid their threats to increase freight rates on farm produce if the compensation for carrying the mail was reduced, and with some members of Congress still shouting that they did not know what it cost to carry the mails, Congress did change the law. In 1916, it provided that the postmaster general could begin to pay the railroads according to the space used to carry the mails rather than according to the weight of the mails. But the victory was not complete. To make certain the railroads would not be hurt, the new law included a provision stipulating that it would finally be left to the Interstate Commerce Commission to decide not only the basis upon which the railroads would be compensated but also how much they were to be paid.

Postmaster General Burleson instituted the new method of

compensating the railroads on 1 November 1916, and the difference this made in postal finances was quickly apparent in the Post Office's ledgers. For the year ending 30 June 1916, according to the postmaster general's figures, the department paid the railroads $62,176,943.05 for carrying the mail; three years later it paid only $54,563,534.49, although the volume of mail in that period had increased considerably.

While the new system of compensating the railroads was still in its infancy, the nation plunged into World War I, and the government took over the management of the railroads themselves as a part of the nation's preparedness program. Then, in the autumn of 1918, as a kind of capstone to a century's struggle between government and private business that revolved about the Post Office, the postmaster general, in compliance with a congressional resolution, took control of the operation of the nation's telegraph and telephone companies.

The ostensible reasons for government management of these private companies were to prevent a threatened strike of telegraphers and to remove from the hands of private companies the transmission of secret government messages in wartime. Obviously this was a wartime measure, but there were many who thought the war was simply an excuse to fulfill an old American dream of government ownership and operation of telegraph and telephone lines. And it may have been. But whatever the reason, the Post Office was at last given the chance to test the theory that the government could improve upon a privately operated business.

The results of the experiment, however, left both friends and foes of government ownership unmoved from their original positions. Testimony before a Senate committee in 1919 indicated there had been no deterioration in service under the Post

Office's management; but neither did it show there had been any improvement. Yet the fact that the postmaster general had been forced to raise telegram rates above those private companies had charged was seized upon by the champions of free enterprise as evidence of the failure of government enterprise. "So it is exceedingly gratifying," said Indiana's Republican senator, James Watson, as he noted the increased cost of sending telegrams in 1919, "to those of us who have always opposed the policy of Government ownership to know that it has been a failure."

On the contrary, the experiment had really proved nothing. The postmaster general had hardly taken control of the lines when the war ended, and Congress, almost as if it were afraid that government ownership might succeed, rushed with lightning speed to return the companies to their owners. This led Postmaster General Burleson to protest that his temporary control of the lines afforded "no more a test of the virtues of Government ownership than could be had through a temporary receivership in a court proceeding."

Progressivism, however, had run its course, and Congress was in no mood to listen to arguments in support of government ownership of business enterprises. The old ideas were once more in the ascendancy and again the Post Office became an object lesson on the inadequacies of a government-owned business. In this mood, Congress not only restored the telegraph and telephone companies to their owners, but in the 1920s even curtailed the effectiveness of the parcel post in order to permit the growth of private express companies.

As for the railroads, they too were returned to their owners, and in time the Interstate Commerce Commission erased the reductions in railroad compensations Burleson had made. Having investigated the matter in 1918 and 1919, the commission came to the conclusion that the railroads should be paid for space used in carrying the mails as the act of 1916 provided, but that the amount paid for space must be greatly increased. And this was so arranged that in the first year of President Harding's administration, the appropriation for carrying the mails by rail was raised from $59,886,822 to $96,000,000.

By the 1920s, then, the American Post Office, after its brief moment in the sun, had once more assumed its traditional nineteenth-century role: a supporter of free enterprise but never a competitor.

VI

Expansionism and the Post Office

"The frequency and rapidity of intercourse," wrote Georgia congressman Thomas Butler King in 1848, "are found to be the surest means of extending and increasing commerce." When he wrote these words, King was arguing for the extension of mail routes into the Pacific Ocean to develop American economic interests in that area, and his statement was one measure of how far the young American Republic had come in its short existence. Sixty years before, the notion that the American Post Office could ever be used to advance the country's economic interests in foreign lands was an idea still waiting to be born. No necessity then existed for using the postal system for such purposes, of course, but even had it, the few letters and newspapers exchanged between the United States and other nations and the clumsiness of the foreign mail service would scarcely have led members of Congress to think of the Post Office as an arm of expansionism.

To mail a letter from the United States to someone in England in those years required the payment of at least three separate postage rates: the inland postage that took the letter from the place of mailing—Athens, Ohio, say—to a seaport such as New York; the sea postage for the transportation from New York to Liverpool; and the British postage to carry the letter to its destination. But to send the letter on to the Continent was even more expensive and confusing. If it went through the British mails, as was usually the case, transit charges were added to take it through England and across the English channel. Once in Europe, the letter was subjected to whatever postage might be charged by the country to which the letter was directed or through which it must pass to reach the addressee.

Since the United States had agreements establishing postal rates with neither England nor any European country, no one knew in advance what the postage would be on a letter when it reached an addressee in Amsterdam, for example, or Hamburg. The prepayment of postage was therefore impossible, and the addressee was stuck with the postage if he wanted the letter.

To this complicated system of exchanging the mail between the United States and foreign countries there was one exception. In 1792 the United States and Canada had made an agreement by which the mails between the two countries would be exchanged at Burlington, Vermont. By this arrangement the Americans permitted the British to send a closed mailbag through the United States to Canada and charged the British government only for the number of letters the British authorities claimed were in the bag. Postage accounts were kept on both sides of the border and settlements were made periodically.

Even here, however, postage was a problem at least for Canadians. American officials had no authority to collect Canadian postage on a letter a Canadian might write to his American cousin, so Canadians had to prepay the postage on their letters as far as the border. Americans, on the other hand, might send their letters unpaid through the United States to any place in Canada, and when Canadian postal officials collected the postage from the addressees, they would remit that part of the postage belonging to the United States for the passage of the letter through its territory to the border.

But postage was only a part of the problem of mailing a letter abroad in the late eighteenth and early nineteenth centuries. There remained the difficulty of transportation. American letters could go abroad with some regularity on the British packets which continued to sail from Falmouth to New York as they had since the colonial period. But they sailed only once a month, touched at Bermuda and in the summer at Halifax, as well as New York, and were therefore a long time coming and going.

The only possibility of faster service was to send one's letter by the transient ships that carried cargo to Europe. And this was done. In the nation's major seaports, mailbags for foreign letters were hung in taverns and other places, and when a transient ship was about to leave, the postmasters announced the sailing time in the papers, so people might deposit their letters in the mailbags at the last minute before sailing.

Whether sending one's letters by transient ships was faster than waiting for the regular British packet service depended upon many things. All ships were at the mercy of the winds, of course, but the transient ship was also at the mercy of its cargo. If it did not have a full cargo at the announced time of sailing it would not sail, or it might sail but make two or three stops along the coast to fill its cargo. Moreover, if it did not sail directly to the port to which the letters it carried were directed, as often happened, there were more delays; thus, by the time the letters finally arrived at the port of destination, the mail packet, though starting later, might have arrived sooner.

Such, in brief, was the foreign mail service in the 1790s and early 1800s. Examination of American diplomatic correspondence indicates that a letter from the secretary of state to an American minister in England or Europe was always more than a month on its way and often as long as three months. Nor were there many improvements in the service until after the War of 1812, when a little group of American businessmen developed a new kind of ocean shipping service.

The new era began in 1818 when the Black Ball Line, a company that drew its name from the black ball its ships carried on their masts, began running a regular packet service between New York and Liverpool. Small but fast, the Black Ball Line's little ships sailed across the Atlantic in twenty-three days going east and forty-one sailing west. They carried both passengers and light, valuable freight, but the most remarkable thing about them was that they sailed on schedule with or without full cargoes, in fair weather and foul, in summer and winter.

Sailing schedules were not new in 1818, of course, but keeping them was, and the new system drastically altered the transatlantic ocean service. Businessmen who had valuable cargoes to send and receive, and passengers too, quickly learned to depend on the speedy, regularly scheduled ships. So successful was the Black Ball Line's innovation that by the 1830s the Atlantic was filled with competitors, and American packet ships were coming and going on schedules as regular as sunrise and sunset.

This improvement in ocean sailing ushered in the golden age of American shipping, and to none was it more important than the postal service. The foreign mails, no longer dependent upon transient ships or even the slower British mail packets, were sent several times a month on the regularly scheduled American packets, and by the 1830s the American ships were carrying not only the bulk of the American mails to Europe but a large portion of the British mails to America.

The new system, along with the growing number of immigrants who came to America each year and wrote back home, dramatically increased the volume of foreign mail and focused Americans' attention on the ineptness of the foreign mail service, which, as far as the Post Office Department was concerned, had not changed appreciably since the 1790s.

In the 1830s, a half-century after the establishment of the government, the Post Office still assumed no responsibility for collecting letters bound for foreign ports. Anyone who wished to mail a letter to a foreign correspondent must place it on board a departing ship himself or deposit it in a private foreign letter office which charged for the service of taking letters to the ships. Nor could any American prepay postage on his letter to a foreign country unless he sent it through William Harnden, whose express company had agents in the various countries and who would, for a price, pay the various postages required to take a letter to its destination.

To compound the difficulties, the British government had no provision for forwarding letters from various countries that piled up in the London post office on their way to America. Since postage was due on these letters and Americans often had no one in England to pay that postage and forward the letters, they remained in the London post office while American businessmen fumed at the inadequacies of the postal service.

In 1836 Postmaster General Kendall recommended making an agreement with England to entrust the foreign mails exchanged between New York and the Liverpool post offices to contractors who would protect them. But Congress ignored this proposal as well as a businessmen's petition of 1839 demanding improvements in the foreign mail service. Not until the developments of the 1840s forced its hand would Congress make revisions in the foreign mail service.

A cluster of events coincided in the 1840s to force Congress to revise the American foreign mail service, but the incident most immediately responsible for the revision was the simultaneous arrival of two British steamships—the *Sirius* and the *Great Western*—in New York harbor on 23 April 1838. The appearance of these two ships in an American port on that spring day opened the age of steam power upon the oceans and signaled the eclipse of the old sailing vessels. Independent of the wind, the steamships could both depart and arrive on schedule and cross the ocean in less than half the sailing ships' time. In short, the steamships could do all the important things the sailing vessel could do in addition to some things the older ships could not do at all.

Quick to see in the development of the steamships a way to wrest control of the Atlantic carrying trade from the Americans, the British government immediately began to subsidize its private steamship companies with lucrative contracts for carrying the mails. These subsidies were to help tide the steamship companies over in the early stages of their development, send them to places they could not otherwise afford to go, and build up trade between England and countries all over the world. In return, the British government received assurances that the private steamships would be turned over to the British navy whenever needed.

Two of the companies entering into such arrangements were

the Cunard Lines and the Royal Mail Steam Packet Company. By the 1840s, the speedy Cunard ships were making regular runs to Halifax and Boston, and those of the Royal Mail ran to Barbados and other West Indian islands and branched off to South American ports and those along the Gulf of Mexico. And, as planned, they were soon carrying the larger portion of the American foreign mail—sixty thousand letters a month from Boston in 1844—and were capturing the passenger and light freight service from the American sailing vessels. Meanwhile, in Europe the British lines plied the English channel from Dover, Edinburgh, and London to Hamburg, Amsterdam, Antwerp, and Ostend, carrying American correspondence along with their own.

This threat to American control of the Atlantic trade came at precisely that moment when Americans were most eager to grapple with it. Driven by their twin compulsions to improve mankind's lot and to make money—both exemplified by the expansionist sentiment that gripped the country in the 1840s—Americans were then busily extending the "area of freedom," as they said, to the Pacific Ocean, perfecting their society with a variety of reforms, and avidly pursuing their economic interests at home and their foreign trade, which had grown increasingly important as their domestic economy had grown. Enormously proud of their young country and its institutions and anxious to retain control of the Atlantic trade, they were not disposed to see England best them without a fight. One member of Congress spoke for many of them in 1846 when he repudiated the "idea that we should supinely remain without making any movements ourselves until all the experiments were tried."

The question was how to meet the British challenge. Ameri-

cans had no privately owned oceangoing steamships and, because of the great success of their sailing vessels, no plans to
build any. The answer, then, since no one had a better, was to
subsidize Americans to build and operate steamships for carrying the mails. In short, the solution was to use the Post Office to
wage economic war against the mother country.

The arguments for doing so were plausible and immensely
appealing to the American spirit of that day. By subsidizing
American companies to carry the mail in steamships, the mail
service between Europe and America would be vastly improved, and the American immigrants, then so poorly served by
the mail facilities, would be able to correspond more freely
with their homelands. American letters and newspapers would
flow in ever increasing numbers to Europe. These would advance American economic interests everywhere and spread "full
and correct information through those populous regions," as a
House report of 1846 noted, "respecting our markets, our resources, and our institutions. Relying no longer exclusively
upon England for information respecting our pecuniary and
moral condition, they will be able to gather, from more direct
and reliable sources, a knowledge of our country and its affairs."
One idealistic American, Elihu Burritt, even argued that better
foreign mail facilities and cheap postage would bring about
world peace.

At the same time, subsidization of American vessels would
eliminate British domination of the American mail service, allow
Americans to spend their postage money on American ships,
stimulate the American shipbuilding industry, and augment the
national pride. But in the opinion of Ohio congressman Allen
Thurman, the "principal inducement to contract for mail steamers, was to obtain vessels for war purposes." By stipulating that

all steamships receiving the mail subsidies must be built so they could be converted to military purposes, and by committing their owners to release them to the navy in case of emergency, the nation's coast, then so vulnerable to the comings and goings of British steamships, could be defended.

This was of the utmost importance to many Americans of the 1840s. Since the late 1830s, a series of incidents—trouble over the abortive Canadian revolution, the Maine boundary dispute, and the Oregon controversy—had embittered Anglo-American relations. Twice in the early 1840s, the possibility of war was discussed on both sides of the Atlantic, and though by 1847 passions had subsided, no one knew when the nation might again be endangered. Perhaps many Americans felt like the New York congressman who warned in 1847 that "as long as we are bordered in the North by the colonies of any European power, we are in constant danger of collision."

Nor could the government ignore the fact that England, according to the 1846 report of the secretary of the navy, had 636 vessels in its navy, 199 of which were steam, while the United States had but 3 steam vessels and only 77 vessels of any kind in its entire navy. Besides, the British steamers sailed up and down the American coast and in and out of American harbors, so that they possessed invaluable knowledge of American defenses or lack of them.

Fortunately, all these problems could be solved, it was believed, at very little expense to the government. According to the plan, the government would give money not for actually building the ships but for carrying the mail. Yet it could insist that the ships be so constructed that they could be converted to naval use. Private enterprise and the government would, then, work hand in hand for this purpose and the interests of both would be served.

Responding to these arguments of the chambers of commerce, various economic interests, and the defense-minded, Congress authorized the postmaster general in 1845 to contract with American shipowners to carry the mail between the United States and foreign countries. Preference was to be given to shipowners who would build steam vessels, and the postmaster general was to proceed whenever he felt the interests of the United States might be promoted thereby. By the next year, Postmaster General Cave Johnson had made a contract with Edward Mills, who formed the Ocean Steam Navigation Company to carry the mail from New York by way of Southampton, England, to the German port of Bremen. This was followed in 1847 with another contract to transport the mail between Charleston, Savannah, and Havana.

But Congress was impatient to confront the enemy in his own backyard as well as elsewhere around the globe. Pushed along by fertile imaginations that could think of a number of foreign posts in which American influence should be felt and by various seaport towns who wanted their own steamship lines, Congress wrote new legislation in 1847, directing the secretary of the navy to contract for more ocean mail steamship routes. Before the year was out, three more routes had been provided for. One was to run from New York to Charleston, Savannah, New Orleans, and Havana, and from Havana to Chagres on the Isthmus of Panama. The mail was to be carried cross the Isthmus, where another steamship route was established to carry the mail up the Pacific coast from the Isthmus to Astoria in Oregon Territory. But the most important of all these lines under the control of the secretary of the navy was the one which was to compete with the Cunard line in carrying the mail from New York to Liverpool.

So by 1847 five steamship lines had been contracted for, three of them at a cost of $784,000 a year. Subsequently, in 1853, largely to appease the South and at the demand of the merchants of New Orleans, one more steamship route was established to run from New Orleans to Tampico and Veracruz and back. "The establishment of this line," argued Texas senator Thomas Jefferson Rusk, "while it is necessary for transporting mail matter, would, in my opinion, shortly more than pay for the outlay, because it would have a tendency to open commerce with Mexico."

To improve the prospects of these routes, however, the laws governing the foreign mail service had to be revised to relieve the foreign-bound mail from as many of the old impediments as possible. Fortunately, Congress had already provided a way of doing this in 1844 when it gave the postmaster general the authority, in effect, to write postal conventions with England, France, and Germany.

With this authority, the postmaster general made the nation's first postal convention with the city of Bremen, not only because American relations were better with Germany than with either France or England at that moment, but because Bremen was to be the entrepôt for American goods into Europe. It was the principal port of embarkation for emigrants leaving the interior of Europe for America—31,016 in 1845 alone—its trade with the United States was greater than that of any European port north of France, and through it American cotton, tobacco, and communications could reach the rest of Germany. "In making these mail arrangements," wrote First Assistant Postmaster

Expansionism and the Post Office

General S. R. Hobbie, who worked out the convention in 1847, "for enlarging the correspondence between this country and the enlightened nations of central Europe, containing a population of forty or fifty millions of people, and extensively engaged in manufactures, it could not escape observation that the increased facilities afforded by it for an exchange of the production of the respective countries, might be more advantageous to the United States than the interchange of mails, and lead to the establishment of a new market for the principal products of this country, of little, if any less, importance than those of England and France."

The Bremen postal convention made the Bremen postmaster the agent of the American Post Office. All the mail from any place in America to any place in Germany and countries north of Germany as well as that from those places to America was to go through the Bremen postmaster. Postage on such matter could either be prepaid or not. If not, the Bremen postmaster collected the postage and made regular settlements with the American Post Office. Perhaps the most important improvement the convention made was the establishment of firm postage rates, so that a German immigrant near Austin, Texas, where a large group of them had settled by 1848, knew that to send his letter to Bremen would cost all together 34 cents; to Hanover, 40; Prussia, 46; and Coburg, 44. If he wished to send it on to Vienna, it would cost 52 cents, and to Stockholm, 70.

Hobbie had hoped to establish a uniform postage rate throughout the Germanies, but in seventeen of the German states he ran headlong into the privileges of the von Taxis family, who had controlled the postal service throughout the area from the feudal period and were reluctant to lower the postage rate in the states under their control. Nevertheless, the Bremen postal convention was a turning point in the history of the American foreign mail service. Though similar to treaties, postal conventions did not have to be ratified by the Senate but could go into operation with the president's signature. Consequently, they could be made easily and quickly, and in the course of years the postmasters general worked out conventions with all the enlightened nations of the world.

The most important postal convention the Americans made in the period, of course, was that with England. This was finally completed in 1848, but only after the Americans had forced the British hand. Relations between the two nations, already strained because of the events of the 1840s, were exacerbated by England's response to the development of the American steamship lines.

When the *Washington*, the first American mail steamship to cross the Atlantic under the new mail contracts, stopped at Southampton on its way to Bremen to drop off the mail for England and France, the Americans learned that the British had issued an order on 9 June 1847 levying the same charges upon the American mails that they would have had they been brought there by a British steamer. Since the postage had already been charged on this mail for passage on the *Washington*, the British order doubled the postage on the mail brought in the American steamer.

George Bancroft, the American minister to London, sent a sharply worded note to the British government protesting against this treatment of the mail carried on an American ship; but neither this protest nor the fact that Americans had not exacted such postage rates for the British mails passing through the states on their way to Canada caused the British to cancel their order. Not until the United States threatened to terminate the agreement of 1844, which allowed the British mails to pass through the United States to Canada, did the British give up their order of 9 June and make possible the writing of a postal convention.

Like the convention with Bremen, this one made it possible for letters on which postage had been paid or left unpaid to pass through the two countries as though they were one, and perhaps it did help inaugurate a new era in the relations between the United States and England. At least this seemed to be the opinion of First Assistant Postmaster General Hobbie, who could hardly control his elation at the success of the convention. "In less than two years," he wrote in 1849, "since this measure was proposed, the hostile policy that it encountered has given way; a liberal reciprocity has succeeded; just and satisfactory terms have been obtained; and our department has entered upon that enlightened . . . career which enables it the better to serve American interests at home by becoming also the handmaid to those abroad—not alone, but in sisterhood with the postal institutions of other countries."

When the convention with England went into effect, it was noticeable at once that in settling postal accounts the United States had to pay much more to England than it received. This was partly because British steamships were carrying most of the American mails, but by 1849 postal officials were looking forward to the time when the American steamships would be in full operation and the unfavorable postal balances would be corrected. Unfortunately, these expectations were never realized. In time, the Post Office had four steamships running from New York to Bremen and the port of Le Havre in France, but though they gave reasonably good service for the time, they sailed neither fast enough nor often enough to steal the mail trade from the Cunard lines. Nor, in the end, could E. K. Collins, the imaginative American who had made a fortune from his line of fast sailing ships and who had contracted with the secretary of the navy for the New York to Liverpool run to compete with the Cunard ships.

Trouble plagued Collins from the start of his venture. Scheduled to begin the service by the middle of 1849, he could not get started until April 1850. He had contracted to build five ships and could build only four; and once begun, his operation was so expensive that he had to appeal to Congress in 1852 to raise the amount of his contract. To add to his difficulties, two of his ships, the *Arctic* in 1854 and the *Pacific* in 1856, were lost at sea. In the former, Collins also lost his wife, daughter, and youngest son.

In spite of all this, however, Collins gave the Cunard line a race for their contract. To the immense satisfaction of the Americans, the Collins steamers were not only bigger and more luxurious than the Cunard ships, but were also faster. The *Atlantic*, the first ship launched, beat all previous crossing records on her second voyage. Moreover, his second ship, the *Pacific*, was the first to fly across the Atlantic in less than ten days. The Americans and the British were making a racetrack of the Atlantic, and the Americans were winning the race.

But all this was not enough. The huge outlay of money for ships that had cost more than British ships, lobbyists who cluttered the halls of Congress seeking subsidies, and the failure of the ships to return significant amounts in postage to the national government convinced many members of Congress in the early 1850s that the subsidization program had been a mistake from the beginning. They complained particularly that it had interfered with free enterprise. Contracts, they charged, had been given to certain select lines which had made monopolies of them and impoverished others.

Some members also believed that the government's priorities were wrong. Instead of using so much money for subsidies that made the rich richer, they argued, the money should have been spent at home to extend post routes so the poor people could have their mail. "And shall we pursue a system longer by which the millionaire shall be enabled to wallow in the lap of luxury and affluence," asked a congressman in 1854 who had not long before been invited aboard the *Baltic*, the luxurious ship Collins had brought up the Potomac to persuade Congress to raise the amount of his contract, "and thereby deprive our own constituents of the benefits which the sum [the subsidy to Collins] so paid would afford them?"

Then, too, as the fear of England's assaults upon the American coasts faded and the need of ships to protect the shores dwindled, opponents of subsidies remembered that they had never believed in the argument that these ships had been built for American defense. Ohio congressman Joshua Giddings claimed he had always considered the idea "sheer humbug, invented for the purpose of giving prestige of war to the matter, to . . . render it more acceptable to the people. . . . The whole truth is," he went on, "this extravagant expenditure has been made for the purpose of national *glory*. . . . Well, sir," he said, "the glory has departed"; and he for one wanted to stop subsidizing ships as soon as possible.

In the Senate, similar sentiments were expressed as the decade wore on, and not a few, turning their backs on the attempt to gain "the first place among the nations of the earth, in a commercial view," which one Senate committee had given as the reason for subsidies, were willing to give up the idea of competing with England. In 1857 Senator Robert Toombs told the Senate he had "heard enough talk about the mastery of the seas; I have heard enough about beating England. That was the pretext under which millions of public money was squandered a few years ago. . . . That is all over now. If England will carry my letters for twenty-five cents, and I cannot carry them myself for less than half a dollar, I will let her do the business."

Against this attack the supporters of mail subsidies marshaled their arguments to demonstrate the great strides the nation had taken under the subsidy program. With pride they noted that "in the great contest for the supremacy of the seas," as one congressman called it, the United States had thus far been victorious. Because of American competition, ocean freight rates had been drastically reduced, and many of those rates were now paid to American rather than British ships, which increased the national wealth. The British monopoly of the steamship trade had been broken, and American foreign trade had increased by millions of dollars as had been predicted. The commerce between Bremerhaven and the United States had grown, it was said, from $3,000,000 to $15,000,000 in the decade since the establishment of the New York to Bremen steamship line. Besides, the competing American steamers had forced England to modify many of her restrictions against the American mails, so that those mails could move to and through England much more easily than they had when England controlled the carriage of the mails.

Beyond all these things, proponents of mail subsidies noted the impetus the program had given to American technology. They recalled that when the first contracts for steamships were made in America, the nation had no machine shops capable of making the huge castings for the great ships. Nor did it have experienced engineers who could handle the powerful engines being built for the new ships. They had had to import both from England. Since then, however, the Americans had learned much about building such ships. They had enlarged their machine shops, and with every sailing of the new ships, they were training engineers who would be the finest in the world.

But the capstone to the argument of the subsidy advocates was that as long as England gave subsidies to its steamship lines, the United States would have to, or "the stripes and stars of our country," as the Senate report of 1852 warned, "which has floated triumphantly on every sea, must grow dim, not only before the 'meteor flag of England' but the standards of the secondary powers of Europe." True, one North Carolina congressman suggested a way out of this dilemma by proposing that the president make an agreement with England that both nations give up subsidies, but this plan was ridiculed and the choice remained: either subsidize the American mail steamers or make "Liverpool, London, Portsmouth, and Southampton the centers of the commercial world," as Senator Jacob Collamer, the former postmaster general, put it in 1858.

In a way, the argument was between the big and little Americans, between those who valued commerce and expansion and those who did not, between the agrarian South and West and the industrial North, as one historian has shown. But only in part was this true. Southerners did lead the attack upon the subsidy program, as both the voices and votes of members of Congress show, but this was not primarily because their region was agricultural. More important to them was their jealousy of the North's commercial growth and their feeling that the subsidies had discriminated against them. "Now, I say, it is not just to the different sections of this Union that this policy should be

continued," said Mississippi congressman Reuben Davis in 1858.
"It is not proper that New York should be allowed the privilege
of three lines; to control the operation of the commerce of this
country; to become the exclusive carrier of letters between the
United States and Europe, to the exclusion of every other portion of the United States."

The South, of course, had a number of steamship routes. For
years the little steamer *Isabel* carried the mail and merchandise
from Charleston and Savannah to Havana solely for the benefit
of the South. The route from New York to New Orleans, Havana, and Chagres was also operated in part for the benefit of
the South. So, too, was the route from New Orleans to Tampico
and Veracruz which had been established because some seventy
or eighty commercial houses in New Orleans had demanded it.
Not only did the South have these routes, but in 1855 Congress
had authorized a line from New Orleans to Mexico and across
the Isthmus of Tehuantepec, and in the late 1850s this route
was put in operation by the southern-oriented Buchanan administration.

No, it was not that the Southerners had no steamship routes
or that they were not interested in them. They had tried as hard
as Northerners to get what they could, and they had, in fact,
obtained much. But they had not received the prize. The bulk
of their trade lay with Europe, not Latin America, and what
they wanted was a route from New Orleans to Europe. So
eager were they for this route that even as late as 1858, when
Congress was preparing to end the subsidy system, a congressman from New Orleans proposed maintaining the subsidies on
the New York routes if subsidies could also be given to a route
from New Orleans to Bordeaux.

Had it been possible in the early 1850s to have linked New

Expansionism and the Post Office

Orleans to Europe with a mail steamship route, the history of the subsidy program might have been different. But this had not been done, and Southerners had so long condemned subsidies because they felt discriminated against that they apparently convinced a majority of Congress that they should be abandoned. In any case, Congress did abandon the system by 1859 after the original contracts had run out and substituted for it a new policy for carrying the foreign mail. Beginning in 1859, the postmaster general would give steamships that carried the American foreign mails only the postage derived from the mails they carried. A foreign steamship would be allowed only the sea postage on the mails it took, but the postmaster general was authorized to give both the sea and inland postage on the mails carried by an American ship.

So the subsidy program came to an end on the eve of the Civil War, but not before its supporters had won some of their objectives, not the least of which was an improved foreign postal service. Forced to grapple with the problem of foreign mails by the American entry into the steamship race, American postal officials had opened conversations on postal affairs with their European counterparts. Out of these came the postal conventions, eight of which had been completed by 1860. By regularizing the mail service between the United States, England, and Europe, the postal conventions provided an improved mail service for immigrants and businessmen, and the better service generated a steady increase in the foreign mails to the United States, as the advocates of subsidies had predicted.

In 1844 perhaps as many as 1,500,000 letters passed between the United States, England, and Europe annually. By 1860 there were more than 6,000,000 such letters. Of these, 1,445,251 were exchanged with Prussia, Bremen, and Hamburg, 1,333,479 with

France, and more than 3,000,000 with the United Kingdom. Obviously, the improved mail service had been useful to American immigrants as the advocates of mail subsidies had hoped, and perhaps it had had some influence on the development of the nation's foreign trade as well. American exports increased by 130 percent between 1850 and 1860.

One can only speculate about the extent to which all these letters inspired immigrants to swarm to the American shores in the 1850s. But beyond question, the subsidy supporters' desire to have the American story told abroad by Americans was achieved. Between 1853 and 1860 the number of newspapers exchanged between the United States, England, and Europe jumped from 1,381,863 to 3,466,077. Of these nearly three and a half million, well over two million were sent rather than received, and only Belgium of all European countries sent more than it received. The eagerness of Europeans to learn about America may account for the fact that more newspapers were sent than received, but whether this was so or not, it did appear that many Europeans were at last seeing America as Americans saw it.

It was significant, too, that from 1861 through 1864, during the course of the Civil War, the North alone, with its postal service intact, blanketed England and Europe with 9,613,155 newspapers. In one year, 1863, the North sent 2,331,764 newspapers abroad, and this was more than two and a half times as many as England and the European countries sent to America. It seems obvious that this outpouring of northern newspapers must have done much to make Englishmen and Europeans see the Civil War through northern eyes and to neutralize the propaganda efforts of Southerners trying to tell their story in England.

Expansionism and the Post Office

This great volume of foreign mails, however, confronted the Post Office Department with new problems and revealed some serious flaws in the postal conventions. Especially troublesome was the failure of the conventions to provide a uniform postal system. Each postal convention regulated postal affairs between the United States and one country only, and each differed from the rest, so that there were neither uniform postage rates for letters sent abroad nor even similar units of measurement by which to weigh the mails. The English and Americans used the ounce as their basic unit for weighing letters and allowed any letter weighing no more than a half ounce to be mailed at the cheapest postage rate. But France used the gram and Germany the loth as the basic unit of measurement, and the conversion of half-ounce letters into grams and loths complicated the exchange of mail.

As for postage, it was still based on inland, sea, and transit rates, most of which were different for each country. Postage rates also varied according to the route over which a letter was sent and the nationality of the vessel carrying it. A letter to Austria from the United States, for example, might be sent directly to Bremen or Hamburg, or by way of England, or by way of France, and the postage would be 15, 30, or 42 cents per half-ounce, depending on which route it had taken and on what steamer.

By the 1860s, then, postage rates had become a tower of Babel and were so confusing that only a handful of people fully understood them. "The whole foreign system, as now established," wrote Postmaster General Blair in 1862, "is too complex to be readily understood by postmasters, and many mistakes and unfortunately delays arise from the complexity."

Almost as confusing as postage rates were the accounts that

had to be kept so that each nation could be credited with the postage due it. Except for Canada, with whom the United States had made a sensible agreement in 1851 allowing each nation to keep the postage it collected, the Post Office Department had to keep minute records of all the postal business it conducted with every nation with whom it had a postal convention. The old letter bills in the postal records, with their maze of columns showing the number of letters and amount of printed matter exchanged, the weights of such letters, and whether the postage on them had been paid or unpaid, are testimonials to how complicated the foreign mail system had grown.

More than most nations, the United States was concerned about the confusion in the foreign mail service. At the very time this service had become so important to immigrants and businessmen, its rapidly increasing volume and complex structure threatened to overwhelm the Post Office Department. Moreover, although the people of the United States sent more letters and newspapers abroad than they received, the United States Post Office, for a variety of reasons, was always in debt at the end of the year to the foreign post offices.

A simplified system, therefore, incorporating some of the features of the Canadian-American convention of 1851, seemed desirable to Postmaster General Blair, who suggested in 1862 the possibility of an international conference to discuss proposals for changing the international postal system. Perhaps Blair was prompted to do this by his first assistant postmaster general, John A. Kasson, whose command of the details of this service was impressive. In any event, when it was agreed to hold the conference in Paris in 1863, Kasson was sent as the American representative.

The principal discussion at the conference centered upon the problem of unifying postage rates, adopting similar systems of weight measurement, and simplifying postal bookkeeping, and in the end, the delegates agreed upon thirty-one rules. But none of the delegates at the conference had the authority to bind their governments to any agreement, and the rules were not formally adopted by the governments represented. Nevertheless, the conference was important. Postmaster General Blair and his successors used the rules as a guide in making new postal treaties, and even old postal conventions were modified to accord with the rules. By 1870, for example, the convention with England was so modified that the postage rate on a half-ounce letter had been reduced from 24 to 6 cents, 2 cents being considered the sea postage and 2 cents the inland postage on each side.

The conference of 1863 also led indirectly to the Berne Postal Congress, which met in 1874 where the General Postal Union, later called the Universal Postal Union, was established. This union was of far-reaching significance. It made all the countries involved into a single postal territory for the exchange of the mails, set a uniform postage rate within the territory, and eliminated the keeping of those complicated accounts of international correspondence. Finally, it made the old individual postal conventions obsolete for every nation that belonged to it.

In the meantime, while the Universal Postal Union was taking shape, Congress wrestled with the old dream of subsidizing American steamships to carry the mail to foreign countries for the purpose of encouraging trade and spreading American influence in those places.

With the collapse of the subsidy program of the 1850s, the emergence of the Civil War, and fear of raids upon American ships by Confederate steamships, which incidently had been constructed by Englishmen who were not averse to injuring the American carrying trade, American steamships had been withdrawn from the Atlantic Ocean. By 1863 the mails to Europe and England were being carried exclusively by foreign ships. But even before this happened, irrepressible American businessmen were already pressuring Congress to subsidize new steamship lines, not to England and Europe, to be sure, but to Brazil and China. Here, where geography had given them a legitimate right to control trade, as Postmaster General Blair claimed, they would make a new start.

True, England already had steamship lines to these places, as she did almost everywhere, and according to Americans who watched such things they had been profitable. Her line to Brazil had enabled her to sell more in that country than she bought, made her the center through which American mails, to say nothing of the American minister, must pass on their way to Brazil, and opened the door to the extension of her political influence in the region. And across the world, her Peninsular and Oriental Steamship Navigation Company took the American mail from Southampton through the Mediterranean Sea to Alexandria, Egypt, overland across the Isthmus of Suez to the Red Sea and Indian Ocean, and on to China—a distance of almost 12,000 miles. More than that, the same line took the gold and silver from the mines of the American West from London over the same circuitous route to pay for products American merchants purchased in China.

But these steamship lines were less obstacles than incentives to Americans, for they furnished expansionists in Congress with their choicest arguments for establishing steamship lines in those places. Americans, too, they said, could in time sell more than they bought in Brazil if only they had a steamship line that would carry the mail there regularly. This line would also end the humiliation of having to send American mail to Brazil via England, and it would counteract European political influence in the region. "Grave political considerations of transcendent importance, are involved in the question of intimate postal and commercial communications with our neighbors upon this continent," said one congressman in 1864. "We need that friendship of these neighboring nations which always follows intercourse."

Even more was to be expected from a steamship line to the Orient. A line from San Francisco to the Far East would shorten the mail route to China by almost half, carry the mail and bullion direct from California to Shanghai, and open the riches of the East to American enterprise.

The Far East! Like a bright jewel shimmering in the sunlight, it charmed and fascinated Americans as it had the Europeans who for centuries had looked for a passage to India through the American continent. Jefferson had been intrigued by it, and Senator Thomas Hart Benton of Missouri had envisoned the American West as the strait to that promised land. Inspired by the same vision, Congressman Thomas Butler King in 1848 suggested establishing a steamship route to China, to go by way of Hawaii, or the Sandwich Islands as they were called, where American whalers put in for rest and recreation and yearned for letters from the homes they had not seen for years.

There had been no opportunity then to establish the line, but in the 1860s the possibility of completing the route to the Orient, even by means of something as unglamourous as mail subsidies, stirred the imagination of excited members of Congress with visions of the East as old as Marco Polo. "There is the East," declared California senator James McDougall in 1862, "and I call Senators' attention to it. . . . There is the wealth of the

Orient, and what wealth is that? . . . It is a country full of wealth." All that was needed to tap it was a mail steamship line, which, combined with the transcontinental telegraph and the Pacific railroad soon to be built, would reduce the travel time to the Orient from some fifty to twenty-five days, give American merchants information on the Chinese market conditions far in advance of the British, dominate the mail service to the East, and, in the words of Massachusetts congressman John B. Alley, "give us vast control over the commerce of the globe," and "make the city of New York the greatest commercial city of the world. Then New York will be what London is now—the great settling point where the exchanges of the whole world are adjusted."

Grandiose as this vision was, it was surpassed by that which foresaw American steamers and American mails fulfilling the destiny to which providence had called Americans in the Far East. "Senators," cried Milton S. Latham, California senator in 1862, "we are the only people of pure Caucasian origin at *home* on the shores of the Pacific ocean; we alone possess a Pacific empire, and we are bound to extend its power and influence morally, if not physically, not only on this continent but on the coast of Asia. This is not only our national policy, but a necessary condition of· our national existence. . . . You of the Atlantic sea-coast have the mission to . . . maintain friendly relations with the Powers of Europe; we on the Pacific coast are called upon to assert moral sway over the Asiatics. We are a most important link in the chain which civilization has drawn around the world, and by which Providence accomplishes His mighty deeds. This is a part of our great mission; and if we fail in it, you of the eastern States, and of the great Mississippi valley are equally involved in the disgrace."

Expansionism and the Post Office

Apparently only a handful of legislators were willing to run that risk. And with no Southerners in Congress to impede the march of destiny, the tiny group of Americans who did oppose the grand vision were swept aside by gusts of expansionist rhetoric. Not even the debt rising from the war gave the expansionists pause. Like the Prussian king who built a fabulous palace at the conclusion of the Seven Years War to prove to his enemies that the war had not exhausted the nation, the United States, too, the expansionists argued, should show those commercial nations of the world who had driven American ships from the seas that Americans, in spite of their war, stood "ready to inaugurate their commercial equality in the face of all obstacles."

So at the close of the Civil War Congress again gave the Post Office Department the duty of directing a new subsidy program aimed at controlling the trade of South America, China, and Japan and extending American influence in those areas. Between 1864 and 1867, it authorized the postmaster general to seek bids from American steamship companies to carry the mail to three areas: from the eastern coast of the United States to Rio de Janeiro via Saint Thomas in the Virgin Islands, Baía, and Pernambuco; from San Francisco to Japan and China; and from San Francisco to Hawaii, where, as one senator explained, so many Americans lived and where the revival of American commerce would have an important political effect.

By 1867 all these lines were in operation, and Americans were waiting expectantly to reap the wealth of the East. In the meantime, however, the renewal of the subsidy program had unleashed Aeolus from his cave. Promoters descended upon Washington like a whirlwind with proposals to carry the mail to any and every port within the possible orbits of American trade.

Expansionism and the Post Office

For six years, the propositions piled up in Congress and members dutifully submitted bills to provide subsidies to carry the mails to such places as Alaska, Venezuela, Columbia, down the west coast of South America, along the Gulf of Mexico, to the West Indies, Mexico, and finally to Europe where Americans might compete head-on with the British once more.

But by 1876 Congress had once more turned its back on the subsidy program. The Hawaii steamship line petered out in 1874 and the line to Brazil in 1875. The next year, Congress refused to renew the Pacific Mail Steamship Company's contract to carry the mails to the Far East.

All this was due in part to the discovery in 1872 that the directors of the Pacific Mail Steamship Company had spent $900,000 trying to artificially raise the company's stock on the market and by the lavish use of money to induce Congress to increase its subsidy to $1,000,000 annually, which, incidentally, had been done. But a more important reason for the termination of the subsidies was the unbelievably tangled interests that webbed every attempt to subsidize American ships in the post–Civil War years.

No sooner were subsidy bills proposed in Congress in these years than the interests fell upon them, either to shape them according to their desires or to kill them. Steamship companies vied with one another for special favors, as did seaports. If New York City was to have a subsidized steamship line, Philadelphia, Boston, Baltimore, and New Orleans wanted one. Then there were differences between shipbuilders and shipowners. An old law dating back to 1789 had stipulated that ships of American registry must be made in America. Shipbuilders naturally wanted to retain the law, but shipowners in many cases would have liked the law repealed so they could purchase ships where they could get them the cheapest. The two political parties, too, held different views. The Democrats argued that lower tariffs would stimulate foreign trade and therefore American shipping and subsidies were unnecessary. But this only exacerbated the long-standing quarrel between the low-tariff Democrats and high-tariff Republicans who wanted subsidies to help both shipbuilders and shipowners as well as to expand foreign markets.

Add to these complications the changed mood of Congress and the country, and the reasons for the failure of the subsidies become more understandable. In the immediate aftermath of the Civil War, the eagerness of Americans to capture the trade of South America and the Far East and reestablish a foothold in the transatlantic carrying trade reflected the expansive sentiment of the administration, whose principal exponent of such a policy was William Seward, secretary of state. Between 1865 and 1868, Seward flirted with the idea of acquiring Santo Domingo and the Virgin Islands, purchased Alaska in 1867, and dreamed, as did so many Americans, of an eastern empire. He supported the steamship mail routes to the Orient and gave his blessing to the acquisition of the Midway Islands in 1867 when Gideon Welles, secretary of the navy, took them over in response to a suggestion from the president of the Pacific Mail Steamship Company that they might make a good coaling station on the China run.

Seward's enthusiasm for expansion rubbed off on the Grant administration, and in the early part of the general's regime some thought was given to taking Santo Domingo and even Canada. Indeed, the unification of the American and Canadian postal systems in 1875 was perhaps a reflection of the desire for union. But by the middle 1870s the nation was moving away from expansionism. Preoccupied with settling the West, with building railroads and an industrial empire, and led by strong-minded Democrats who had returned to power in Congress eager to economize and with very little interest in whether the old flag flew over the oceans or not, the nation turned inward. It was not, in fact, merely coincidental that the subsidy for the Pacific Mail Steamship Company was killed in the House of Representatives in 1876, the very first time the Democrats had controlled that body since 1860.

Still the issue would not go away. Shipowners and shipbuilders continued to pressure Congress for subsidies for mail steamships, and with each passing year more and more businessmen joined the list of advocates. The nation's industries were growing rapidly, surpluses were accumulating, and manufacturers were beginning to feel the pressure for markets for their goods. "We have crossed the Rubicon," said one impassioned congressman in 1879. "We are no longer a nation which can live within itself. We must sell our surplus commodities abroad, for when a nation has reached that state of productive development that she can supply any portion of the rest of the world, it is because she produces a surplus, or has the capacity to do so; it is because she has grown from within until from her own fullness she has burst the barriers which surround her, and as neither men nor nations can remain stationary, she must sell abroad or retrograde."

Lamenting this state of affairs in 1873, the poet Sidney Lanier wrote, "O Trade! O Trade! Would Thou wert dead!" but this would not exorcise the evil even in Lanier's own backyard in the South, where the clamor for trade was enough to force a number of southern legislators to desert the Democratic opposition to steamship subsidies. "We have the beginning of a new era in the South," said Georgia senator Benjamin Hill as he discussed the Post Office appropriation bill for 1880, "and it is a very marked one. Our whole industrial system has been changed. We were formerly only an agricultural people. . . . Now, we expect in the future to become a manufacturing people, a very large manufacturing people. . . . Now we want markets. . . . We think that South America and Central America, and the West Indies are our proper markets."

One certain way to obtain these markets, it seemed, was to establish steamship lines in the new areas, and Southerners like Hill were willing to team up with Northerners to get them. But they could not take the lead in the fight. The brunt of the battle had to be borne by the Republicans.

Because they could not reduce tariffs without forsaking one of their cardinal principles or allow shipowners to purchase ships outside the United States without injuring shipbuilders, the Republicans were stuck with the subsidy program as a means of solving the shipping crisis and building up a merchant marine. This was what made the postal service important to them. For just as it had been used to serve the interests of other groups, the American Post Office could with some justification be made to serve the interests of expansionists, shipping interests, and national pride.

There was, of course, truth in the argument that the expansion of the foreign mail service and the expansion of foreign trade and commerce went hand in hand. John Kasson, the first assistant postmaster general and later congressman from Iowa, who represented the United States in the postal conference in Paris in 1863, had learned from this experience that "in proportion as you develop rapid communication between two countries engaged in commerce, in the same proportion, or greater, you develop commercial transportation."

Expansionism and the Post Office

And there was something more than rhetoric in a Kansas senator's view of the relationship between the mail service and expansion. "Give a handful of Americans in the Argentine Republic, in Uruguay, in Paraguay, steamers that will carry to them the mails which are necessary to their businesses and conveniences there," he said as he argued for the establishment of steamship lines to those areas in 1887, "and the handful of men will become colonies, and the colonies will become a great people, and there will be a connection, not merely of a commercial character, but a connection by blood, by similarity of institutions, by all that communicity of interests which bind together remote populations."

Furthermore, tying the ship-subsidy program to the mail system made it possible to argue that government payments to steamships were not really subsidies but compensation for carrying the mail. This was no small point, considering that the word "subsidy" evoked an image of scandal and tarnished reputations as useful to those who opposed giving help to steamship lines as the image of the old flag floating over American ships at sea was to their supporters. Even such an estimable man as New York's Democratic congressman Abram Hewitt came at last to support compensation to ships for carrying the mails on the grounds that such payments were not subsidies but "reasonable compensation for service" which the people were demanding.

The nation's postal policy was also useful to the expansionists, who never denied their critics' charges that they were more interested in developing steamship lines with mail subsidies than they were in carrying the foreign mails. They argued instead, and not unreasonably, that compensating ships for carrying the mail was only an extension to the sea of the postal policy the nation had always followed upon the land. On land, they said, railroads and stagecoach lines were subsidized to carry the mail. Why not, then, compensate ships for doing so and equalize the service? Of course this would help the shipping interests just as railroads and stagecoaches had been helped, but was this not all in the national interest? The trade that would flow along the new shipping lanes, the estimated $200,000,000 annual freight bill that could be paid to American rather than foreign steamship lines to help give the nation a favorable balance of trade, to say nothing of floating the old flag over the seas once more, were these not all worthy ways to use the nation's wealth? Besides, much of the money needed to compensate American ships for carrying the mails could be taken from the profits made from postage on foreign mails, which was estimated in 1890 to be $2,000,000. And as important as all these things was the expectation that there would be no extra expense in administering a subsidy or compensation program to build up steamship lines. The Post Office Department could do it, as it had in fact already done.

Finally, not the least of the postal service's contributions to the drive for steamship subsidies were the annual Post Office appropriation bills which gave friends of steamship compensation a chance to provide indirect subsidies when direct subsidy bills were impossible to bring before Congress. The importance of this was suggested by the history of steamship legislation in the post–Civil War period. Three times in those years bills to give direct subsidies to steamships reached the talking stage in Congress. But each time they met with such opposition that Republicans were forced to fall back upon the Post Office appropriation bills as their only hope for keeping the issue alive and securing something for the shipping interests.

Acting on this wisdom, the Senate, which was as Republican

in the Gilded Age as the House of Representatives was Democratic, almost annually for fifteen years amended the Post Office appropriation bills as they came from the House to include some scheme for subsidizing mail steamships. Sometimes the amendment was in the form of a general proposition such as the one of 1882 to classify American ships and pay them for carrying the mails according to their classification; at other times, it was only to carry the mails to the Orient, Australia, New Zealand, or merely to Mexico and South America. Once, in 1879, the Senate agreed upon two monthly mail routes to Brazil, one to leave from New York and the other from New Orleans, with the stipulation that if either should fail for lack of freight the other must also be stopped. This was the South's price for its support. "Come," Senator Hill told northern senators, "if you use the New Orleans line to start the New York line, then use the New York line to keep the New Orleans line going. That is what we want. That is fair."

But almost always, the Senate amendments failed in the House of Representatives, where two Democrats, William Holman from Indiana and Georgia's James Blount, took the lead in blocking efforts to make large payments to American shippers for carrying the mails. The two men were much alike. Both represented rural constituencies, both made their reputations in Congress by naysaying, and both were economy-minded agrarians in a world rapidly becoming industrialized. Of the two, Holman was the more vigorous foe of subsidies. Vowing that he was "now and forever against" them, he eliminated Senate subsidy amendments to the Post Office appropriation bills with dispatch, usually by parliamentary tactics that prevented the House from even voting on them. Once, when he had refused to permit consideration of a subsidy amendment, the Senate tacked the amendment to the post roads bill. The House then killed the post roads bill for that year.

Only once between 1877 and 1891 did Congress successfully enact a subsidy bill. That was in 1885, when Congress, in an attempt to pay steamship companies the same for carrying the mail on the sea as was paid for carrying the mail over the star routes on land, authorized the postmaster general to make contracts with steamship companies to carry the mail for fifty cents a nautical mile over both the outward and the inward voyage. But this was passed just as the Democrats were coming into control of the executive branch of the government for the first time since the Civil War, and President Cleveland's postmaster general, Vilas, refused to make the contracts.

Stymied by the Democrats at every turn in their efforts to obtain subsidies for mail steamships, the Republicans were forced to wait until 1891, when they controlled Congress and the White House, before they could push through a subsidy bill. Then they enacted a law similar to the proposal made in 1882. The postmaster general was authorized to make contracts with steamship companies to carry the mails whenever in his judgment they would "best subserve and promote the postal and commercial interests of the United States," and he was to pay them according to the tonnage and speed of the ships upon which the mail was sent. A steamship of eight thousand tons, for example, with a speed of twenty knots, could be paid as much as four dollars a mile annually for carrying the mail for each outward voyage.

Perhaps this act, passed as the spirit of American nationalism soared and near the year that marked the end of the American frontier, reflected the nation's new mood as it moved rapidly into the whirlpool of world politics, propelled by the foreign mail service, which had grown mightily over the years in which the mail steamship controversy had been debated.

The nation's foreign mail service in the post–Civil War period bore almost no resemblance to its antebellum counterpart. By 1872 the service had already grown so large that Congress had been compelled to provide a superintendent of foreign mails, not only to route the American mails around the world on numerous steamship lines but to supervise the many postal services being added to the system.

Between 1869 and 1881, arrangements had been made with all the major western powers for the exchange of money orders, and similar agreements were being made with other nations annually. By that time, too, the registry service was being widely used in the foreign mail, and after 1872, when they were adopted in the United States, so were postal cards. Parcels of sample goods were going through the international mails in large quantities, and by the turn of the century parcel post conventions creating parcel post systems through which merchandise other than samples could be exchanged had been written with a number of countries. Strangely, these conventions gave Americans, for a time at least, a better international than domestic parcel post.

Mail transportation to distant lands too, though poor in some areas of the world, was excellent on the Atlantic. Virtually all of the mail here was carried by foreign ships merely for the price of sea postage, but so many steamship lines from England and Europe to America competed for the trade that by 1874 the mails could be dispatched to Europe four days a week, on the swiftest ships afloat. That year the Post Office began what was to be a long-standing practice of keeping a record of the crossings of various steamships and assigning the American mails to the speediest of the available ships leaving port at any given time. Then in 1890, to speed the delivery of the mails once they reached New York, Postmaster General Wanamaker, the master innovator, put sea post offices on some steamships. On these the mails were sorted on the voyage and made ready for instant delivery once they reached the harbor.

The greatest change in the foreign mail service, however, resulted from the operation of the Universal Postal Union, which the United States government, in spite of its tendency to look inward in the period, had readily joined. By 1876, when France became a participating member, all western European countries belonged to this amazing confederation that made their nations one great postal district, and each year more nations joined until by 1891 only China, Cape Colony, the Orange Free State, and a few isolated islands remained outside.

Under the union's direction the postal systems of the various nations were so well integrated that foreign transit mail passed from country to country as smoothly as if it were domestic mail. The complicated postal accounts were eliminated, and important above all else, the international postage rates were reduced. In 1875 a letter could be sent from America to England or any place in Europe for five cents, and a postal card or newspaper for two.

Because of these changes—the speed of new ships that brought Europe and America within 176 hours of each other by the fastest steamer, the efficient postal service, and the reduction of postage—the American postal service was building a bridge of words and ideas between Americans and foreigners, as the postal statistics indicated. The year the Civil War ended, Americans exchanged nearly 7,500,000 pieces of mail with those living outside the country. Only fifteen years later, in 1880, that figure was 106,981,414, and by 1900 it was 252,021,124.

Letters of all kinds composed more than 34,500,000 pieces of all this material in 1880 and 129,473,874 in 1900. By far the greatest number of these throughout the years to World War I, almost half in fact, were exchanged with Great Britain, which might have suggested to diplomats the continued close ties between England and the United States in spite of the popular American pastime of "twisting the lion's tail." But the mail that came in the foreign mailbags also indicated the diverse origins of Americans and the changing composition of the American society as the new immigration from eastern and southeastern Europe debouched upon the American shores in the late nineteenth and early twentieth centuries and the newcomers began to write back home.

In 1880, next to England, Americans sent most of their correspondence to Germany, France, and Sweden in that order. Italy ranked next, but barely above Norway and Switzerland, and correspondence to Austria and Russia was apparently too sparse to record. Twenty years later, however, Italy ranked third in the number of letters received from the United States, and France fourth. Close behind France was Austria, then Russia, and finally Sweden. Norway and Switzerland had fallen far behind. By 1905 the pattern was even more remarkably changed. Americans were now sending more letters to Italy than to Germany, which after so many years had dropped to third, just above Austria and Russia. France now ranked sixth and Sweden seventh in the number of letters received from America.

Not only did the statistics drawn from the American foreign mail service suggest how rapidly the new immigrants were filling up America, but the number of letters they sent back to the old world indicated that they were possibly more literate than many native Americans believed. They also showed that the new immigrants were prospering in their chosen land.

In 1880 not quite 7,000 money orders were issued in the United States to be sent to Italy, even though that nation ranked third, behind England and Germany, in the number sent. None were recorded for Austria and Russia. But in 1914, more than 600,000 money orders valued at $22,124,768 were issued in the United States for Italy alone. In the number of money orders issued in the United States for all countries, Italy ranked next to England and was closely followed by Russia and Austria. Even Hungary, which now ranked sixth, was not far from Germany in the number of money orders received from the United States.

It was remarkable, too, that the total value of money orders issued in the United States for Italy that year surpassed by some $8,000,000 the total value of the more than 1,000,000 money orders sent to England from America. All together, in 1914, 1,875,403 money orders valued at $58,356,978 were issued in the United States for the five European countries from which the new immigration came. By contrast, 113,331 money orders worth only $6,132,453 were issued in those countries for people living in the United States. That year, the excess the United States had to pay over what it received through the exchange of money orders was $78,957,343.

By making possible the exchange of all letters and money orders, to say nothing of the books, parcels, and more than 109,000,000 newspapers, articles, and commercial papers exchanged in 1900 alone, the American Post Office was perhaps giving Americans a better understanding of their world and shattering their isolation as well. At the same time it was indeed spreading American influence in the underdeveloped areas of the world as the expansionists had intended.

As ubiquitous in the world's distant lands as the proverbial Singer Sewing Machine agent and the American missionary, the American postal service carried the American message around the world. From the 1880s on, no nation in the Universal Postal Union dispatched more of its newspapers and commercial papers to foreign countries than the United States. More than 29,000,000 pieces of such mail were sent out in 1880, and over 61,000,000 in 1898. Along with millions of letters and postal cards, they went to every corner of the world, and one could read the growth of the American presence in the various parts of the globe in the postal statistics.

The weight of letters and newspapers sent to Japan in 1880 was 10,210,206 grams, 9,229,309 of which was composed of newspapers and commercial papers. That year the mail sent to Hong Kong weighed 3,495,976 grams and that to Singapore 63,815 grams. More than 34,000 letters were sent in 1880 to Shanghai, where the American consul kept a post office for American missionaries and businessmen and where after 1887 all classes of mail including unsealed packages were being exchanged with San Francisco. By 1900, however, the mail sent to Japan weighed 106,840,639 grams, that to Hong Kong 14,382,380, and that to Singapore 463,492. Mails weighing 41,548,789 grams were exchanged with Shanghai that year, and in 1900 more than 131,000 grams of mail were even sent to the obscure land of Cochin China. In just fourteen years, from 1886 to 1900, the weight of the mails sent to the British Australasian colonies from the United States jumped from 24,800,925 grams to 114,898,584.

Expansionism and the Post Office

Closer to home, the American mails were also penetrating the Latin American countries, in spite of sporadic mail service to many of them. In South America, where American businessmen coveted markets, the weight of the mail sent to Brazil, Argentina, and Venezuela increased between 1880 and 1900 from 5,807,770, 1,462,840, and 1,107,550 grams to 70,153,740, 49,483,-960, and 28,335,375 grams respectively. Moreover, the aims of the American businessmen in this area were further served by the Democratic administration when in 1887 the Post Office Department announced that it would soon complete "parcel-post conventions with several West India Islands and South and Central American states, for the purpose of dispatching through the mails merchandise parcels of declared value, through which the Department will . . . obtain new facilities, for increasing the trade relations with our South American neighbors." By 1901 nineteen such conventions had been written with countries in the western hemisphere, and that year more than 76,000 packages of merchandise weighing some 252,000 pounds were sent through the mails from the United States to foreign countries.

Throughout the years, the postal service was also of some importance in drawing into the American orbit the islands that would become the nation's possessions and protectorates by 1898. From the 1840s the mails had been sent regularly to Cuba and irregularly to Hawaii. After the Civil War every effort was made to develop good mail service to both islands. By 1896 Hawaii had a trimonthly steamship mail service from the United States and the weight of the mails being sent there had increased from 7,197,045 grams in 1882 to 48,254,173 by 1897.

To Cuba there was much better service. In 1880 the second assistant postmaster general noted the demand for a fast mail service to that island, to advance, as he said, "the commercial interests of the United States." Five years later, when the Democrats in Congress and the Cleveland administration were decrying subsidies to steamships, so important did the mail service to Cuba seem that Congress declared the Cuban mails to be a part of the inland rather than the foreign mail service and authorized the postmaster general to subsidize, in effect, a steamship line to carry the mails from Tampa to Havana. More than that, Congress even permitted the extension of a fast mail train to Tampa to connect the mails from New York with those going from Tampa to Havana. Consequently, in the eleven years between 1886, when the service went into effect, and in 1897 the volume of mail to Cuba and Puerto Rico rose from 31,927,486 grams to 51,469,927.

As an agent of expansionism, the postal service was also helpful in Americanizing the island possessions once they came under American control. In a gesture that, according to the postmaster general, gave "the people of those islands another practical evidence that they were under the flag of the United States," the postal rates to the new possessions, and Cuba also, were reduced to the United States domestic rates in 1899. Quickly, too, American postal laws and organizations were established in Puerto Rico and Hawaii, and even in Cuba the postal service was completely Americanized before it was returned to the Cuban government on 20 May 1902. The Philippine mail service, on the other hand, was never integrated into the American system or paid for from the regular Post Office appropriation bills. Yet even here many of the American postal practices were put into effect by the former American postal officials who went to the Philippines to take charge of the service.

Expansionism and the Post Office

By the turn of the century, then, the American Post Office had, with great effort, served the interests of the American expansionists in many ways. But it had not yet secured all that supporters of steamship interests desired. The act of 1891, in fact, which had authorized the postmaster general to subsidize ships for carrying the mail, had been thoroughly disappointing to the expansionists, shipping interests, and even postal officials. For the subsidies offered by the act had been so meager that by 1900 the postmaster general had been able to keep under contract only six sea steamship routes, after once having advertised for fifty-three.

In the aftermath of the Spanish American War, however, all signs pointed to the likelihood that supporters of steamship interests would be able to wring additional subsidies from the government. The war itself had produced arguments for increased subsidies. On the one hand, the need for more ships had been dramatically indicated when some American troops had to be transported to Cuba aboard a British vessel. At the same time, the fact that four mail steamships operating under the act of 1891 had been converted into auxiliary naval vessels and had made a valuable contribution to the war effort seemed to prove the wisdom of the 1891 law and argued for its extension. Then, too, the acquisition of a colonial empire that reached halfway around the world made the building of a strong merchant marine seem imperative. Finally, the Republicans, who had always favored subsidies for steamships, were in control of both Congress and the White House.

Under such favorable circumstances, the Republicans launched their drive for steamship subsidies in December 1898, when President McKinley made a plea for American steamship lines to connect the United States with her colonies, and presented their first subsidy proposal in the Senate in 1900. From then until 1910 they waged an aggressive campaign for ship subsidies that was more notable for its persistence than for its success.

So confident were the Republicans as they began the battle that they had not even bothered in their first proposal to suggest that the purpose of the bill was to compensate ships for carrying the mail. Instead they offered a direct subsidy measure. The complete failure of this bill, however, apparently convinced Republicans that if they wished to have ship subsidies they would have to relate them to the mail service. So between 1902 and 1910 they presented Congress with three more bills to subsidize steamships, and all of them were to promote the ocean mail service.

No effort was spared in promoting this legislation. Both President Theodore Roosevelt and President Taft supported the fight enthusiastically, and top administration officials were also thrown into the battle. In 1906 Elihu Root, secretary of state, just back from a trip to South America, gave a much publicized address to the Trans-Mississippi Commercial Congress at Kansas City, emphasizing the need for better communications between the United States and South America as a means of developing trade. "It is absolutely essential," he said, "that the means of communication between the two countries [continents] should be improved and increased. This underlies all other considerations and it applies both to the mail, passenger, and the freight services." He noted that "not one American steamship runs to any South American port beyond the Caribbean Sea," and that the mails between Europe and South America were "swift, regular, and certain," but were "slow, irregular, and uncertain" between the United States and South America. "Six weeks," he said, "is not an uncommon time for a letter to take between Buenos Aires or Valparaiso and New York. The merchant who wishes to order American goods can not know when his order will be received or when it will be filled."

Republican postmasters general, too, from 1898 to 1912, vigorously supported the subsidy program in their annual reports. They argued that America's new position in the world demanded that she have an ocean mail service equal to those of England and Germany, and they warned that more and more of the American mails were being carried under foreign flags on ships over which the postmaster general had no control. They alluded often to their inability under the act of 1891 to contract with steamship lines to carry the mails to South America south of Venezuela or to the Orient and noted the loss the nation sustained because of this. "The foreign trade of South America is $1,500,000,000 and is increasing at the rate of $100,000,000 a year," the postmaster general wrote in 1909, "yet this country has only two contract routes to that continent, both of them to Venezuela. The Orient offers vast opportunities for trade, yet there is no contract service between the United States and the ports of the Philippines, Japan, China, or Australasia."

But all their efforts were fruitless. Not even Republican majorities in both houses of Congress could push through larger subsidies than those already afforded by the act of 1891. Perhaps the times had much to do with their failure, for the dangers of subsidizing special business interests loomed large in the Progressive years when millionaires sat in Senate seats and large-scale private enterprises were so often suspect.

It was also apparent that southern Democrats and midwestern Republicans did not care any more for the glories of empire after the Spanish American War than they had before. Their minds were on other things. In 1906 the Grange let it be known that it was opposed to subsidies, at least until the nation had been covered with rural free delivery mail routes. And southern Democrats scoffed at Republican attempts to use the Post Office Department as a buffer to conceal their efforts to secure ship subsidies, which seemed unconstitutional to many Southerners. Besides, the farmers for whom they spoke had no vital interest in sending ships to South America and the Orient. Their produce went across the Atlantic, and on that ocean there were plenty of ships to haul their crops.

So the long Republican campaign to use the Post Office to subsidize steamships as it had been used to subsidize railroads came to an end by 1910. Perhaps the Republicans had been to the well once too often, and maybe the very fact that the railroads had exacted such heavy tolls through the years was one reason steamships could not. But whatever the reason for their failure in 1910, the Republicans had the last word.

Pleading for steamship subsidies in 1902, Senator Mark Hanna from Ohio had called the Senate's attention to the fact that when the British had withdrawn their fast steamers from the Atlantic in 1896 to use in the Boer War, freight rates had doubled and quadrupled. "What," he asked, "would be the condition in this country if the opponents in that contest had been England and Germany or France?" It was a pertinent question, but those who were determined to crush the subsidy movement were not to be dissuaded by such hypothetical propositions. Then, suddenly, in 1914, Hanna's supposition was a reality. England, France, and Germany were at war, their ships were being withdrawn from the Atlantic trade, the American farmers' products were without transportation, and the Democrats who were then in power had a problem. Rarely in history was a political party more rapidly converted. While Republicans looked on in amazement, the Democrats, using the arguments Republicans had gathered for more than half a century, wrote their own steamship bill in 1916.

True, the Democrats established a government corporation to purchase, construct, operate, and lease steamships instead of giving private companies an outright subsidy, and the Republicans called it socialism. But when World War I was over, Congress made provisions in 1920 for the gradual shifting of the ships to private owners with the promise of mail contracts that were to be arranged largely by the postmaster general.

But this was not the end. The shipping interests were still dissatisfied and in 1926 began a campaign to induce Congress to grant enlarged subsidies for steamships. Two years later, the Republicans at last secured a mail subsidy bill designed to develop a merchant marine capable of carrying the greater part of the nation's commerce. The Post Office Department was made the principal agency for achieving this goal, and by 1929 the postmaster general, with plenty of money at his disposal, had made twenty-five contracts with steamship companies to carry the mail to South America, Europe, and the Orient.

VII

Guardians of the
Nation's Mails and Morals

Probably no people in the world expected more of their Post Office than Americans. Aside from subsidizing their businessmen, newspaper and magazine publishers, railroads, stagecoaches, and steamships, they expected their postal system to provide them with a safe and regular mail service over vast distances and all but impassable post roads at cheap postage rates; and they took it for granted that it would carry their money as well as their mails across the nation as safely as they could themselves. After the Civil War, when their society grew more complex, they looked to the Post Office to uphold the nation's moral standards and protect them from the misuse of the mails by unscrupulous members of their society.

In striving to fulfill all these expectations the Post Office Department did a much better job than Americans had a right to expect, considering that the government was slow to enforce the laws it passed to protect the nation's mails and morals and that the Post Office was so accessible to the purposes of the dishonest.

Of all branches of the government, as Postmaster General Holt was to point out in 1859, none offered so many opportunities for dishonesty as the Post Office. Thousands of postmasters had ample opportunity to juggle their accounts and return less money to the department than was due. Mail contractors could easily find ways to make fraudulent bids or omit portions of the routes they had contracted for. Citizens, too, could send messages to friends on newspapers to avoid paying letter postage, wash and reuse canceled stamps, open and read other people's mail, exaggerate the population and business activity of their towns when they petitioned Congress for extensions of their mail facilities, and use the mail to defraud the American public with deceptive schemes that promised much but gave nothing. And nowhere in the nation through most of the nineteenth century was there a better chance for successful thievery than that offered by the postal service—first because the mails carried most of the money that circulated through the country, and second because the risks involved in such robberies were small.

The American mail service had not been designed to carry money, and its troubles would have been significantly reduced had it never done so. But because they had no alternative and because they assumed it was the Post Office's duty to carry it, Americans sent their money by mail, then demanded that the Post Office protect it, never realizing the burden this placed upon the department. Letters with money in them were passed from post office to post office where they were handled and rehandled by postmasters, clerks, and mail carriers, and even occasionally by unauthorized people, and were a constant test of the postal employees' honesty that not all of them could pass. In addition, the isolated post office, the lone postrider, and the mail stagecoach, traveling along the nation's empty roads, were easily robbed by those given to making their living by the sweat of other men's brows.

To prevent all these things from happening Congress passed laws, of course—many laws—but unfortunately for years it provided no way to enforce them, and the postmasters general were left to find their own way of doing this. At first they relieved their assistants from their duties in the department, paid them two dollars a day for expenses, and sent them off as troubleshooters to inspect the service, correct abuses, and enforce the laws. By the early 1800s, however, the violations of the postal laws and the bottlenecks in the service were already too numerous to be investigated by the assistants, and the postmasters general began hiring men on a temporary basis to do this work.

In the first half of the nineteenth century, these employees were called special agents and were often referred to as the "eyes and ears of the department." Their duties were as varied as the troubles that plagued the postal system, but basically they inspected the service from top to toe, instructed postmasters and mail contractors in their duties, and made whatever recommendations were necessary to provide for the "celerity, certainty, and security" of the mails. In practice this meant recommending the removal of incompetent postmasters, clerks, and mail carriers, fining mail contractors for failure to perform service, suggesting changes in post routes and even post office sites, and settling as best they could community postal squabbles. Increasingly, as more and more letters with money in them entered the mails, it also meant tracing missing letters, investigating robberies, and tracking down mail depredators and bringing them to justice for their crimes.

Little is known about crime in the young American Republic

and no statistics are available to trace its course. But the postal records suggest that men were as inclined then to steal when the opportunity afforded as they would be in the years to come. In 1792 and 1794, when the first postal laws were written, the mails had already been plundered so often that Congress included in those laws capital punishment for anyone convicted of stealing letters containing money. Even in Jefferson's virtuous Arcadia, the president was forced to conclude in a letter to his attorney general in 1808 that then was a poor time to ask Congress to eliminate corporal punishment for postal crimes because robbery of the mails had "become so frequent and great an evil."

This problem was to worsen in the wake of the War of 1812, when postal robberies not only increased but were frequently perpetrated by outsiders. Before the war, most of the robberies seemed to have been the work of postal employees—postmasters or postal clerks usually—who had direct access to the mails and could remove valuable letters either before or after they were placed in mailbags without arousing immediate suspicion. But as the nation approached its fourth decade, the mails were often being attacked by highwaymen.

The increase in postal depredations in those postwar years apparently reflected a general increase in crime, and puzzled Americans speculated on its cause as they were to do so often in the future. Postmaster General Meigs, like so many of his countrymen who were to follow him, blamed the immigrants. The end of the European wars, he wrote in 1819, had brought a "migration to our shores of numbers of desperate characters," and those, mingling with the "profligate of our own nation," and all "being indisposed to self-support by honest means," were quick to seize the property of others.

But some thought the trouble lay deeper. The editor of the

Niles *Register,* among others, suggested that the mail robberies had resulted from the rapid deterioration of the national character, and he could think of nothing Congress could do to protect the mails. "That which formerly guarded it—a sense of moral rectitude," he wrote in 1821, "has greatly ceased to operate in favor of its safety through the pressure of the times." Wistfully, he added: "It will take us many years to get back to the state of confidence we formerly enjoyed—when every one, by honest labor could *furnish himself* with a competency of the good things of life."

The pressure of the times was at the root of much of the trouble. A financial panic had struck the nation in 1819, but more than that the nation was moving rapidly from its simple agrarian ways toward becoming a business-oriented world, and the increased postal crimes reflected in part this transformation of the economy. The growth of business activity brought more money into the mails and made them more tempting to thieves. Some ninety thousand dollars, for example, an astronomical sum for the time, was involved in the robbery of the Great Eastern Mail stagecoach in 1818. At the same time, the expansion of the postal service made its supervision more difficult. Yet even in the 1820s, Congress had provided the Post Office Department with no permanently employed special agents to supervise the system. Instead, in 1821 the department had eight agents scattered from Pennsylvania to Mississippi and as far west as Vincennes, Indiana, acting as its eyes and ears but employed only occasionally for special missions.

Suggestions for the improved protection of the mails had been made through the years, of course. In 1818 the Senate raised the possibility of placing armed guards on all mail stagecoaches, but Postmaster General Meigs, still thinking of the virtuous Republic, could not bring himself to agree to hire armed guards to protect the mail, "to the distrust of the civic virtues and moral energies of the people." Even before this there had been suggestions that special agents be employed on a permanent basis. But fear of increasing the postmaster general's power by adding to the number of people he appointed to office kept Congress from permitting this.

So in spite of the need, it was 1830 before the postmaster general established the Office of Instruction and Mail Depredation in the department, and not until 1836, when the Post Office Department was reorganized, that Congress authorized the regular employment of special agents. Acting on this authority, Postmaster General Kendall reorganized the Office of Instruction and Mail Depredations, called it the Office of Inspection, placed it under the direction of the third assistant postmaster general, and employed special agents full time. Four years later the office had an appropriation of $22,000 for the year.

Unfortunately, the new Office of Inspection had scarcely been established before its troubles with Congress, which were to restrict its work and adversely affect its appropriations until World War I, began.

The Office of Inspection's special agents necessarily had to be given considerable power in order to do their jobs. Their commissions authorized them to inspect a postmaster's records, open mailbags and inspect the mails at any point along the post road, make arrests, make recommendations of all kinds, and require postal employees to assist them in their work. Because of their power and the fact that they represented the national government, the agents were often treated with deference and even regarded with awe when they visited a community to inspect a post office or settle a postal problem. James Holbrook, special agent in the 1850s, recalled that once when the people learned he had arrived in their community to settle a quarrel over the location of a post office they were so excited that they dropped out of a funeral procession to talk to him. "Compared with the post-office question," he wrote, "the grave was nowhere, and funerals were at a discount."

It was inevitable, however, that men with such power and such duties would make enemies. Occasionally they would abuse their power and ruffle a citizen's feelings. More than that, their recommendations for solving community feuds over the mail service were certain to alienate someone. Inevitably, too, they were bound to become involved in politics. They were, after all, employed by the party in control of the government, and the recommendations they made regarding the locations of post offices and the dismissal of postmasters were not often made without political considerations. Besides, they were given outright political chores to do, and it was this that led them into their first great clash with Congress in the 1840s.

In 1841 Charles Wickliffe, postmaster general for the newly elected Whig administration, ordered his special agents to make a full-scale inspection of the postal service, which was no doubt badly needed. But it soon became apparent that the agents were "politicking" as well as inspecting. They not only urged postmasters to support this or that candidate for election, but even helped in political campaigns themselves.

Proof of this was brought to the country's attention in a sensational way in 1843 when the postmaster general's own nephew, Robert Wickliffe, avidly supported by Special Agent Brown, was running for Congress against the incumbent Garrett Davis. On 1 August, Wickliffe was speaking at Russell's Cave Spring in Fayette County, Kentucky, when Brown and

Cassius Clay, a Davis supporter, exchanged words, then blows. Disregarding the bullet that Brown fired at him point-blank, Clay charged upon Special Agent Brown with his bowie knife, severed the agent's left ear and a piece of his skull, pierced his right eye, cut his nose in two, and threw the senseless body down a creek bank.

Brown, who was the special agent for New Orleans, had apparently made this trip to Kentucky with the approval of the postmaster general himself, for when Davis accused the postmaster general of conniving with Special Agent Brown to defeat him, Wickliffe did not directly deny it; nor did he challenge Davis when the latter called his actions cowardly. But however it was, the affair convinced many congressmen that the men who were supposed to be protecting the mails were only protecting politicians, and some members of Congress were reluctant to appropriate money for them. Twice after this affair the postmaster general tried to get Congress to raise the agents' salaries from $1,000 to $1,500. But the most it would do was to increase them to $1,200, and when an attempt was made in 1844 to get more, a number of congressmen led a movement to eliminate the agents altogether.

The next year, Cave Johnson, President Polk's postmaster general, did remove all the agents shortly after he came into office, probably as much because they belonged to the wrong political party as because they were politicians. To do their work, Johnson returned for a time to the old system of hiring agents only when a specific investigation was to be made, and the appropriations for special agents and mail depredations dropped from $30,000 for 1846 to $12,000 for 1849.

But both the country and the Post Office were changing too rapidly to return to the old ways. As the nation hurried through its biggest boom and bust period in the 1850s toward the Civil War, the postal service was extended to the Pacific coast and the postage rates were lowered. The mails were now laden with more letters and more money than ever before, and the rifling of letters increased accordingly. In 1849 alone, the department received almost two-thirds as many complaints of mail depredations as it had in the three years between 1841 and 1844, and the postmaster general's letterbooks were filled with communications concerning postal depredations.

The post offices themselves, as much as stagecoaches and post-riders, were now being held up in such numbers that by 1859 the New York *Times* called it an epidemic. "The recurring accounts of these forays upon the mails," ran the paper's editorial, "suggest the idea that the sacredness of the mail-bag has departed, and that a post-office is little better than a panel-crib." It was even less during the Civil War, particularly in the border states, where no post office was safe from armed men. In 1863 the postmaster general estimated that there had been one hundred attacks upon post offices that year, with losses as high as $6,000. Suspicious as it was of the Office of Inspection and its agents, Congress could not ignore the threat to the mails posed by the changing times. Even Postmaster General Johnson had reemployed special agents before he left office, and in the course of the 1850s Congress gave them at least grudging support. Their salaries were increased to $1,600 a year in the early part of the decade, and the annual appropriation for agents and mail depredations rose from $12,000 for 1849 to $60,000 for 1865. This permitted the department to raise the number of agents from the eighteen it had in 1853 to thirty-three and to station men on the Pacific shore, in the Southwest, and throughout the more populous areas of the nation.

Guardians of the Nation's Mails and Morals

Congress tried, too, in those years to reduce the number of depredations with new legislation. It regularly made large appropriations for new mailbags and for new locks to secure them. When it learned in the early 1850s that ingenious Americans had found still another way to rob the mails by opening mailbags with duplicate, or counterfeit, keys, as they were called, Congress made it a felony punishable by ten years in prison for anyone convicted of having any part in the making of keys for this purpose. Three years later, in 1855, after more than a half-century of carrying money through the mails without special provision for its protection, the registry system to safeguard valuable letters was provided. Finally, in 1864 the money-order system was created, so that Americans could at last mail money without actually putting it in the mail.

But the value of these laws was somewhat offset by the postmaster general's decision in 1864 to abolish the old Office of Inspection and place the special agents under the supervision of the second assistant postmaster general. Unfortunately, as it turned out, this decision deprived the government of an office that was badly needed to meet the changes that confronted the nation in the post–Civil War period.

At the heart of these changes was the swift growth of American industry, which amazed the world. In one generation, the United States had changed from an essentially agricultural country to the leading industrial nation of the world. By 1900 it had more miles of railroads than all of Europe and Russia combined, and its steel production was twice that of England and almost double that of Germany. Its national wealth had grown from just over $16,000,000,000 in 1860 to more than $88,000,000,000 in 1900, and its per capita income from $514 to $1,165. In the same period, its population had more than doubled, as had the percentage of its urban population, in spite of the fact that thousands of Americans had gone West to farm and to close out the American frontier on the Great Plains.

Rapid industrialization brought more wealth to American homes and more creature comforts, and made life easier for more people, more varied, and more interesting. But it was also accompanied by a startling increase in crime. Between 1860 and 1890, the number of men and women in prison for every 1,000,000 inhabitants increased from 607 to 1,315! These figures do not, of course, tell the number of crimes committed in the nation in 1890, but they do suggest that the amount of crime in this period had at least doubled as urbanization and industrialization became the new way of American life.

The American Post Office reflected all these changes, and like the economy it had expanded enormously to keep pace with westward-moving Americans and the nation's burgeoning businesses, which were so dependent upon it. Between 1870 and 1890, the nation's post offices increased from 28,492 to 62,401, and the number of miles the mails were being carried annually by rail from 47,551 to 215,715,680. Some $34,000,000 worth of money orders were issued in 1870; twenty years later those orders amounted to $114,462,757.

Registered letters, too, whose only protection for the mails before the war, according to Postmaster General Holt, had been to draw the thief's attention away from the nonregistered mail, came into their own. Perhaps no more than 500,000 such letters had been mailed in 1870 compared to a total of 14,749,081 domestic and foreign parcels and letters registered in 1890. In this registered mail passed everything from stamps and national bank notes to gold coins and even gold bullion. In 1890 the Post

Office and Treasury departments alone sent more than a billion dollars worth of stamps, postcards, national bank notes, and national bonds by registered mail.

At the same time as the postal statistics mirrored the growth of the nation's economy, they confirmed the surging crime rate the census figures suggested. In 1870 the postmaster general listed 3,071 complaints of missing letters and losses due to depredations of the mails. Approximately 1,500 of these involved registered mail. Two decades later, the department received 51,745 complaints of missing or rifled ordinary letters and 7,369 complaints of registered letters. The first time the postmaster general listed post offices robbed in 1879, they numbered 98; eleven years later, 862 had been burglarized and 358 burned, and so numerous had become such crimes and so heavy the losses that Congress had been compelled in 1882 to permit the postmaster general to reimburse postmasters for losses they sustained because of burglary, fire, or some other accident for which they were not responsible.

Besides the depredations upon post offices, the nation also endured an epidemic of mail stagecoach and train robberies. In 1879 fifty mail stages had been held up. The number of train robberies that year was not recorded, but only the year before, four years before the death of Jesse James, the frequency of such robberies in Texas and Missouri had inspired an excited Texas congressman to sponsor an amendment to the Post Office appropriations bill. He wanted to authorize the postmaster general to "call upon the Secretary of War for a guard to accompany and protect the mail on any post-route in Texas, Missouri, or in any of the territories," when he felt it was necessary. The congressman proposed, too, that the postmaster general offer a reward of $1,000 for the "capture, dead or alive, of each and every person who shall by violence rob or attempt to rob the mail." Congress refused to provide a guard, but such was its temper that it did appropriate $20,000 to be used for reward money. From then through the early twentieth century, the department had a standing reward for the capture and conviction of stagecoach and train robbers.

The Post Office did more, however, than reflect the rise of crime; it was in some measure responsible for it. The very expansion of the postal service that brought the mails to so many eager and demanding Americans and the very postal innovations that made the service more useful to them enlarged their opportunities for plundering letters, burglarizing post offices, and robbing trains and stagecoaches. The rich treasures pouring through the mails in registered letters and parcels made them especially attractive to the dishonest, and numerous scattered post offices made easy prey for desperadoes, as did the postal cars along the lonely miles of railroad tracks. Even the money orders, which were thought to be the ultimate in safety, fell victim to the practice of forging signatures.

Furthermore, the great expansion of post routes and the rapid transit of the mails by rail that made mass communication possible, and the cheap postage for second class mail matter designed to promote the diffusion of knowledge, scattered nationwide obscene and fraudulent materials which violated postal laws and sharply increased the number of postal crimes.

Frauds were not unknown, of course, before the Civil War, but for every fraudulent scheme Americans had known then came dozens in the postwar period—everything from convincing Americans they were heirs to European fortunes to selling counterfeit money to a bewildering variety of games of chance. Take, for example, the lottery. In colonial America, and even in the early national period, this scheme of enticing people to buy tickets in the hopes of winning a prize had been used to raise money for public purposes. But in the reform period beginning in the 1830s, lotteries were condemned as dishonest, immoral, and the sure path to the corruption and degradation of young people. Consequently, most states had outlawed them before the Civil War.

After the war, however, lotteries again became popular in some states, particularly in Louisiana, where they were legalized and where the Louisiana Lottery Company of New Orleans was granted a charter in 1868. This company was to flourish for years, reaping millions of dollars in profit and returning very little in prizes, largely because the mails provided a national market for the sale of its lottery tickets just as they did for the sale of obscene literature.

In antebellum America, obscene pictures and publications, like monarchies, seemed for the most part to have been something Americans had left in the old world. Several of the states, it was true, had antiobscenity laws in the early nineteenth century, indicating that obscene articles were not unknown. But the national government had no such law until 1842, and when it was passed it was directed against the importation of obscene objects—paintings and prints—from foreign countries, not against the domestic production and circulation of such things. This law was strengthened in 1857, and in 1865, at the request of Postmaster General Blair, Congress for the first time enacted a loosely drawn law outlawing the mailing of obscene and scandalous materials.

But it was after the war, when the cheap second-class postage rates led to the great outpouring of licentious matter from the nation's presses and the postal service scattered it throughout the country, that obscenity became a problem. By then, Charles Goodyear's vulcanization of rubber had made possible the manufacture of cheap contraceptives, and these, plus a mixture of dubious devices for inducing abortion, were being widely advertised in the numberless newspapers and pamphlets that moved through the mails. Moreover, an almost unbelievable mass of paperback novels whose settings gradually moved, as the population did, from the forest and open fields to the cities that seemed more in keeping with their plots of murder, blackmail, confidence games, and conspiracies to ruin young girls, circulated at cheap postage rates through the mails into every cranny of the nation.

Besides this, the postal system made it possible for peddlers of pornography to reach the nation's young people secretly, particularly those who lived at boarding schools and colleges. The usefulness of the mails for this kind of salesmanship was disclosed in 1873 by a report that 15,000 letters, all of them presumably from young people and all of them ordering obscene matter, had been seized from the publishers of such material.

The man who had seized the letters and who was largely responsible for arousing the American public to the perils of pornography, obscene objects, and fraudulent schemes circulating through the mails was a young drygoods clerk named Anthony Comstock. After the Civil War he had come to New York fresh from a farm in Connecticut, and he knew pornography when he saw it. Greatly agitated by what he believed were the effects of this material upon the young people he saw at his boardinghouse and elsewhere, he began a one-man crusade in 1872 to wipe it from the face of the earth. Using a recently enacted New York law forbidding the publication and manufacture of obscene articles, Comstock seized and destroyed, among other things, 182,000 obscene rubber articles and more than 700 pounds of lead molds for manufacturing these articles.

By the 1920s, when the first critical biography of Comstock appeared, his name had become synonymous with repression, censorship, and Puritan morals, and indeed, like most reformers convinced of the righteousness of their cause, he sometimes forgot in his zeal for reform that others had rights. But had it not been Comstock who led the fight, it would likely have been another, for Comstock's was a crusade whose time had come, and it drew the support of middle-class Americans who shaped public policy.

Already disturbed by the rapid changes they saw about them —the rolling tides of immigrants sweeping in upon their shores, industrialization, urbanization, and the rise of crime—middle-class Americans saw in the mass circulation of fraudulent and obscene material one more blow to the moral fiber of the nation. A sparsely settled people, taught to believe in the sanctity of marriage, the chastity of women, and the sacredness of life and the act from which life sprang could scarcely be expected to look with equanimity upon the mass distribution of newspapers and pamphlets advertising devices for preventing conception and producing abortion. Especially was this true when they considered the effect these advertisements and other obscene publications, including dime novels, had upon the lives of their children.

What effect this material did have upon the young and the rise of crime, no one really knew. Young people in prison frequently pointed to the reading of obscene literature as the cause of their downfall, and important Americans testified to the harmful effects of racy books upon the young. Comstock, of course, was emphatic upon this point, and in his book *Traps for the Young*, published in 1883, he observed that the lust roused by the reading of obscene literature was *"the constant companion of all other crimes."* The use of such material, he wrote, was a favorite device for luring young girls into brothels.

True or not, it was easy for Americans to jump to conclusions when they saw the growth of such publications on the one hand and on the other the increase of assaults upon young women in the cities. Indeed, so frequent were these attacks by the 1880s that the Woman's Christian Temperance Union and the Knights of Labor petitioned Congress in 1887 to protect young girls. To this Congress responded in 1889 with a law making it a felony in Washington, D.C., for any person to "carnally and unlawfully know any female under the age of sixteen years."

The sense of alarm with which many Americans viewed what was happening to young womanhood in their cities could be deduced from the remarks of New Hampshire senator Henry W. Blair, who supported the law in Congress. "I may say in this connection," he said in 1887, "that our civilization seems to have developed an almost unknown phase of crime in the annals of the race, and today the traffic in girls and young women in this country, especially in your large cities, has come to be more disgraceful . . . than ever was that in the girls of Circassia."

Given these conditions, and considering that their abhorrence of pornography was so deeply rooted that it would be a century before their legislators would become inured to it, it is not surprising that Americans were as ready to use their Post Office to protect the nation's morals as they were to have it support their business interests. At their insistence, Congress passed a series of laws between 1868 and 1890 aimed at ridding the mails of both fraudulent and obscene material. In 1868 it declared all letters and circulars relating to lotteries to be nonmailable, and five years later it passed the so-called Comstock Law that forbade the mailing of all obscene, lewd, lascivious, and indecent writings and all articles or advertisements of articles to prevent conception or induce abortion.

But it was toward the close of the 1880s and early 1890s, as fraudulent and obscene material continued to find its way into American homes and the crime rate still soared, that the moral crusade reached its apogee. In 1888 Congress strengthened the Comstock Law by stipulating that sealed mail would be no protection for obscene material. The following year, it attempted to put an end to the pernicious "green goods" fraud by closing the mails to all communications relating to the sale, advertisement, or sending of counterfeit money. One year later, in 1890, after the courts had made the law of 1868 for controlling lotteries ineffective, Congress enacted a vigorous statute that made it possible to destroy those lotteries that depended upon the mails for success. Finally, even this law was strengthened by an amendment in 1895. That middle-class Americans as a whole were behind these laws was suggested by the southern congressman who called the passage of the act of 1890 "a great moral act in the interests of the best people and the best sentiment of the country."

The courts, like Congress, also reflected the sentiments of the country by rendering decisions that generally supported the laws against the mailing of obscene and fraudulent material. Particularly important was the case of *ex parte Orlando Jackson* in 1878, in which the court affirmed that Congress could determine what could and what could not be carried in the mails.

Whatever the merit of all these laws, their enactment created new postal crimes, and these, together with a massive increase in the violations of the old laws, placed such an impossible burden on the department's special agents that they had to be completely reorganized. By the early 1880s they had been renamed post office inspectors and placed in a new office called the Division of Post Office Inspectors and Mail Depredations, presided over by a chief inspector. Some fifty-six of them had been scattered throughout the nation in six inspection divisions, each of which was supervised by an inspector-in-charge. The Division of Post Office Inspectors and Mail Depredations was placed under the direct control of the postmaster general in 1875, where it remained until World War I, except between 1891 and 1906 when it was located in the office of the fourth assistant postmaster general.

Until the early 1900s, some inspectors were assigned to the railway mail, money-order, and free delivery services, and drew their pay from those branches of the Post Office Department. But by 1911 all inspectors, including those who had been laying out rural free delivery mail routes in the country and had once been assigned to the superintendent of free delivery, were placed in the Division of Post Office Inspectors and Mail Depredations, making a total of more than three hundred inspectors.

In spite of their political connections, the post office inspectors were, as a group, the most competent men in the postal service. Chosen with care, usually from the elite corps of railway mail clerks, they were experts on postal law, discreet, well-trained, and completely professional in their approach to crime detection and criminal identification. They used, for example, the Bertillon system of identifying criminals according to their physical characteristics. This was the most up-to-date system of criminal identification in those days before the techniques of fingerprinting were developed in the early 1900s, and the postal inspectors' reports were filled with "Bertilloned" men they had arrested.

Even more important than this reorganization of the structure of the Division of Post Office Inspectors and Mail Depredations were the changes made in the division's day-to-day operations. By the late 1870s, every complaint against the mail service that reached the division was placed in a category labeled A, B, C, or F, and sent by the chief clerk to the various clerks in charge of each category. In time, complaints became so numerous that they overflowed these categories and new ones had to be added, but originally all complaints relating to the registered mail were marked A, and all those concerned with the loss or rifling of ordinary mail, as well as highway, train, and post office robberies, were put in category B. Category C included all miscellaneous problems—neighborhood quarrels over postmasters and post offices, for example—as well as routine work orders establishing or discontinuing post offices, making post office inspections, and all cases involving obscene and fraudulent mail. To the class F clerk went all complaints involving foreign mails.

Once the clerks received a complaint, they jacketed it, gave it a number, and sent it to the inspector-in-charge of the division where the offense had supposedly been committed. From there it went to an inspector in the field for investigation, and word was sent to the complainant that his problem was being investigated. The B clerk, for example, made up the following jacket for a robbery that occurred near Mineola, Texas, in 1886:

Ordinary

Case N. 36,242   B

Post Office, Mineola, Wood County, Texas

Robbery of the mail

Date: Nov. 20th, 1886

Hour: _____

Loss of: Mail between Quitman and Mineola
   robbed about two miles Mineola.

Report of P.M., Mineola.

To Hollingsworth, Nov. 25, 1886

While this report was on its way to Hollingsworth, inspector-in-charge of the Texas division, word was sent to the assistant attorney general for the Post Office Department that a robbery had been committed and that he would be informed of the results of the investigation. If in due time the robber was arrested and the case solved, the case on file would be marked "closed," and the name of the arrested person sent to the arrest desk where it would be recorded in another file.

With this organization and a force that by 1900 still numbered fewer than one hundred men, the postal inspectors, like Saint George confronting the dragon, went out to battle the offenders against the postal laws whose violations, together with the routine work of inspection, had increased so enormously that the number of cases the inspectors were given jumped from 29,569 in 1880 to 197,996 in 1900. Obviously this was more than those guardians of the nation's mails and morals, whose ranks grew slowly in these years, could handle, and each year hundreds of cases went untended. So much of the routine work of inspecting post offices had to be left undone, in fact, that in 1891 the postmaster general bemoaned the inefficiency in the little post offices across the land that could not be inspected because inspectors were too busy elsewhere.

Nevertheless, by working day and night the inspectors did investigate thousands of cases each year with such efficiency and dispatch that the number of those they arrested for violation of the postal laws rose from 577 in 1880 to 1,526 in 1900 and 2,818 in 1914. In addition, large sums of money alleged to have been lost through the rifling of letters were either recovered or found never to have been lost. In 1891, a fairly typical year for this period, the Division of Post Office Inspectors and Mail Depredations received 6,906 complaints of lost or rifled registered letters. But so successful were the postal inspectors in tracking down both real and alleged losses that only about one in every 8,872 pieces of registered mail was actually lost.

Postal inspectors were particularly adept at ferreting out postal employees who violated postal laws. They often watched suspected employees from concealed positions in the post offices and caught them in the act of rifling letters. And they continued, as they had done from the early days of the service, to use decoy letters to trap those employees who could not resist the temptation offered by a letter containing money. But whatever method they used, they rarely failed to find the dishonest postal employee, a fact that had much to do, no doubt, with the postal workers' record for honesty, which—as the postal statistics of 1891, for example, suggest—was good. Of all the losses in the registered mail that year, only 287 were traceable to the dishonesty of postal employees. Considering that nearly 135,000 employees handled the registered mail that year day in and out, this was a creditable record and possibly one unequaled by private enterprise.

In any case, it seemed clear that the number of dishonest

postal employees was significantly smaller, proportionately, than the number of dishonest patrons they served insofar as rifled letters were concerned. For when it came to investigating complaints of lost or rifled letters, both registered and ordinary, postal inspectors learned to investigate first the people who complained.

Most of the complaints of lost or rifled letters were made in good faith, of course, but inspectors discovered that many Americans claimed to have sent letters they never sent and not to have received letters they did receive. Thy would swear that their registered letters had been rifled when they themselves had pocketed the money contained in the letter. Or, to pay a bill, they would send a registered letter to their creditor, fail to enclose the remittance, and then argue that the letter had been rifled. An inspector once found a woman who had sent her neighbor a registered letter to pay a debt but had made no enclosure. When confronted with this, she declared that as far as she was concerned the debt was paid and her neighbor would have to look to the Post Office Department for the money.

The extent of this practice was suggested by the number of false claims made each year. In 1890, to take but one example, 328 claims were made of rifling of letters in which, in fact, no rifling had taken place, and in 143 instances senders had included no remittances when they should have. "Many of the investigations . . . have demonstrated," wrote the chief inspector in 1891, "that there is a class of people, I am sorry to say, who make use of 'Uncle Sam' to pay (?) their just debts." Inspectors even ran across people who, when rebuked by their friends for not writing, would claim to have written and blame the Post Office for losing letters they had never sent.

Most such cases could be easily settled. The honest mistakes were soon cleared up, and even those who made false claims often admitted as much when they were asked to sign affadavits swearing they had told the truth. Much harder to solve were the kinds of cases such as those involving "green goods," or counterfeit money, in which the postal patrons became the victims of their own avarice.

The "green goods" game was played in a variety of ways. In the 1890s, one sharpster passed himself off as a representative of the secretary of the treasury and a cabal of well-known citizens who for political and private reasons were anxious to issue spurious government money. All one had to do to obtain this money was to pay a fee for membership in a secret society. The confidence man discovered that men from every walk of life were tempted by his scheme, but the most susceptible, he thought, were Populists.

Normally the "green goods" men began their pitch with a letter. "I am desirous," one would write to some small-town resident, "of obtaining a shrewd agent in your locality to handle my 'Goods.' . . . I have a very superior article of the kind. . . . I warrant each and every note to be perfect as to Paper, Coloring, Vignette, Printing, Engraving, and Signature, and when made to appear as having been used or handled much, I defy the best bank clerk or expert to tell them from genuine."

The percentage of Americans who answered such teasers was no doubt small, but there was always someone, often respected in his community, who would send money for the "goods." In time he would receive a package that, alas, contained only newspapers or sometimes sawdust. But although he had been roundly cheated, he could not report the incident without revealing that he was as dishonest as the person who had sold him the "goods," and this obviously hampered the inspectors' efforts to trace the counterfeiters. Nevertheless, they did. One of their most celebrated cases occurred in 1895 when they rounded up a "green goods" gang that had moved from the city to the quiet of the little village of Hillsdale, Michigan.

The "green goods" fraud was only one of hundreds of swindles perpetrated through the mails; in fact, the genius of Americans for devising schemes to separate their fellow citizens from their money through the use of the mails was truly awe-inspiring. The number of different kinds of guessing games alone reached into the hundreds by 1903 and involved hundreds of thousands of dollars.

Occasionally there were periods when certain frauds, like the gold brick and mining stock swindles of the early 1900s, were particularly popular, but even then these were only a part of a vast array of dishonest dealings. In 1912 the chief inspector listed the names of those who had been convicted that year of nearly seventy different kinds of fraud, including everything from the fake detective agency to the sale of states' rights by the Balancing Attachment Company of Mount Vernon, Texas. That year, ten clairvoyants, thirty-one blackmailers, and seven fake real estate dealers were convicted of using the mails for fraudulent purposes.

No less amazing than the American ingenuity for inventing swindles was the American gullibility that led them in 1911 to invest an estimated $77,000,000 in fraudulent schemes. Why Americans of all classes, both the wealthy and the poor, should spend their money on obviously risky gold mine stock and astrologers like the "Wizard of the Stars," who promised to help people "maintain friends, avoid enemies, obtain health, make money, win fame, and secure a position in business and social life," was a great mystery. Americans had a strong inclination to believe whatever they saw in print, and aside from their hope of quick riches, perhaps their inability to understand that men would cheat in print accounted for their readiness to believe fraudulent advertisements. This may have been why one observer noted in 1911 that, as a class, the most numerous victims of fraudulent schemes were ministers and priests.

To stop the flow of this fraudulent material, the postmasters general for years issued fraud orders, authorized by the laws of 1890 and 1895, against those who sent such matter, and between 1890 and 1909 over three thousand such orders were issued. By this device, all letters and money orders directed to anyone against whom a fraud order was imposed were marked "FRAUDULENT" and returned to the sender.

Such orders were based primarily upon the investigations made by the postal inspectors. Once a charge was made against a dealer in fraudulent schemes, he was invited to answer the charge in a hearing and show cause why the fraud order should not be issued. After that, the attorney general, having considered all the evidence, recommended either approval or disapproval of the fraud order to the postmaster general, who usually followed the attorney general's recommendation.

Fraud orders were effective instruments for stopping frauds, and the fact that in all the years from 1890 to 1909 only two court injunctions setting aside fraud orders were issued—both of them on legal technicalities, not on the merits of the case—suggests how careful the department had been in using its considerable power to stop a man's mail. But the accused had rights, too, and friends in Congress, and in the early 1900s they raised a great hue and cry about the violations of their rights. They complained that at the hearings where they were asked to show cause why a fraud order should not be issued against them they were not shown the inspector's full report, which was apparently true. Moreover, since the fraud orders were not subject to court review, they had no ready recourse against an order of the postmaster general. Instead, as one congressman explained, they were branded as dishonest in the eyes of the public for no more than slightly exaggerated advertisements of their products.

Some members of Congress took up the cause of the accused swindlers, blasted the department's procedures, and forced the department to run for cover. In 1910 the postmaster general stopped issuing fraud orders on the ground that too much of the evidence that would have to be used in subsequent criminal trials had to be revealed at the fraud order hearings. This obviously jeopardized the chances of securing a conviction. In place of the fraud order the postmaster general attempted to bring criminal charges against those who perpetrated frauds. But while the criminal proceedings went on so did the frauds, and by the beginning of World War I fraud orders were once more being issued to protect people who somehow could not protect themselves. Even so, the number of frauds continued to mount at such a pace that the postal inspectors could do no more than stop the most obvious.

As difficult as it was for postal inspectors to build a case against the tricksters who made their living through the fraudulent use of the mails, it was no harder than to capture those who robbed mail trains, stagecoaches, and post offices. Thanks to the protection given the mails by national laws and to the Post Office Department's standing reward for the capture and conviction of highwaymen, desperadoes often robbed trains without touching the mails. Moreover, when they did rob the mail train, they usually robbed the express car too, so that in running down the bandits, postal inspectors might have the help of the

Pinkerton detectives who were employed to protect their property.

No such help was available, however, for the capture of post office robbers, and in this work the inspectors fought a lonely battle. Sometimes they were aided in making an arrest by an unusual occurrence that, in a rural community, was quickly noticed. In 1896, for example, a farmhand near Sterling, Missouri, was arrested for robbing a post office because he changed a quarter in the hardware store, and no one knew where he could have gotten so much money unless he had stolen it.

Not often, however, was a postal inspector's task that easy, as the tally of post office robberies and arrests through the years suggests. In 1900, to pick one year, 1,587 post offices were robbed and 258 robbers arrested. Obviously this record was nothing to boast about, but it was understandable in light of the postal inspectors' two principal problems: their inability to reach the scene of the crime before the robber's trail was cold and the unwillingness of the local people—the sheriff and others—to help find those who had robbed their post office.

Local law officials did, of course, sometimes arrest the man who robbed their post office before the inspector arrived on the scene. But if the suspect fled across the county line they were reluctant to go after him, knowing that it would be expensive and that they were not likely to be reimbursed for their trouble. Besides, they tended to be apathetic about a post office robbery. Possibly this was a reflection of a general American attitude toward government property. The stolen stamps and money were, after all, Uncle Sam's property, and stealing from the government, a long-standing American practice, did not seem as serious an offense somehow as stealing from one's neighbor. They knew, too, that their postmaster would be repaid for his

Guardians of the Nation's Mails and Morals

losses and that a postal inspector would be sent out whose job it was to track down the thief.

To add to the inspectors' woes, there were those perverse Americans in the nation's little villages and towns who would not help the inspectors because their sympathies were with the thief. They were not numerous, apparently, but they were important enough for the chief inspector to call attention to them in 1891. "There is . . . a sort of sentimental sympathy with criminals of all grades and conditions," he wrote, "from the red-handed murderer to the petty thief, and violators of postal laws are not exceptions to this feeling on the part of some persons."

To overcome this apathy toward post office robberies, the postmasters general began to recommend in the 1880s that Congress offer rewards for the capture and conviction of post office robbers as it did for highwaymen. Not until 1894, however, after such burglaries had increased by some 247 percent in ten years, did Congress finally begin appropriating $25,000 annually for rewards so that postal inspectors might purchase the people's cooperation, which they could not secure voluntarily.

The postmasters general claimed in their annual reports that the rewards did help in the capture of post office robbers, but they did little to reduce the number of robberies in the last decade of the old century and early years of the new. Between 1890 and 1907, the number of post office robberies tripled, and post offices had become the victims of professional thieves as well as "weary Willies" who wandered about the countryside. Organized gangs, operating under the direction of a chief whose headquarters was in the city, toured the countryside, broke into post offices and post office safes with burglar tools and dynamite—just then coming into popular use—stole stamps, money-order blanks, and money, and returned to the city to divide the spoils.

In the early 1900s, the professionals were followed by "yegg-men," poor imitations of the professionals, who carried with them only a bottle of nitroglycerine, a fuse, and a cap. Whereas the professional used a drill and a little explosive to force entry into a safe, the "yeggman" tamped the safe's joints with soap, put in glycerine to percolate behind the soap, lit the fuse, and blew the safe open with a great crash. He sold the stamps he stole to a fence in the city, and the fence disposed of them at a discount to businessmen who, much to the disgust of the chief inspector, never asked why they were sold at less than their value.

Post office burglaries kept postal inspectors busy not only writing reports fixing the responsibility for them so that the postmasters' claims for losses might be allowed if they were in no way to blame, but also tracking down the depredators. On this task they might spend weeks or even months if there seemed reason to suppose they would eventually capture the suspect.

Because of this work, postal inspectors were sometimes de-risively called "thief-catchers," a term the chief inspector took exception to in 1892, since catching thieves was only one part of their job. But if most Americans thought this was the in-spectors' principal duty, it was probably because nothing else they did received so much publicity, unless it was Anthony Comstock's continuing crusade against obscenity.

After the enactment of the Comstock Law in 1873, Comstock was made a postal inspector, and in the course of years he waged a mighty campaign against obscene publications, even though he served without pay. But he did not engage the enemy alone, as the publicity accompanying his activities made it appear. In 1896 alone, the chief inspector's report listed 531 obscene and scurrilous mail cases, and nearly all of these were handled by the regular inspectors without any fanfare at all.

Comstock's biographers have placed so much emphasis on the reformer's relentless attacks upon freethinkers who wrote off-beat sociological and medical tracts as opposed to outright pornography that they have obscured what the postal inspectors' reports make clear: much hard-core pornography was being published in that age of the horse and buggy and Victorian morals. Not only was it published, it was perhaps of equal quality with the unfettered variety of the 1960s. There is apparently a limit beyond which writers of pornography cannot go without being monotonously repetitive, and in such titles as *Courting on Compton Hill*, an obscene poem that went the rounds in 1895, and a book, *Only a Boy*, the authors had obviously reached the limit. *Only a Boy* was especially popular. It appeared on many lists of obscene publications picked up by the postal inspectors and was so avidly read that one inspector, writing from a small town in Ohio in 1891, noted that it had only been in that town from Monday evening until Wednesday noon and was already badly worn from numerous readings.

These and thousands of other pornographic books, photographs, poems, and songs were quietly seized by postal inspectors, but even so, only a small part of their obscenity cases were concerned with such publications. They spent much of their time tracking down the senders of contraceptive materials —advertisements and devices—and the makers of fraudulent abortifacients whose advertisements brought soul-searching letters from harried pregnant women who ordered the fake medicine to abort the children they did not want but sought assurance that there was a Christian way to do it.

Most of the obscenity cases the inspectors had to investigate, however, came from violations of the laws designed to protect a person from receiving or being injured by obscene or scurrilous letters and postcards. According to the postal laws, one could mail no envelope or postcard on which was written, for all the world to see, anything "intended to reflect injuriously upon the character or conduct of another." Interpreted, this meant that one could not request a person to pay an overdue bill on a postcard or send a bill in a black-bordered envelope, thereby denoting a person's previous failure to pay. Neither could obscene letters be sent through the mails, even though they were sealed.

Yet much of this kind of material appeared in the mails in those years before World War I, particularly in anonymously written letters. Indeed, judging from the number of such letters the inspectors investigated each year, it appeared that the nation was filled with people who felt the need to vent their pent up emotions anonymously by writing scurrilous and obscene letters. Many of these were written by women to their rivals for a man's affection. Some were sent to young girls by lonely old men, and some to older women by young boys with youthful fantasies. Some were also exchanged between consenting adults, as it were; yet even so, if these letters were somehow turned over to the inspectors, as many of them were, the inspectors had to find the writers and bring them to trial.

Obscene and scurrilous letters were not the products of the poor and uneducated only. "Both men and women of high rank and station in life," wrote the chief inspector in 1896, "and of apparently good breeding and refinement, have been discovered to be senders of the most shocking examples of this class of matter, and the revelations have, in some instances, led to acrimonious dissension, resulting in the division of communities." He cited one case in which the membership of a prominent church in Cambridge, Massachusetts, was torn friend from friend by the scurrilous postcards some members received, which the postal inspectors finally traced to the minister himself.

The frustrations the postal inspectors endured to protect people from obscene and scurrilous letters were endless. Guilty parties would be arrested after a long investigation only to have witnesses fail to respond at the last moment. Legal maneuvers delayed trials for months and sometimes years. Not uncommon was the case of the man who wrote obscene letters to three young ladies in an Iowa town in 1891 but was not sentenced for his crime until 1893. Moreover, sentences given for these offenses were grossly uneven. In one case, a man was sent to prison for six months for trying to arrange an assignation with two women through the mails; but in a similar case, the judge quashed the indictment saying he knew of no United States law "making penal the mailing of letters intended . . . for procuring such assignations."

Then, too, many sentences given were so light as to make the labor of investigation and arrest seem useless. In North Dakota, a woman arrested in 1894 for writing a most obscene letter was acquitted, and the disgusted postal inspector wrote that it was "virtually useless to attempt to convict a woman in this portion of the country no matter what the crime." But this was almost universally true across the nation as far as obscene letters were concerned. Women might sometimes be fined for their obscene letters, but they were rarely sent to jail.

In spite of their frustrations, the postal inspectors tried earnestly to investigate all the obscenity cases given them, but they could no more keep pace with these offenses than they could with those relating to fraud and post office robberies. Particularly was this true in the early 1900s, when they were faced with a mounting importation of obscene material from France and with additional homegrown varieties of obscenity.

In the great stream of newspapers, pamphlets, and magazines flowing through the mails at the turn of the century were countless advertisements of medicines to cure all kinds of sexual malaise. These advertisements contained detailed descriptions of bodily functions which, if not obscene, were indecent in the view of many Americans. For a time, the Post Office was reluctant to ban such material from the mail, particularly after 1895 when the Supreme Court ruled in *United States* v. *Swearingen* that the obscenity laws referred only to sexual impurity. But by 1903 postal officials had concluded that these advertisements were not only obscene and indecent but promoted fraudulent cures as well.

From then until World War I, they drove them from the mails either by denying the use of the mails to publications that carried such advertisements or by issuing fraud orders against those who manufactured the fraudulent cures.

Though the Post Office Department had found a way to attack these particular advertisements, it could not, with the laws at its disposal, rid the mails of many other kinds of writings that people found obnoxious in those years when the nation was moving so rapidly from the old agrarian order. For this reason, many Americans demanded stronger antiobscenity laws than those on the books, and their demands were reflected in Congress, where from the 1890s to World War I numerous bills were introduced to strengthen the old Comstock Law.

Guardians of the Nation's Mails and Morals

In this bag of miscellaneous legislation were proposals to add the words "loathsome and disgusting" to the descriptions of nonmailable matter and measures, like the one of 1892, to ban from the mails publications primarily devoted to "criminal news, police reports, or accounts of criminal deeds, or pictures and stories of immoral deeds, lust, or crime." In 1894 the Society of Friends of Genesee, New York, petitioned Congress to bar from the mails any newspaper carrying an account of a prize-fight, and in 1910, when accounts of such things were becoming more and more common, bills were proposed to prevent depositing in the mails publications carrying stories of divorce proceedings, rape, adultery, or seduction cases.

But there was a limit to how far Congress would go in protecting American morals. It did eventually add the word "filthy" to the descriptions of unmailable matter, and in 1908, in response to the spread of anarchist literature, it temporarily declared all mail matter tending to "incite arson, murder, or assassination" indecent and nonmailable. Six years later the Senate also approved a treaty designed to suppress the mailing of obscene literature in foreign mails.

Even when the crusade for purity was at its height, however, in the fading years of the nineteenth century, Congress had indicated its reluctance to go as far as many people wished in legislating against obscenity. Rejecting "the theory," as one senator put it, "that all the morals of the people must be directed from this central point by agents selected" by the postmaster general, it had refused to employ more inspectors to investigate post offices in 1892. That same year, Congress refused to strengthen the Comstock Law, and from then until World War I, except for the amendment of 1895, it steadily rebuffed all efforts to put more teeth into the antiobscenity laws.

Guardians of the Nation's Mails and Morals

Some members of Congress no doubt resisted demands for stronger laws because they were genuinely concerned about the freedom of the press even though the Supreme Court had ruled in *ex parte Rapier* in 1892 that barring the mails to publishers did not prevent publication and was therefore not censorship. On the other hand, pressure was probably as strong from those who wished to pollute the mails as from those who wanted to purify them, and influence from those who wished to advertise their products as they pleased may have been one important reason for the lack of additional antiobscenity legislation. Occasional official blunders also, such as banning the report of the Chicago Vice Commission from the mails in 1911, may have helped convince legislators, and even middle-class Progressives, that the antiobscenity laws were strong enough. Perhaps, too, Congress hesitated to enact new laws because it was reluctant to hire more inspectors to enforce them.

For a number of reasons Congress had never adequately supported postal inspectors, and in the post–Civil War period it had doled out money to them as if every penny came from each member's own pocket. Budgetary problems for the inspectors began in earnest in 1869, when Congress learned that Postmaster General Randall had spent some $34,000 more to hire inspectors than his appropriation had allowed. Enraged by this discovery, Congress reduced the department's request for postal inspectors for 1870 by $18,000 and forbade the postmaster general in the future to spend more for inspectors than was specifically budgeted for that purpose.

From that time, as postal crimes mounted, Congress toyed with the appropriation for postal inspectors and mail depredations, sometimes raising it slightly, then lowering it, but rarely vigorously supporting the inspectors whose work was increasing so rapidly. Once, in the decade of the 1870s, the appropriation reached $160,000, but when the Democrats took control of the House of Representatives in 1876 it fell to $135,000, and there was even talk of doing away with inspectors altogether. By 1883 the amount appropriated had reached $200,000, only $100,000 more than it had been fourteen years earlier, and there, with one exception, it remained until 1890.

The financial pinch the Division of Post Office Inspectors and Mail Depredation suffered from Congress's skimpy appropriations could be seen from the list of items these small appropriations had to be used for. From the lump sum appropriated each year the postmaster general had to pay not only the salaries and per diem expenses of the postal inspectors but the salaries of the division's clerks, the fees of the United States attorneys when they were used, as well as those federal marshals, clerks of local courts, and lawyers who aided the inspectors in the apprehension and conviction of mail depredators.

Aside from Congress's unwillingness to spend money, one reason for its parsimonious appropriations for postal inspectors was, as it had been before the war, politics. Because of the nature of their jobs and the fact that the postmaster general could send them at government expense to any place in the country at any time, postal inspectors had become key political figures in the days when the spoils system was at its peak. All members of Congress who knew anything about politics in the Gilded Age knew this, and those who belonged to the party out of power made every effort to restrict appropriations for postal inspectors lest the country be overrun with the administration's political agents at election time.

Fortunately for the "outs" this was made easier because the

Guardians of the Nation's Mails and Morals

Congress was divided between the Democrats and Republicans through much of the last half of the nineteenth century. Therefore, no matter what the administration might request for postal inspectors, one branch of Congress or the other could trim it if it wished to do so. That this was what happened was indicated by the fact that from 1876 to 1896, with one exception, increases in the appropriation for postal inspectors and mail depredations were made only when one party controlled both houses of Congress and the presidency. Two illustrations indicate how the system worked.

In 1890 and 1891, Republican majorities in both houses of Congress raised the inspectors' appropriation. But in 1892, when the House of Representatives was again in control of the Democrats, the appropriation was considerably reduced, because, as one Democratic congressman argued, the Republicans were trying "to get an extra lot of people to run over the country to manage the campaign" of 1892. A year and a half later, when the Democrats took possession of both houses of Congress and the presidency too for the first time since the Civil War, the appropriation for inspectors was raised from $235,000 to $300,000, over Republican protests. "This is properly known in the Post Office Department, Mr. Chairman," said a Republican congressman from California, "as the 'slush fund.' . . . Of course that will provide places for fifty or sixty good Democrats."

But politics was not the only reason Congress failed to appropriate the money to hire enough inspectors to enforce the laws it passed. From 1897 to 1911, the Republicans controlled both houses of Congress and the White House too. Yet never in all those years was enough money appropriated to make it possible for the Division of Post Office Inspectors and Mail

Depredations to catch up with its work. In 1901, for example, the chief inspector summed up the condition of his division for the previous five years by pointing out that an average of 13,000 cases a year had gone untouched because there were not enough inspectors to handle them. Four years later, out of the 221,836 cases given the inspectors to work, almost 114,000—enough "to keep the present force employed for nearly seven months," according to the chief inspector—had been neglected.

Not that Congress had done nothing to relieve the situation. Between 1897 and 1912, it did increase the Post Office Inspectors and Mail Depredation appropriation from $300,000 to more than $1,000,000, an increase that perhaps reflected the rising cost of crime throughout the nation. The number of inspectors was also raised from approximately 100 to 390. But most of these additions had been made early in the 1900s, so that in 1912 the chief inspector could justly complain that from 1905 to that date there had been no real increase in the number of traveling inspectors. Yet these were the years when the total number of cases inspectors were expected to handle rose from 221,836 to 311,545.

The plain fact was that the Republican Congress had supported postal inspectors with scarcely larger appropriations, considering the increase in their work, than had those Congresses that had been divided between the two parties. Obviously, this was not attributable to politics. Rather it was in part a reflection of Congress's uneasiness over the work and power of the inspectors.

Members of Congress had always been wary of public officials who had to pry into people's private affairs to enforce the laws. But of all those who did this kind of work in the nineteenth century, like secret service agents and federal marshals, the members were perhaps most aware of postal inspectors. Because they snooped about a community, asked questions, wrote secret reports, and sometimes arrested prominent citizens, postal inspectors stirred up trouble and made innumerable enemies. "An agent in the discharge of his duty is certain to make enemies," wrote a special agent in 1875, "often of a dangerous character, and may consider himself fortunate after finishing his work in any section of the country if he escapes the severest criticism from those in sympathy with the rogue caught in the commission of crimes or of officials whom he has reprimanded for dereliction of duty."

Such criticisms as were made of postal inspectors naturally found their way back to Washington and predisposed members of Congress to regard the inspectors' work with suspicion. Moreover, as the postal service grew and postal crimes and laws to prevent those crimes increased, the inspectors' activities multiplied until they seemed to some legislators a threat to freedom itself.

Particularly obnoxious to members of Congress were many of the investigations the inspectors made. In 1896, for example, their spying upon city mail carriers who were falsifying their daily service records in order to collect overtime pay touched off an uproar that reverberated in Congress. Even more exasperating, however, were the inspectors' investigations that led to the issuance of fraud orders.

Such investigations had to be extraordinarily thorough, of course. In making them the inspectors had to interview numerous people and include in their files much hearsay evidence as well as hard facts. But these investigations, and the secretiveness that accompanied them and the fraud orders that followed them, often involved important people, frightened some Americans, and elicited strong statements from members of Congress that indicated their deep-seated reservations about postal inspectors. "Now I think inspectors are clothed with too much power," said Indiana congressman Edgar Crumpacker in 1905, as he argued against an increase in their numbers. There were, he thought, already too many of these "emissaries who go about the country looking after the business of the Post Office Department, and incidentally by dark-lantern methods, make inquiries into the reputations and the business carried on by every citizen, every association and every corporation throughout the land. Who knows," he asked, "how many secret reports that may reflect upon the character of individuals, associations, or business concerns are now sleeping in the archives of the Post-Office Department that have never come to light, put there by confidential reports of these emissaries?"

That much of this animosity toward postal inspectors and their "dark-lantern" methods had rubbed off on the legislators seemed apparent in 1907, just two years after Crumpacker's speech, when President Theodore Roosevelt's attorney general, Charles Bonaparte, asked Congress for funds to employ investigators in the Department of Justice. Coming as it did when Congress was already troubled by the postal inspectors' secret reports and fraud orders, Bonaparte's request was, to say the least, badly timed. Arguing that they wanted no general system of espionage such as older governments had had, members of Congress not only refused to appropriate money to employ investigators for the Department of Justice, but the next year they forbade the attorney general to use the Treasury Department's secret service men for his investigations as he had always done.

Left with no way to carry on a part of his official duties, Bonaparte hired a number of investigators—the nucleus of what was to become the Federal Bureau of Investigation—on his own authority. To this Congress reacted so violently that President Roosevelt felt compelled to reply with a dramatic defense of his attorney general. Determined to show the need for agents to make certain kinds of investigations, the president did what had rarely, if ever, been done before: he made public a report written by two post office inspectors revealing that Senator "Pitchfork" Ben Tillman, a foe of the Bureau of Investigation and Roosevelt's implacable enemy, had, in fact, been involved in a land grab scheme in Oregon.

Charges were bandied about that the postal inspectors had rifled the senator's desk to obtain letters and information for their files. They were not true, but the publication of the inspectors' report may have confirmed Crumpacker's warnings about the inspectors in the minds of some members of Congress. Certainly the report did nothing to endear inspectors to Congress or to prompt that body to increase appropriations for their work. Nor did it move Congress to enact stronger antiobscenity laws.

So partly because of their fear that the inspectors' work endangered American liberties as well as their concern with politics and the expense of hiring inspectors, members of Congress not only refused to enact more antiobscenity laws but would not employ enough inspectors to enforce the laws they had already passed. The result was that the Division of Post Office Inspectors came to the summer of 1914 understaffed and overworked, with more than 130,000 cases from the previous year still unprocessed.

Obviously Congress had decided that it was better to develop a certain tolerance to the violation of postal laws than to fill the land with inspectors to enforce those laws, which, insofar as the postal system was concerned, seemed to be the better part of wisdom. But that the decision had to be made at all was one more indication of the unique nature of the American Post Office.

Had the Post Office been merely a business, Congress might have demanded that it provide only for the "celerity, certainty, and security" of the mails instead of legislating on their contents. But this was the people's Post Office, and Congress, bowing to the American passion for passing laws to establish the good society, insisted that it protect the people's morals and save them from fraudulent schemes.

To do this, however, cost more in one way or another than Congress was willing to spend, and the people, having expected more, were left to complain about the mailing of obscene and fraudulent mail, lost letters, and the Post Office's delays in reimbursing them for their losses that the postal inspectors were often too busy to prevent.

VIII

Politics and the Post Office

One of the enduring assumptions nineteenth-century Americans held about their Post Office was that whatever was wrong with it was traceable to its connection with politics. Though more often proclaimed than proved, there was enough truth in the assumption to make it believable to most Americans. Politics was a factor, certainly, in creating postal deficits. It also produced massive periodic turnovers in postal employees, hampered efforts to change the structure of the system, and increased the number of employees needed to operate the postal service. But if politics was the source of all these problems, it also sped the growth of mail routes to the far corners of the land, promoted postal innovations, inspired needed postal legislation, preserved the familiar relationship between patrons and postmasters, and made the Post Office a public servant instead of a mere business. For better or worse, politics also compelled the Post Office to serve the needs of the nation's politicians as it did those of businessmen and of newspaper and magazine publishers.

Politics and the Post Office

Aside from Congress's control of the Post Office, which subjected its management to pressures from the people, the connection between politics and the Post Office sprang primarily from three sources: the development of national political parties, the president's constitutional power to appoint federal officeholders, and Congress's interpretation of that power. At first glance there seemed little to interpret in the president's appointive power. According to the Constitution, Congress could by law give the president, or his department heads, the sole power to appoint officials holding inferior positions in the government. Other officials, however, such as ambassadors, certain public ministers, consuls, and Supreme Court judges, were to be appointed by the president with the advice and consent of the Senate.

All this was clear, but except for the Supreme Court judges, who were to remain in office during good behavior, the power to remove the officeholders the president had appointed was left hanging in the air. Did the president have the sole right to dismiss the officers he had appointed or must he obtain the Senate's consent for their removal as he had for their appointment? On this the Constitution gave no direction, and the first Congress debated the matter at length in 1789 when it considered the measure creating the Department of State.

A handful of members warned of the danger of placing this power in the hands of the president, but awed by Congressman James Madison's arguments, Congress ignored the naysayers. It gave the president the sole authority to remove officeholders and so augmented his power while diminishing somewhat the value of the Senate's right to consent to appointments.

For most members of Congress this seemed logical, and probably even those who opposed it did not foresee how it would

Politics and the Post Office

affect the Post Office. That department had not yet been permanently established, and when it was, three years later, it was regarded as a semi-independent organization created to carry the mail, not to help politicians. To be sure, the president was to appoint the postmaster general with the advice and consent of the Senate. But the power to appoint, and presumably to remove, postal employees was vested in the postmaster general, and there was some doubt that the president had any right to interfere at all in the appointments the postmaster general made.

The idea of an independent Post Office and postmaster general gained strength in the Republic's early years because the first two presidents did not generally interfere with postal appointments. They had no need to do so. The Post Office was small, office-seekers, though present, were not numerous, and neither Washington nor John Adams had to worry about removing officeholders who belonged to a different political party from their own.

But in 1800 Jefferson's Republican party defeated the Federalists in the presidential race, and the Republicans' victory, along with the rapid growth of the postal system, brought politics into the Post Office for the first time and led eventually to the eclipse of the independent Post Office.

The man at the center of the Post Office in the new regime was Gideon Granger. A Connecticut Yankee, Granger served both Jefferson and Madison, remained in office longer than any other postmaster general, and was the first one to represent a political party different from his predecessor's. Undoubtedly he would have liked to follow the lofty example set by the Washington and Adams administrations of removing only the incompetent and appointing only the best qualified, but this, if possible, was not practical. For the postmasterships were filled with Federalists, many of whom hated Jefferson passionately, and Granger felt compelled to replace the most obdurate of these with good Jeffersonian Republicans.

Jefferson obviously agreed with his postmaster general's policy and believed it was necessary to strike a balance between Federalist and Republican officeholders, but there is no evidence that he interfered with Granger's appointments and removals. Nor for years did Madison. By 1814, after nearly thirteen years as head of the postal service, Granger had appointed more than 2,500 postmasters.

Because of his long tenure in office, the number of officeholders who were beholden to him, and the independent position he had maintained, Granger had accumulated so much power that he apparently felt strong enough to defy even the president. Early in 1814 he appointed Dr. Michael Leib, a United States senator and a political foe of the president, to the lucrative postmastership at Philadelphia against Madison's wishes. This was more than Madison could bear, and using the power Congress had given the president to remove officials without the consent of the Senate, he removed Granger and appointed Return J. Meigs in his place.

President Madison's removal of his postmaster general established, at least indirectly, his control over the appointment of postmasters and struck at the independent position of the postmaster general, but it had no immediate repercussions in the postal service. By this time, there was only one effective political party and therefore no need to make many changes in the Post Office. Congress apparently took little notice of Granger's removal, and presidents Monroe and John Q. Adams went out of their way to avoid interfering with the appointments and removals of their postmasters general. Unlike Madison, Adams would not remove his postmaster general, John McLean, even when he had reason to suspect McLean was appointing his political enemies to office. "Some think I have suffered for not turning my enemies out of office," the old Puritan confided to his diary. But he could not bring himself to use the postal service for political purposes.

This was not true, however, of his successor. For when Andrew Jackson became president in 1829, he abruptly altered what had become more or less the standard policy on appointments and removals. No longer was there to be any hesitation in removing men from office; nor were there to be half-hearted apologies, such as Granger had made, for doing so. Under the new dispensation, the removal of the old officeholders and the appointment of the new were to be reforms, not scandals. "In a country where offices are created solely for the benefit of the people," Jackson told Congress in 1829, "no one man has any more intrinsic right to official station than another. Offices were not established to give support to particular men at the public expense. No individual wrong is, therefore, done by removal, since neither appointment to nor continuance in office is a matter of right."

President Jackson's justification for removing government officeholders, which was not without merit, was swiftly translated as "to the victors belong the spoils" by one of his followers, and, practically speaking, it amounted to that as, one after another, government employees unfriendly to Jackson were removed. And in no department of the government were removals as numerous as in the Post Office.

Apparently Jackson had marked postal employees for removal while he was still president-elect. Having discovered some time before he took office that John McLean, the man slated to continue as postmaster general, was reluctant to remove politically minded postmasters, he elevated McLean to the Supreme Court and made a more pliable man, William Barry, postmaster general. At the same time, and probably in recognition of the Post Office's rapidly growing importance, he made the postmaster general a member of his cabinet, a position which, in effect, further weakened the postmaster general's independent status.

In Barry, Jackson found the right man to carry out his rotation policy. A warm-hearted believer in the common man, Barry had his own philosophy for removing officeholders. "If the great body of public officers are to be retained," he wrote his daughter, "why change the head of the nation? Those who prefer the calm of perpetuity in office, would certainly be better pleased that the Executive head be made permanent. This will not suit a republic." So with a ruthlessness inspired in part by his belief in the justice of his cause, Barry removed incumbent postmasters without regard for their length of service or the quality of their work. The exact number of postmasters who fell that first year is unknown, but it was probably more than four hundred, and the work was still going on in 1830.

This blatant departure from the ideal of selecting the best man for the job gave Jackson's lengthening list of enemies ample opportunity to attack him, and perhaps nothing was more responsible for his being branded "King Andrew" than his rotation in office policy. Unable to touch Jackson directly, however, the anti-Jacksonites fell upon Postmaster General Barry. Twice in six years they investigated the Post Office Department, uncovered some corruption, which may, in fact, have had some connection with the spoils system, and in the end forced Barry, the most loyal of all Jackson's followers, to resign.

Politics and the Post Office

Besides the resignation of the postmaster general, Congress's politically inspired investigation led to the postal law of 1836, which not only revamped the operation of the Post Office but also attempted to bring the appointment of important postmasters under the control of the Senate. By this act, Congress made all postmasters whose salaries were more than one thousand dollars a year presidential postmasters. They were to be appointed by the president, not the postmaster general, with the advice and consent of the Senate, and were to serve four-year terms unless sooner removed by the president.

But this law could no more contain the forces Jackson had unleashed than it could crush a politician's lust for office. It did not touch the president's removal power, although it was hoped that it would induce a president not to remove a presidential postmaster at least until his four-year term was completed. Neither did the law say anything about the growing army of postmasters who made less than one thousand dollars a year, nor about postal clerks in the department in Washington and in the country's larger post offices. These were still to be appointed, and removed, by the postmaster general, with the president, of course, finally responsible for whatever policy was adopted.

So the spoils system began, and although President Jackson and his postmaster general have been given credit for it in its traditional form, it was really less Jackson's inspiration than a product of the times. For the election of 1828, in which Jackson had defeated his old enemy, John Q. Adams, in a bitter political campaign, marked the reemergence of two political parties and the first time in almost thirty years that one political party had wrested control of the government from a rival party. This meant that when Jackson became president he found his predecessor's appointees, many of them men who had campaigned against him, holding government jobs.

It was to replace these enemies—especially those postmasters who had attacked his wife's good name or distributed the coffin handbills that portrayed him as a murderer—that Jackson began what came to be the spoils system and justified it with the rotation-in-office argument. Aside from justifying his action, he was only doing in 1829 what the Jefferson administration had done years before and what another man in his position would likely have done. And had the political situation been the same in Jackson's day as in Jefferson's, the spoils system might well have ended as soon as Jackson's enemies had been removed. But the situation was not the same. Through the years, particularly from 1816 on, state after state had stripped away voting restrictions, given universal suffrage to white adult males, and created a mass electorate that sent a new spirit of democracy racing through the land.

In this new era, instead of one political party, two had risen from the rib of the old Jeffersonian party, and both were needed to shelter opposing political opinions and provide vehicles to carry on the new democracy. And, as if Providence had willed it, the control of the government alternated between these two parties, Whigs and Democrats, from 1840 to 1856, thereby fastening upon the nation the spoils system Jackson had begun. Because the Whigs in power in 1841 were eager to do what the Jacksonites had done, and the Democrats returning to power in 1845 were anxious to undo what the Whigs had done, postmasters and postal clerks came and went with each change of administration like waves upon the shore, until in less than a decade the spoils system had been institutionalized within the Post Office Department.

Politics and the Post Office

Typically American in its development, the spoils system was as practical as politics and altogether essential to the politicians who were organizing the new political parties. With no leisure class to support them and no money to hire political workers, they were provided through the spoils system with government employees who could do political chores and work for the government at the same time. By this means political expenses were transferred to the government, so that it was, in effect, the government—largely through the Post Office, whose revenues came largely from the people—that underwrote the expense of promoting democracy through the two-party system; and if this was not the cheapest way to do it, it was at least a way that worked, which in America was the crucial test of any system.

Because the Post Office had more to offer the politicians than any other branch of the government, it became the handmaiden of the new political parties and was both nurtured and extravagantly used by them. No other department of the government, for example, could carry the speeches of senators and congressmen, government documents, and sundry political pamphlets to the nation's printers and the folks back home. Such a service was of vast importance to the politicians of the nineteenth century, and, unlike television, was eminently fair, at least to all incumbent members of Congress who, no matter how rich or poor, had the franking privilege and could send their constituents whatever political material they desired free of charge.

How much the frank cost the government across the years is lost to history, but there is no reason to doubt that by carrying the politicians' mail free the Post Office bore the major campaign expenses in election years. In just six days of the waning summer of 1848, when Zachary Taylor, Lewis Cass, and Martin

Van Buren were all running for the presidency and the nation was torn section from section over the question of slavery in California and New Mexico, 450 bags of free matter weighing 35,000 pounds were mailed at the Washington post office; and from December 1847 to October 1848, members of Congress sent approximately 5,000,000 copies of speeches and other materials and about 170,000 public documents through the mails in addition to their letters. Waiting still to be sent in October were one-half the public documents Congress had ordered printed at that session of Congress. Although this staggering load had been sent in a presidential election year, similar burdens were thrown upon the mails during congressional campaigns. When the desperate Stephen A. Douglas ran for reelection to the Senate against Abraham Lincoln in the summer and autumn of 1858, he blanketed the state with 345,000 speeches and pamphlets at the expense of the postal service. True, he used the mails more than any other senator that year, but all together senators distributed approximately 1,160,000 pieces of political material at a cost to the department of nearly $35,000.

The party in control of the government could also use the Post Office to win the political support of local newspaper editors by paying them to print in their newspapers the lists of unclaimed letters at local post offices and advertisements for bids to carry the mails. The amount of postal printing one paper might receive was often small, but it was eagerly sought and sometimes made the difference between publishing and closing shop to editors who ran their newspapers on a shoestring.

Some notion of how extensively government printing was used to build up a party press can be deduced from a Senate committee report of 1844 showing that the growth of favored printers had grown from about 100 in John Q. Adams's administration to 529 in Andrew Jackson's. The Van Buren regime had given government printing to 729 publishers, and the Tyler administration to 671.

But the most important contribution the Post Office had to make to the political parties was its employees. No other government department had as many workers as the Post Office or had them as conveniently deployed throughout the country. In 1830 more than 8,000 postmasters were dispersed in cities and villages, country stores, taverns, and log cabins; in 1840 there were almost 13,500, and in 1850, nearly 18,500, a force which made the Post Office Department so valuable to the politicians that had it not existed, they might have had to invent it.

To be useful to the politicians this great body of men had to be politicized, and one of the most significant results of the Post Office's connection with politics and the spoils system was to transform them from postmasters to postmaster-politicians. The first to feel the effect of this process was the postmaster general. Once the independent administrator of postal affairs, the postmaster general became, after the Jackson years, the president's right-hand man and arch politician, whose job it was to reward faithful party workers with postmasterships; and the alacrity with which he undertook this assignment, even while the memory of Washington's more seemly policy was still fresh in men's minds, underscores the irresistible political pressures generated by the surging tide of the new democracy.

Within seven years of the close of Van Buren's administration in 1841, two Whig and one Democratic postmasters general had changed virtually all the nation's postmasters twice, and Cave Johnson, President Polk's postmaster general, a man who had himself appointed more than 13,000 of the country's 16,159 postmasters by 1848 and best represented the changed role of the postmaster general, was asking Congress to free the Post Office from political influence and party contests. He suggested that the postmaster general be nominated for a specific number of years, that he be removed from the cabinet, and that he be removable from office only by impeachment. Subordinate officers too, he thought, should be given specific terms and be removable only for good and sufficient reasons which must be reported to the Senate each session.

Political realities being what they were, no one could have expected the Whigs in the midst of their victory of 1848 to have taken Johnson's recommendations seriously; nor did they. Neither did the Democrats when they returned to office in 1853, nor the Republicans in 1861. President Lincoln and his postmaster general, Montgomery Blair, in fact, proved to be the greatest manipulators of the spoils system the nation had seen. In a four-year period they had appointed an estimated 21,000 postmasters, a task so immense and frustrating that a story went the rounds that President Lincoln was less worried about the Civil War than the "postmaster at Brownsville, Ohio."

Besides rewarding the party faithful, the postmaster general's purpose was to use the patronage in such a way as to secure the renomination and reelection of the president he served. The notable lack of success some of the postmasters general had in this, however, suggests the limits of the postmasters' usefulness. Postmaster General Wickliffe, for example, was unable to build a party for John Tyler, and Postmaster General James Campbell could not swing Franklin Pierce's renomination. Perhaps the most notable failure was Postmaster General Alexander Randall's attempt to create a groundswell for the reelection of Andrew Johnson. Still, it was significant that by 1866 the spoils system was considered so powerful a weapon that fear of President

Johnson's use of it led his enemies in Congress to consider ways of depriving him of it. Their deliberations led in 1867 to the Tenure of Office Act which did restrict the president's right to remove officeholders without the advice and consent of the Senate.

By the Reconstruction period, then, if not before, the postmaster general had become the key political figure in his party's organization, and in time new political chores were added to those he already had. While the first assistant postmaster general and later the fourth assistant took over the appointment of all nonpresidential postmasters and so became important political figures themselves, the postmaster general became the president's principal advisor on political affairs, campaign manager, and liaison between the president and Congress. Finally, in the early 1900s, it became customary to make the postmaster general, the man most closely identified with the spoils system, the chairman of his party's national committee.

While the postmaster general was being made over into a master politician, so also were the local postmasters. In fact, even before the spoils system began in earnest, members of Congress had demanded and were given a voice in the appointment of postmasters in their districts. At first, congressmen who belonged to the political party in charge of the government were merely consulted in the appointment of their postmasters; but by the 1850s it had become the practice for such congressmen to name their postmasters. If a district were represented in Congress by a congressman not affiliated with the party in power, however, a senator of the administration party recommended the postmasters. But if neither of the state's two senators belonged to the controlling party, a local politician of that party picked the postmasters.

Politics and the Post Office

Appointed through political influence, these men learned the rules of the game quickly, knew what was expected of them, and understood that their survival depended not only on how well they handled Uncle Sam's mail but also on how well they handled voters; and in this many of them became adept.

The political potentialities of the local postmaster, only dimly perceived in the Jeffersonian era, were cultivated under Jackson and refined in the years that followed until the postmaster became one of the politician's most valuable assets. The urban postmaster was, of course, the most important to the politician, not only because he worked where votes were heaviest but also because he had to have clerks and mail carriers to handle the heavy mails. Since each additional employee meant another potential party worker, the urban postmaster with his corps of workers formed a small political machine of considerable influence. Moreover, an alert postmaster was able to increase his staff as his mails grew, so that his own time could be used to attend political conventions, organize political rallies, and collect money from his clerks and carriers for the party's treasury. He could inform his congressman or senator of the drift of political affairs in his community, and if he happened to be the editor of the city paper, as he often was, his publication became the voice of the administration in his town.

Control of urban postmasters, therefore, was considered essential to the party in power, and it was just because they were so important that Jackson's opponents had attempted to limit the president's power over them in 1836 by forcing the president to seek the approval of the Senate in making their appointments. Important as they were, however, there were only 433 of them in 1860, and but 2,738 in 1890. The rest, more than

28,000 in 1860 and over 70,000 in 1890, were to be found in the small towns and at the crossroads of rural America, where they too became politically important.

Rural postmasters were likely to be country storekeepers, editors of country weekly newspapers, or simply politically oriented farmers in their areas. If they were editors, they might expect to secure government printing for their papers; and if they were storekeepers, they profited from the trade the post office, usually located in their stores, drew to their business. But whether they were editors, storekeepers, or farmers, the post office brought them prestige which was immensely important to them.

Through much of the nineteenth century postmasters had the franking privilege, which was at once a monetary fringe benefit and a badge of distinction in small communities. Furthermore, they were generally respected by their neighbors, in part because they were usually the only representatives of the national government in their communities and partly because their positions suggested they were better educated than their neighbors.

Their prestige was enhanced, too, by the supposition that they knew important people outside their communities and by their apparent knowledge of everything that went on in their villages and surrounding countryside. Few people, in fact, knew the residents of their communities as well as the local postmasters, who read their neighbors' postcards and the addresses on their outgoing and incoming letters and kept an eye on the kind of reading material that entered their homes.

As a whole, rural postmasters were a gregarious group, interested in people and party affairs, and the very kind of persons who made good politicians. Because they lived in a political world, they were not averse to talking politics with their patrons and beating their party's political drums when the opportunity offered; and the fact that it was necessary to have a postal regulation in the post–Civil War period stipulating that "a postmaster must not allow his post-office to become the resort for loungers or disorderly persons, or the scene of dispute or controversy," indicates the extent to which local post offices were gathering places for political palaver. "The post-offices of the county were the head centers of the community," wrote an observer of the political campaigns of the late 1870s and early 1880s; "and there clustered in them on week-nights and on Sundays the floating voters to accept their money and managers to take their instructions. Postmasters were largely the chairmen of ward, township, county, or district committees. They handled the mails with a view to party advantage. Their employees, every one, were of their own political faith. No man held a position for a moment who didn't work and vote for the political principles of the party in power."

Rural postmasters did not confine their political work to their post offices, however. In the heat of political campaigns they organized political rallies at local schoolhouses or the Grange hall, helped their congressmen campaign in their areas, attended district and state political conventions, and used their newspapers, if they were editors, to punish their enemies and reward their friends. Their post offices were places of deposit for the huge stacks of government documents members of Congress sent for them to distribute where they would do the most good. And, although the law of 1836 forbade it, postmasters could, and sometimes did, delay the mails of the opposition while pushing through the pamphlets and newspapers of their own party as speedily as possible.

Politics and the Post Office

The cost of these postmaster-politicians to the government was not as great as was sometimes suggested or as many Americans may have supposed. A survey of the compensation laws of the nineteenth century gives little evidence that members of Congress were unable to resist the importunate demands of postmasters for higher wages because of the political relationship between themselves and postmasters. On the contrary, postmasters rarely put great pressure on Congress to change their pay, and even if they had wished to do so, unlike other postal workers of the late nineteenth century, they had no real organization through which to achieve such an objective.

This is not to say that politics played no part in increasing postmasters' pay, for postmasters did benefit from their peculiar connection with members of Congress. But politics was a two-way street, and if there were members of Congress who were anxious to raise their postmasters' salaries, there were those of the opposite party who were not. The result was that the laws regulating the postmasters' compensation, though changed no less than ten times between 1853 and 1883, were moderate and even reformatory in nature. They did, it was true, tie the postmaster general's hands so that, unlike executives of other big businesses of the nineteenth century, he was not free to hire his workers for the least amount they would work for, which served the postmasters' interests and may have made the postal service more costly than it otherwise might have been. Neither was he free, on the other hand, to play politics with postmasters' salaries by lowering or raising them for political purposes.

In colonial times, postmasters had always received a certain percentage of the revenues produced by their post offices for their pay, and Congress continued this method of paying postmasters when it established the permanent Post Office in 1792.

Politics and the Post Office

By 1825 the postmasters' share of their postal revenues had been set by Congress at a scale ranging from 30 percent of the first $100 worth of postal business they did each quarter to 8 percent of all above $2,400 until their commission reached $2,000, which was the maximum they could earn.

For more than two decades these percentages remained the same. But when the postage rates were lowered in the 1840s, thereby reducing the amount postmasters could earn under the percentages set in 1825, Congress doubled the percentage postmasters could take on their first $100 worth of business. This was done, however, over the objections of the postmaster general, who argued that he could hire postmasters for less and complained in 1855 that the new pay scale had cost the department more than $300,000 in one year. But Congress, realizing that cheaper postage meant increased mails and more work for postmasters to do in addition to their political chores, refused to reduce the postmasters' pay even when the postal deficit doubled, then tripled, on the eve of the Civil War.

By that time, postal authorities were more concerned with the method of paying postmasters than with the amount they were paid. From the 1790s on, the department had kept track of the commissions each postmaster was entitled to by the quarterly returns he sent the department. When the postal system was in its infancy, this was a manageable arrangement, but by 1861, when the returns of more than 20,000 postmasters had to be scrutinized in Washington each quarter, the battle of the paperwork was rapidly being lost. To improve the system, in 1862 Postmaster General Blair recommended substituting shorter and less frequent returns for the quarterly reports and replacing quarterly commissions with annual salaries for postmasters.

The proposal provided for the classification of postmasters

into five salary groups, with each postmaster's classification to be determined by his annual average compensation for the two years preceding the inauguration of the plan. If, for example, a postmaster's compensation, based on the percentages prescribed by the law of 1854, had averaged $2,345 over the two-year period, he would be placed in the second class, which would include all those making between $2,000 and $3,000 a year, and his salary would be $2,300. Once this salary was established, only periodic checks of the postmasters' returns would be necessary and the lengthy quarterly returns could be eliminated.

The plan was sound and badly needed, but for nearly two years Congress withheld its approval while members worried that the proposal might give the postmaster general too much control over the postmasters' salaries. As originally drawn, Blair's scheme gave the postmaster general the option of reviewing a postmaster's salary every two years to determine whether it should be raised or lowered in accordance with an increase or decrease in business at his office. Some members of Congress thought this option would put the postmaster general under pressure from the most politically powerful postmasters to raise their wages; others, who understood the penny-pinching ways of most postmasters general, believed they would raise few salaries if they were given the option. So Congress waited, and only after the proposition had been modified to force the postmaster general to review all postmasters' salaries every two years was it accepted.

The classification system went into effect on 1 July 1864 and provided the basic framework for the organization and classification of postmasters that has been used ever since. Except for New York City's postmaster, who was to receive a higher salary than the rest, all postmasters whose compensation for the two years preceding 1864 had been between $3,000 and $4,000 became first class. Those who had made between $2,000 and $3,000 were put in the second class, and those from $1,000 to $2,000 in the third. Everyone in the first three classes, therefore, was automatically a presidential postmaster. The nonpresidential postmasters who made less than $1,000 a year—the vast majority—were lumped together in the fourth and fifth classes until 1874, when the fifth class was eliminated.

The new law did simplify the method of paying postmasters, as it was designed to do. At the same time, it also greatly improved the salaries of presidential postmasters. But this had not been its primary purpose, and Congress could not have foreseen, when it passed the law, how rapidly these salaries would increase.

In the busy aftermath of the Civil War, the nation's booming economy enlarged the postal business in towns and cities and inevitably augmented the postmasters' salaries that were tied to the amount of business done. And because Congress had forced him to review postmasters' salaries every two years whether he wished to or not, the postmaster general had to push more and more postmasters up the scale from fourth- to third-class post offices, third to second, and second to first as business increased each biennium. In 1865 there were only 712 presidential postmasters; ten years later there were 1,547. In the same period, the annual appropriations for postmasters' salaries rose from $3,000,000 to $6,000,000, and it was estimated that the salaries themselves had increased 65 percent from 1868 to 1875.

Not all presidential postmasters, however, fared equally well; for the law, whether deliberately or inadvertently, favored postmasters in the middle-sized towns rather than those in the big cities. Because Congress had given the postmaster general no administrative power to prevent it, more and more postmasters had approached the $4,000 maximum salary, which led to the preposterous situation in which in 1873 the postmaster at the little mining town of Central City, Colorado, made as much as the postmaster at Philadelphia. At the same time, Congress's failure to provide the postmaster general with rigid guidelines on the employment of clerks in post offices led to other inequities.

Clerk hire was permitted by law at first- and second-class post offices and certain other places on the basis of need, but it was left to the postmaster general not only to determine need but to dole out the money Congress appropriated for clerk hire as he saw fit. As might have been expected, giving the postmaster general this discretion invited postmasters to make continual demands through their congressmen for additional clerks. The result was that in many cases political influence as much as need became the determinant in assigning clerks to postmasters, so that some postmasters had more than they needed and others not as many as they should have had. In this matter, too, postmasters in small and medium-sized towns usually fared well, for most of the nation's most influential congressmen in the nineteenth century represented these towns rather than the large cities.

Though politics had much to do with the appointment of clerks to post offices—and clerks were often little more than political workers—the reasoning behind the appointments was sound. Obviously, clerks were needed to take care of the ever increasing mails, and it is probably true that, overall, more post offices were shorthanded than were overrun with politically minded postal clerks, as was often implied. Many congressmen could tell tales about their poor postmasters, struggling with the daily mail and having to pay clerks out of their own pockets, and in many instances they were probably true.

Nevertheless, the prosperous condition of the presidential

postmasters in the medium-sized towns and the inequalities between them and the large city postmasters had become a problem to Republican members of Congress, whose party had written the postal laws and appointed postmasters. In town after town, postmasters whose educations had not extended beyond the country school and whose primary qualification for their jobs was political know-how, were earning upward of $1,000 a year. In 1873 some ninety of them were making the maximum $4,000 annually, and many more nearly as much. For those times, these were excellent salaries and placed postmasters, unjustifiably, many thought, on a par with the educated professional men, so that a postmaster in a town of 20,000 in Maine, it was claimed, made more than the governor of the state!

With their plush salaries and clerks to do much of their work, and with their rent, fuel, and lights paid for if they were in first- or second-class post offices, the impression generally made was that presidential postmasterships were the nearest things to sinecures the government had to offer. "A man is appointed to a $4,000 post-office," remarked Congressman James Garfield in 1875, "with power to employ an almost unlimited number of clerks; he has as deputies men who are entirely competent to do business for him; his rent is paid by the Government; his office is lighted and warmed at public expense; and he has about the 'softest' thing in the way of a political office that I know of in the United States."

During the panic that began in 1873, the presidential postmasters' salaries looked all the better, and Republicans thought seriously of adjusting postmasters' salaries according to the size of the towns they served in order to eliminate the inequality between large- and small-town postmasters. They also talked of reducing the postmasters' salaries generally. But they did nothing until the Democrats forced the issue in 1876.

Politics and the Post Office

In that year, for the first time since the Civil War, the Democrats were enjoying control of the House of Representatives, where they had charge of the appropriations bills. Still committed, as they had been before the war, to the principle of states' rights, they had no program for commending their party to the people except to stress economy in government and view Republican extravagance with alarm.

To make a record for economy, they severely cut almost all appropriations bills for the next year, 1877, including the Post Office bill, in which they proposed a 22 percent reduction in the salaries of presidential postmasters. This was a shrewd political maneuver. Democrats did not have to worry unduly about Republican postmasters, particularly presidential postmasters, who were few in number in the Democratic South and West, and by suggesting such reductions, they could put the country on notice that the Democratic party was the party of economy.

At the same time, they could embarrass the Republicans. For Republicans, too, in that presidential year were anxious to appear dollar-conscious, but they were also reluctant to reduce their postmasters' salaries by such a large amount at the very time they were most needed. The result of this conflict of political interests was that the House bill was rewritten in the Republican Senate, and the postmasters' salaries reduced by only 10 percent.

After 1876 the Democrats, eager to prove they were tight-fisted administrators of the public money, dominated the House of Representatives and for a time the Senate too, until 1881, and boasted in the presidential campaign of 1880 that they had reduced public expenditures by $40,000,000. In those years, there were, of course, no salary raises for postmasters; instead each year, in order to give the impression that they were economizing, the Democrats appropriated less money than was needed to pay postmasters' salaries, then, when no one was looking, passed deficiency bills to make up the shortages. Neither did the Democrats attempt to eliminate the inequalities between the large- and small-town postmasters or change the method of paying postmasters, even though the system in use, in spite of the improvements classification had made, was still inordinately complex.

The trouble was that postmasters' salaries were still based ultimately on the old 1854 law that established different percentages for different amounts of postal business done—60 percent on the first $100 worth of business, 50 percent on the next $300, 40 percent on that between $400 and $2,000, and so on. Every two years when salaries were readjusted, these varying percentages had to be figured to arrive at a postmaster's salary, and the computation was so complicated that "necessity herself," according to one postmaster general, "though admitted to be the mother of invention, could not invent a more cumbrous or complex method of adjusting salaries."

Perhaps the Democrats made no move to change the procedure for paying postmasters because they did not control the administration and were not as aware of all the administrative difficulties as were the Republicans. Or it may have been their reluctance to increase the salaries of big-city postmasters or even their negative attitude toward change that stayed their hand. They were not given to making changes in the Post Office, and it was perhaps indicative of the power of politics to effect some changes in the postal system that the Republican party, which was always more politically involved in the Post Office than the Democratic party after the war, made every important innovation and improvement in the service from 1860 to World War I, with the possible exceptions of rural free delivery of mail and airmail. And even these were really developed by Republicans.

Whatever the reasons for the inaction of the Democrats, their failure to modify the postmasters' compensation laws left the matter up to the Republicans after they regained control of Congress in 1881 and had before them the recommendations of President Arthur's postmaster general, Timothy Otis Howe.

This old politician, irritated by having to make decisions on such matters as the number of clerks to give postmasters and the amount of money to allot for rent, fuel, and lights, and exasperated by the mountain of paper work involved in determining a postmaster's salary, wanted changes made. He recommended that Congress eliminate the allowances for rent, equalize the sums given for clerk hire, and base salaries of presidential postmasters on the gross receipts of their post offices rather than on the sliding scale of percentages of the various amounts of business done.

Of all these recommendations, the only one accepted by the Republican Congress was the proposal to base postmasters' salaries upon the gross receipts of their offices. A bill embodying this idea was passed in 1883, along with provisions for raising the maximum salaries postmasters could earn from $4,000 to $6,000 annually and for reviewing all salaries annually instead of biennially.

This legislation so simplified the method of figuring the salaries of presidential postmasters that it was remarkable it had not been thought of before. Moreover, it eliminated the inequities in compensation between city and small-town postmasters. But whether it was enacted more for the sake of efficiency than for rewarding politicians who manned the urban post offices was impossible to determine. Passed by a Republican Congress just as the Democrats were about to regain control of the House of Representatives, rushed through in the closing days of Congress with almost no time for debate, the bill may have passed mainly because it was, as one disgruntled Democratic congressman charged, "an ingenious method to effect a long-standing effort to increase the salaries of postmasters all along the line."

If this was not the correct interpretation of Congress's purpose, it was at least the result of the law. At post offices where gross receipts were between $40,000 and $600,000 and above, postmasters' salaries now ran from $3,000 to $6,000, except at New York City where the postmaster received $8,000 annually. Gross receipts from $8,000 to $40,000 gave second-class postmasters salaries of from $2,000 to $3,000, and in the third-class offices salaries went from $1,000 to $2,000 on gross receipts beginning at $1,900 and running to $8,000.

This pay scale remained essentially unchanged from 1883 through World War I. In that time the growth of urban life, the increase of postal business, and the annual instead of biennial salary adjustments swelled the ranks of presidential postmasters to more than 14,000 by 1916. At the same time, the postmaster appropriations rose from $8,800,000 to more than $30,000,000.

Probably the salaries paid presidential postmasters were more than those paid bank and express company employees whose responsibilities were similar to those of postmasters. This charge was occasionally made in the nineteenth century, and there is no doubt that presidential postmasterships, with their fringe benefits of postal clerks, rent, fuel, and lights, were much sought after. Even so, these salaries, tied as they were to the amount of business the post offices did, were not unreasonable, and if they cost the Post Office Department somewhat more than they might have, the great host of fourth-class postmasters cost the department very little, in spite of the fact that they too were often active politicians.

Unlike the presidential postmasters, the fourth-class postmasters had not prospered from the classification law of 1864. Most of them could never hope to do enough postal business to upgrade their post offices to the third class, but immediately after the 1864 law was passed a number of them tried to do so by sending in fraudulent returns of their business. Since many of these were postmasters in newly established post offices on the frontier from which no previous returns were available for comparison, it was difficult to disitnguish between the fraudulent and the honest returns, and between 1866 and 1872 the postmasters general rejected almost all of them, both good and bad. The result was that the country postmasters eventually put in claims for their lost compensation. In 1883 Congress ordered the postmaster general to pay those claims whose validity could be determined, but this proved so difficult that many claims were still not adjusted at the outbreak of World War I.

The practice of sending in fraudulent claims led Congress to reestablish the commission system for paying fourth-class postmasters in 1874 and to revert to the use of the old quarterly returns to determine the postmasters' commission each quarter. At the time this change was made, Congress, anxious to do what it could for these servants of the post and politicians, allowed them to base the amount of their commissions on the amount of stamps they sold rather than upon those they canceled as had always been done. But when they began selling their stamps for less than the standard price, as they were legally entitled to do, and drawing trade from businessmen from the nearby towns and cities, thereby costing the department thousands of dollars a year in lost revenues, Congress rewrote the law in 1878 and forced them to derive their commissions once more from the stamps they canceled.

After this, the fortunes of the rural postmasters declined. In 1883, when it was legislating for presidential postmasters, the Republican Congress tried to improve the compensation of fourth-class postmasters by giving them all the rentals from their post-office boxes and all of the first fifty dollars worth of postal business they did each quarter. Even this did little good, however, and in the 1890s thousands of them were making less than fifty dollars a year.

Through the decade of the nineties and into the early twentieth century, the fourth-class postmasters made some effort to increase their pay. A small weekly newspaper, apparently subsidized by these postmasters, took up their cause in Washington by urging Congress to allow fourth-class postmasters allowances for the rent, fuel, and lights of their post offices and an annual salary of one hundred dollars. This was as close as postmasters came to bringing organized pressure on Congress, but in spite of the old political relationship between themselves and members of Congress, their efforts were fruitless. The department broke up whatever organization there was, and Congress refused to make any changes in the law. Consequently, by the early 1900s some twenty thousand rural postmasters were making less than fifty dollars a year and as many as forty thousand less than one hundred dollars, which meant that the rural mail service must surely have been as inexpensive as if politics had never been associated with the Post Office.

If postmasters, particularly country postmasters, derived few financial benefits from their political connections with members of Congress, it was also true that this relationship was not an unmixed blessing for members of Congress. The process of appointing men to postmasterships consumed a considerable portion of their time, and because so many people in the districts clamored for the few postmasterships available, they were bound to alienate someone when they made their selection. Besides, the appointment system was always a sword poised above a congressman's head; for though precedent gave him the privilege of naming the postmasters in his district or city, it was a privilege that could always be removed if he displeased a president.

Because of the trouble a bad appointment could cause them, wise congressmen usually appointed as postmaster the man the people of the community petitioned for. This was James Garfield's practice, for example, and it is probable that the system worked as well as it did because so many members of Congress followed his example. Still, a number of legislators through the years tried in one way or another to get rid of the problem altogether by divorcing politics and the Post Office.

One of the earliest solutions to the problem of selecting postmasters was to have the people elect them. First proposed in the 1840s, it was written into the platform of the Free Soil party in 1848, and during the Civil War, when so much trouble arose over the appointment of postmasters, it was seriously debated. The debate ended, however, with the argument that the Constitution did not permit the people to elect postmasters, and though the proposition was revived from time to time, most of those who wished to sever the connection between politics and postmasters joined the movement to reform the entire civil service.

From the beginning of the spoils system there had always been those who opposed it, but no serious movement developed to reform the system until after the Civil War. Then, led by Thomas Jenckes, a Republican congressman from Rhode Island who was supported by a number of disenchanted politicians and a strong battery of periodicals such as the *Nation, North American Review,* and *Harper's Weekly,* a reform movement gathered strength in the 1870s. In the early 1880s the reformers, using President Garfield's assassination by a disappointed spoilsman to rally support, pushed through the same Congress that had raised postmasters' salaries in 1883, the Pendleton Civil Service Act. This act established a Civil Service Commission and made appointment to at least some government jobs dependent upon competitive examinations instead of politics.

The movement had been led by upper-middle-class Americans who despised the raffish types churned up by the spoils system and who dreamed of recapturing the golden years of the Republic when the government seemed purer and men served the nation without expecting rewards. They were spurred on, too, by what they believed was corruption in the civil service, by waste and extravagance, and especially by their idealization of private businesses, which they believed were models of efficiency, frugality, and wise management. Private businesses, they thought, hired employees on the basis of men's capabilities, not their politics, and set an example the government should follow in hiring its own workers.

Beyond this, the reform movement gained support in Congress from the logical supposition that the escalating number of government workers would one day make it impossible to replace the vast army of officeholders each time the administration changed hands from one party to the other. Predicting the complete collapse of the postal system if a new administration should attempt to change all postal employees, New York senator Warner Miller warned that no party could hope "to manage the patronage of the Government in its present magnitude and maintain itself before the people."

Politics and the Post Office

Strangely, Senator Miller's remarks were one of the few direct references to the Post Office in the campaign for civil service reform. Since the postal service, more than all other branches of government, was the stronghold of politicians, one might have expected that reformers would have made an all-out attack upon it to prove the necessity for change and to persuade Congress to vote for the Pendleton Act. True, Postmaster Thomas James's reform of the New York City post office was used as an example of what might be done, but one searches in vain to find advocates of civil service reform alluding to the inefficiency and corruption of the Post Office to support their position. Not even the story of the star route frauds, which broke in 1881, disclosing that the Post Office had been bilked out of thousands of dollars by politicians who had conspired to raise the price of carrying the mails over the long routes in the West, was used, at least in Congress, to strengthen the case for civil service reform.

Nor did the Pendleton Act itself make many changes in the postal service. No postmasters were placed under the new civil service regulations by this law, and only clerks and workers in the Post Office Department in Washington and in post offices employing more than fifty persons were made to take competitive examinations to obtain their jobs. In 1884 this meant that only 5,599 employees at Washington and 23 post offices throughout the country were covered by the new rules.

The civil service law, however, empowered the president to extend the new regulations to other government jobs and so lengthen the list of employees classified under the law. Not only that, he could fill nonclassified jobs with political appointees, then put them under civil service regulations and so presumably prevent their removal by his successor even though they had not taken examinations to get their jobs in the first place. As it turned out, this discretion given the president, though probably not planned that way, became an important incentive for adding government employees to the classified lists.

Just as the Whigs and Democrats, alternating in control of the government, had fastened the spoils system on the nation, so the Republicans and Democrats, sharing the White House in the 1880s and 1890s on an alternating basis, extended civil service reform. Each party, as it came to power, made political appointments, then covered them with civil service rules, so that the classified list grew from about 15,000 employees in March 1885 to more than 87,000 in 1896, near the end of Cleveland's second administration. This included 25,724 postal workers but no postmasters. By this time it was generally assumed that presidential postmasters were nonclassifiable under the law because the president appointed them with the advice and consent of the Senate as he did judges and other high officials. But of the 72,371 classifiable but unclassified jobs still left in government service in 1896, 66,825 were fourth-class postmasters!

A word from the president was all that was necessary to put these politicians of the countryside under civil service rules, but no president dared give it. President Cleveland, supported by Republican mugwump reformers who had deserted their party for him in the election of 1884, had come to office in 1885 pledged to civil service reform, and it might have been expected that he would classify fourth-class postmasters. But no; he simply replaced them with Democrats, then refused to classify even the newly appointed Democrats, probably because that would have eliminated them from participation in politics at a time when members of his party desperately needed political workers.

In two years' time Adlai E. Stevenson, Cleveland's first assistant postmaster general, removed more than 12,000 postmasters and accepted the resignations of more than 16,000 more. This amounted to more than half the number of country postmasters and led Postmaster General Vilas to write "that a change of administration, resulting from the success in the election of a political party for a long period previously excluded from participation in Government service, naturally constitutes a peculiar epoch in the course of appointment of postmasters."

It must have been so, for in four years' time the Cleveland administration filled almost all the postmasterships, presidential and fourth class, with Democrats. To be sure, the president issued a famous order in 1886 saying that "office holders are the agents of the people, not their masters," and warning them against trying to control politics in their local communities; but after having appointed a host of postmasters to do just that, the order seemed more like a belated effort to redeem campaign pledges than to stop postmasters from controlling politics.

Nor was Cleveland's civil service record much better in the other branches of the postal service. His postmasters general were the first to discover that classified workers, though protected from removal for political reasons, could be dismissed for dereliction of duty, and in one year, 1887–88, 376 classified employees—209 of them in the New York City post office alone—were removed. Moreover, by 1889 he had replaced with Democrats almost all the Republican railway mail clerks, an elite and efficient group of postal workers of whom the Republicans were especially proud, and had tried to squeeze them into the classified service. Unfortunately, the classification was mistakenly ordered for 15 March 1889, eleven days after he had left office. The result was that President Harrison's incoming postmaster general, Republican John Wanamaker, held up the classification long enough to fill the railway mail service with Republicans once more and then permitted them to be brought under civil service rules.

Wanamaker's maneuvering here was only a sign of things to come. "In every hamlet," one observer wrote in 1890, "at every cross-roads, each man asks his neighbor: How long will it be after the new president comes in before the old postmaster goes out?" The answer was "not long." In his first year in office, Wanamaker removed or accepted the resignations of more than 16,000 postmasters, which was about 30 percent of the total number. And, like his predecessor, he removed classified personnel in urban post offices for dereliction of duty.

So the Post Office remained the great conspicuous example of the spoils system, and civil service reformers who had avoided assaulting it before the passage of the Pendleton Act, except in a general way, now attacked it furiously in the pages of their journals, and the persistent image Americans had of a corrupt, inefficient, wasteful, and scandal-ridden postal service, whose troubles sprang from its connection with politics, owed much to the polemics of the civil service reformers in the 1890s and 1900s.

The postal service, they claimed, had been demoralized and corrupted by the great struggle for postmasterships. In the upheaval in country post offices, men had been made postmasters without regard for their ability; many of them could neither read nor write, and the service's efficiency had been greatly impaired for the sake of partisan politics. One former postmaster general wrote in 1889 that the nation could never have an efficient postal service until it was divorced from politics, and the *Nation* editorialized in 1892 that "everybody knows that insecurity of tenure makes the highest efficiency difficult if not impossible."

That the removal and reappointment of country postmasters undertaken in the Cleveland and Harrison administrations were time-consuming, troublesome, and perhaps wasteful exercises was too obvious to be disputed. But that they had led to corruption, inefficiency, and demoralization of the postal service was not so apparent. What the reformers meant by corruption was never clear. Apparently they did not mean that the new appointees corrupted the actual service, but that the process by which they received their appointments with the understanding that they would do political as well as postal chores was itself corrupt.

Nor did they cite specific examples of inefficiency in the service that was supposed to have resulted from the spoils system. The postal service was not perfect, of course. Postmasters did make mistakes and many kept poor records, but there was no breakdown in the service. The postmasters took care of all the mail there was, and it is unlikely that the service had ever been better than it was in the 1890s, particularly during Postmaster General Wanamaker's administration. Wanamaker, who was bitterly attacked by the reformers, was an expert administrator and made more improvements in the postal service than perhaps any other postmaster general, with the possible exception of that other great spoilsman, Montgomery Blair.

On this point, the reformers themselves seemed confused. One writer in the *Forum* magazine, who had lived off and on in the United States for twenty-five years and lamented the chaotic rotation in postmasterships, admitted that never in all those years, as far as he knew, had he "missed a letter through the fault of the Post Office, not even when it was addressed to him at 'Cornell University, America.'" Even the editor of the *Nation*, at the very time he called Wanamaker a failure as a postmaster general, agreed that he had made improvements in the postal service.

The reformers' exaggerations about the demoralization and

impaired service in the postal system were the result, of course, of their dismay at the failure of civil service reform which was made so obvious in the removal of fourth-class postmasters during the changes in administrations. As they saw it, the removal and reappointment of fourth-class postmasters threatened the whole program of reform. "So long as politicians habitually regard sixty thousand post offices . . . as legitimate party plunder," one journalist wrote, "they will look upon the evasion of the civil-service act as worthy of censure only when performed so bunglingly as to be detected by the opposite party. In civil-service we must get the whole before we can have assurance of keeping a part."

The attack of the reformers upon politics in the Post Office did produce some attempts at reform short of classifying rural postmasters. Postmaster General Wanamaker himself, noting in 1890 that there were then 59,000 rural postmasters—almost double the number of sixteen years before—suggested eliminating some of them and placing the rest of them in postal districts to be watched over by district supervisors. Applicants for fourth-class postmasterships were to be examined and graded by postal inspectors who were then to certify the top man to the postmaster general for appointment.

Though this would scarcely have eliminated politics in the appointment of country postmasters, some civil service reformers, perhaps realizing that no president was ever likely to classify these public servants outright, jumped at Wanamaker's suggestion as a possible method of separating postmasters from politics. The House Committee on Reform of Civil Service presented a bill to Congress containing the suggested appointment plan, but Congress refused to act on it.

The same fate awaited a later attempt to reorganize the rural postal service by making fourth-class post offices substations of larger post offices. By doing this a classified person from the central post office would become a clerk at the substation and the fourth-class postmaster could be eliminated. Actually, the postmaster general had long had the authority to create substations, and where cities had pushed into rural areas a number of these had been established. But in 1896, when Cleveland's postmaster general, William L. Wilson, sought more sweeping authority to do this, Congress balked, and the debate on this proposition in the Senate revealed why it was so difficult to change the status of fourth-class postmasters or reorganize the rural mail service.

Politics was the paramount reason, of course. The Committee on Reform of the Civil Service might complain—as it did—that the only reason for the political appointment of fourth-class postmasters was "the bold assertion that the machinery of government shall be diverted from legitimate public objects to the service of a faction or a party," but that was the way it had been since the development of the two major parties, and politicians could not imagine what would happen to them if they did not "divert the machinery of government" to help them. As they saw it, "the fate of the party and the Administration lay in the crossroads post offices," as one Democratic politician put it.

Congress also had another reason for its refusal to reorganize the rural mail service and change the status of fourth-class postmasters. By 1890 the Post Office, like some complicated modern machine, was guided by more than a century's accumulation of laws, regulations, and traditions, many of them designed to protect the peculiar relationship between the American people, their postmasters, and their post offices, and Congress hesitated to change any of them, even for efficiency's sake, lest that relationship somehow be disrupted.

In their efforts to save their fourth-class postmasters, members of Congress made the most of this relationship and surely exaggerated its importance. But when they argued against the consolidation of country post offices, as one senator did in 1896, because they were places "of resort" that answered "the purpose of a clubhouse, in a certain way," for the people of a neighborhood, tradition was on their side. And when they objected to the replacement of fourth-class postmasters by clerks from larger post offices because this might destroy the special relationship between the postmaster and his patrons, they had not only tradition but the law on their side.

To safeguard that relationship, Congress had declared in 1863 that postmasters must reside in the communities their post offices served, and for this reason the man selected for a postmastership in a rural community was usually someone born and raised in the neighborhood where his post office was located. He knew all his patrons personally, and they knew him. Often they had helped him get his job with their letters and petitions, and they did not hesitate in turn to ask him to help them fill in legal papers, speak to their congressmen for them, or help them write a letter. In short, the rural postmasters served some of the same functions in the country that machine politicians did in the cities. "The people have looked to the small post office," said Maryland senator Arthur Gorman in 1896, "as the only place through which they come in contact with the officers of their government." What they wanted, he continued, was a place where "as American citizens they may go and tell their postmaster what they desire, and let him communicate with the Postmaster General."

It was to preserve this intimate relationship between patrons and postmasters in a world rapidly becoming urbanized, centralized, and impersonalized that members of Congress said they opposed consolidation of rural post offices. Even Senator Joseph Hawley from Connecticut, who had presented the Pendleton Act to the Senate in 1883, thought that to consolidate the little post offices under one great central office was to gather "them into one ship like hands in a factory or the soldiers in a company, to be under a central discipline," and he was opposed to it. "It is," he said, "against the feeling, the old-fashioned feeling of what the post-office ought to be."

It may have been that in trying to classify rural postmasters and join small post offices to large ones in the name of efficiency civil service reformers had overreached themselves. Much could be done for the sake of efficiency in a land as enamored of business techniques as America, but not everything, and those who represented rural America in Congress rebelled against putting efficiency ahead of personal relationships, especially when it involved taking away political workers. In any case, instead of broadening the authority of the postmaster general to consolidate fourth-class post offices, Congress wound up forbidding him to discontinue any post office in a county seat and restricted his power to eliminate any country post office. Furthermore, the angry argument over fourth-class postmasters and post offices stirred up a vigorous assault upon civil service reform.

Probably the Pendleton Act was never seriously endangered by this attack, but throughout the 1890s its supporters were on the defensive. Congress twice made critical investigations of the system, and a number of bills calling for the act's repeal were thrown into the congressional hoppers. The platform of the Democratic party in 1896 carried a veiled threat to the reform, and although the Republican platform stood foursquare behind it, President McKinley's administration, beginning in 1897, took what critics called "the first backward step" in civil service reform when it declassified some 10,000 government workers and reinstated a number of those who had been thrown off their jobs by President Cleveland. To make matters worse, the president's first assistant postmaster general, Perry Heath, a perfervid Republican, appeared to undermine Cleveland's old order of 1886 with a directive to postal employees saying that "individual interests and activity in political affairs are by no means condemned."

With civil service reform apparently on the run and postmasters still unclassified, the nation passed the century mark. President McKinley was reelected in 1900, then assassinated in 1901. This brought Theodore Roosevelt to the presidency, and one of the many problems this outspoken civil service reformer had to confront was a major scandal in the Post Office.

In spite of all the talk about politics breeding corruption in the Post Office, only two prominent scandals had occurred in the service before 1900. One was in the Jacksonian period and the other was the star route frauds of the early 1880s. Neither of these could be attributed solely to politics. Both involved collusion between postal officials in the department in Washington and mail contractors, which could easily have happened had no politics whatever been involved. Besides this, hundreds, perhaps thousands, of postmasters had juggled their accounts through the years and had cheated or tried to cheat the government in much the same way as bank clerks embezzled money from employers. But again this was more because of the lack of supervision than because of politics.

Actually, considering the magnitude of the postal enterprise, the method of hiring employees, and the difficulties of supervising them in a land as large as the United States, the Post Office had been remarkably free of corruption. A brief comparison of the long lists of defalcations in private business listed in the indexes of the New York *Times* with the records of postmasters in the 1870s and 1880s suggests that had private enterprise been operating the postal service, it would have been no freer from corruption than it was and might have been worse.

Nevertheless, politics was perhaps more involved in the scandal of the early 1900s than it had been in the other two. The corruption began before the Spanish-American War, was linked to the American mail service in Cuba, and stretched across the country involving congressmen, some postmasters, and departmental officials in Washington in post office rental manipulations and wasteful, if not corrupt, use of money for clerk hire.

For the most part, the illegal activities were confined to the department in Washington, where prominent postal officials in the first assistant postmaster general's office, from Perry Heath down, were engaged in one scheme after another to pad their pockets at the expense of the government. Mostly they made money by receiving kickbacks from contractors who sold the government such materials as ink, leather straps for mailbags, and office machinery. But their schemes were as varied as their opportunities for pilfering. George Beavers, chief of the Salary and Allowance Division, took kickbacks from clerks whose salaries he increased, and August Machen, superintendent of free delivery, deftly robbed the government as he was endearing himself to congressmen by the development of rural free delivery, the new turn-of-the-century service for farmers that was nurtured in a political hothouse.

Perhaps no postal service had ever been as popular or so much in demand when it began as the free delivery of mail to farmers, a fact of which congressmen were well aware. Every mail in the early 1900s brought to their desks petitions from farmers demanding rural free delivery mail routes, and a congressman's standing in his community in those years, and indeed his reelection in some areas, depended upon the number of free delivery routes he could get for his constituents.

In a way, there was nothing new in this. From the 1790s on, members of Congress had been in the business, partly for political reasons, of securing post routes and post offices for their districts, and throughout the nineteenth century many a post road over which letters or newspapers were rarely sent ran expensively to some isolated corner of the nation because of a congressman's concern for his constituents' demands. But the establishment of a rural free delivery route was more expensive, more appreciated, more dramatic, and altogether more politically profitable than the old post roads had been.

Besides pleasing the farmers, rural mail routes were also politically important. For each route there was a rural mail carrier who eventually became more politically powerful than the fourth-class postmaster whom he replaced. Riding along his route, he saw most of his patrons every day instead of once or twice a week, talked politics with them, did favors for them, and built such a rapport with them that it was often said he could make or break a congressman. Even if this was not true, congressmen acted as if it were, for they protected the rural mailmen and made them the pets of the postal service. In return, the rural mailmen helped their congressmen and became the most frequent violators of civil service political rules in the days before World War I.

So politically valuable were the new rural mail routes that congressmen indulged in a mad race after 1900 to get as many for their districts as possible. In the race, the Republicans had the inside track, of course, partly because their party was in power during most of the years when the system was built and partly because August Machen, who was in charge of free delivery, was willing to play politics with the building of the service. Republican congressmen wrote freely to him, particularly at election time, of their pressing needs, confident that their requests would be honored. "Do not as you value your life," wrote one anxious Republican congressman to Machen in September 1902, "fail to get the service started by Oct. 1st. It would cost me hundreds of votes if it did not go in according to promise." And back came the routes, hundreds of them for the hard-pressed Republicans while other areas were temporarily denied them because not all requests could be answered immediately.

There was nothing really illegal in Machen's giving rural mail routes to political favorites first, but this, along with payoffs he was known to have received on postal supplies and the corruption uncovered in the other bureaus of the Post Office, gave civil service reformers the opportunity they had been waiting for, and they made the most of it. The *Nation* and other like-minded magazines were certain that corruption had "honeycombed the whole service," and that behind it all was the political appointment of officeholders. So vicious was that practice, according to the *Nation*, that because of it even an honest president like Theodore Roosevelt could not prevent corruption. "A political system which, really representing only a minority of the party," the magazine argued, "controls nominations to elective office, and, through them, dictates the nominees to appointive office—there you have the origin of that coil of corruption in which President Roosevelt finds himself entangled."

Bad as it was, the corruption in the Post Office was not as

far-flung as the *Nation* and other magazines made it out to be; nor was it clear that the political appointment of postmasters and other officeholders was to blame. The scandal involved, for example, virtually no fourth-class postmasters. But the reformers, who had so long wished to divorce politics and the Post Office, were not to be denied their interpretation of the source of corruption. And in the Progressive period civil service reforms did come at last to the Post Office.

Rural mail carriers were put under civil service regulations in 1904, and in December 1908, after his successor had been elected, Theodore Roosevelt classified all fourth-class postmasters east of the Mississippi and north of the Ohio River. This was not as courageous an act as it might have been, for it did not touch the Republican organization in the South and West, where the party desperately needed postmasters to run political chores, and it left unclassified almost 40,000 country postmasters, to say nothing of those in the presidential class. But the *Nation* hailed it as a great assault on the last bastion of the spoilsmen. "From time immemorial," ran its account, "the village postmaster has been the chief local dependence of the party in power. Often the only Federal employee in town, he has used his office to the full. . . . Henceforth, if other Executives are as earnest in keeping Federal employees of the classified service out of active politics as Mr. Roosevelt had been, the political effect of his last order will be far-reaching."

After Roosevelt's order, speculation went the rounds that the rest of the fourth-class postmasters would be classified, and this proved correct. In October 1912 President Taft, perhaps sensing the defeat of the divided Republican party in the upcoming election, classified the remaining country postmasters. Not to be outdone, President Wilson, although he could not classify presidential postmasters under the civil service rules, ordered all those applying for such postmasterships to take an examination before they could be appointed.

But the old connection between politics and the Post Office had been too long in operation to be completely destroyed by presidential pronouncements, and perhaps total separation was not really intended. In any event, the civil service regulations governing the appointments of these servants of the service were made porous enough to let politics in or out as the need existed. President Wilson's order, for example, was only a gesture. Presidential postmasters by law had, like politicians, to stand for reappointment every four years, and examination or no examination, they had little chance of retaining their offices unless their party was in power when their terms expired.

As for fourth-class postmasters, only those who made more than five hundred dollars a year had to take a civil service examination to win an appointment. All the rest, a majority even after World War I, were appointed by the postmaster general on the recommendation of a postal inspector, which was about as nonpolitical as having the congressman make the recommendation. But even when examinations were taken, the postmaster general was allowed to appoint to office any one of the top three candidates certified by the Civil Service Commission, and if none of these would do, new examinations could be requested. This "rule of three," as it was called, applied also to rural carriers and was an open invitation to politically minded administrators to manipulate the appointments when political necessity demanded it. Furthermore, in appointing rural mail carriers the wishes of the people they served had to be considered, which made a strict enforcement of the civil service laws impossible.

Politics and the Post Office

Civil service rules were applied much more satisfactorily to those workers in the urban branches of the postal system like postal clerks, city mail carriers, and railway mail clerks. Here the turnover in personnel was reduced, and urban post offices gradually lost the political aura that had always enveloped them. But even among these workers, reformers' hopes that civil service regulations might eliminate politics in the Post Office and improve efficiency were not entirely fulfilled.

As long as they were dependent upon politicians for their jobs, the urban postal workers' loyalties were attached to their party and the postmasters they served. But once they were classified their new civil-service status fostered a community of interests among them they had not had before, and in the early 1890s, when so many economic groups were organizing to get what they wanted, postal workers too began to organize. Between 1890 and 1891, they formed the National Letter Carriers' Association, the National Association of Railroad Postal Clerks, and the National Association of Postal Clerks. And to the alarm of the reformers, they began to make demands on Congress they would never have made before.

In the 1890s the railway mail clerks, by taking "advantage of their fixed tenure of office," as *Harper's Weekly* put it, forced Congress to rescind the postmaster's ruling that they must live along the railroad lines they served. And a short time later, the city mail carriers persuaded Congress to reject the postmaster general's request for more postal inspectors to supervise the work of the mail carriers. The editor of *Harper's Weekly* was certain that all this was an attempt to ruin civil service and if allowed to continue "the new system of corruption," he thought, was "likely to be worse than the old spoils system."

In time, the postal workers' associations did win concessions from Congress. An eight-hour day, vacations with pay, pay raises, and classification laws for postal clerks were all tributes to the effectiveness of their organizations. But these victories were costly to their organizations. Surprised by this unexpected result of civil-service reform, government officials could not get used to representatives of postal labor unions buttonholing congressmen and acting for all the world like lobbyists for big business, and in 1902 President Theodore Roosevelt issued his famous "gag" order and reaffirmed it in 1906.

This order forbade government employees "either directly or indirectly, individually or through associations, to solicit an increase of pay or to influence . . . in their own interest any legislation whatever either before Congress or its committees," and touched off a battle between postal workers and the administrations of three presidents that lasted from the early 1900s through World War I.

In 1910 President Taft amplified the "gag rule" by forbidding government employees even to respond to Congress's requests for information on their pay or working conditions unless authorized to do so by their department heads. And when Taft's administrators discovered that railway mail clerks were joining secret lodges, they issued a directive warning the employees that such action was "inimical to the interests of the government," and dismissed one man from the service when he continued his association with the lodge after the warning was given.

So a little reign of terror prevailed in the postal service in the Progressive period, and never, even in the worst days of the spoils system, had the morale of postal employees been so low. The workers were effectively muzzled, and had it not been for a paper called the *Harpoon* the terror might have lasted longer than it did. But this little paper, telling its appalling story of the unsafe and unsanitary wooden postal cars in which hundreds of railway mail clerks were killed or maimed each year, caught the ear of Congress. In 1912 that body stepped in to curtail the power of the postmaster general with a law that protected the postal workers' right to join labor organizations, defended them against arbitrary dismissal from the service, and broke the "gag rule." Unfortunately, even this did not prevent Postmaster General Albert Burleson from continuing the attack upon postal workers' organizations during the Wilsonian years until their usefulness as labor unions had all but ended.

Not the least of the results of the Post Office's attack upon the postal workers' unions was the disruption, if not the permanent impairment, of the employees' efficiency which was supposed to have been improved by civil-service reform. Few arguments in support of the Pendleton Act had been more often repeated than that this would increase the employees' efficiency, and perhaps it did. Both the Civil Service Commission and the postmaster general reports made much of statistics showing that postal railway clerks, at least, made fewer errors and handled more pieces of mail after they were classified than they had before. On the other hand, better working conditions and improved mail-handling techniques may easily have accounted for the difference.

In any event, the case for the postal workers' improved efficiency under civil service had never really been proved, and after the harsh attacks upon the associations and the attempt to force larger work loads upon the postal railway mail clerks, the service came very near breaking down in some areas during the winter of 1910 and 1911. Moreover, by World War I there were those who believed that making the postal worker's job permanent under civil service rules had diminished, not increased, his efficiency. "The protected employee," wrote a journalist in the *Forum* in 1916, "often travels along the ragged edge of his work—he will not do any definite act which will warrant a discharge, but at the same time he will measure the lowest known standard of efficiency."

By 1916, then, civil service reform had reduced the mad scramble for public office somewhat and brought order to a chaotic method of appointing postal workers; but it had apparently neither appreciably increased the efficiency of postal workers nor completely divorced politics from the Post Office. Regulations to remove the appointment of postmasters and rural mail carriers from the clutches of congressmen had been easily circumvented, and urban postal workers had formed powerful unions that were able to generate more pressure on Congress than postmasters had dreamed of. And so at the beginning of World War I civil service reformers were left to wonder what more could be done to free the Post Office from politics, which they believed, as did many Americans, was at the root of the service's problems.

Exasperating as political postmasters were to the reformers, however, it was not true that politics was the source of all the deficiences they saw in the postal service. Nor was it likely that the Post Office would have served the American people as well had it been free of politics. For politics in the Post Office, like leaven, was the ferment that forced changes in the postal system, made the service responsive to the will of the people, and made the Post Office a mechanism for developing the nation's political system. Even the agitation for the control of the small post offices in the little communities across the land nurtured a healthy interest in politics among the people. "It is complained," said Senator Gorman in 1896, "of the agitation about the small post-office, at the corner grocery, with the people excited and struggling for office. This right is the very corner stone of our form of government. It is the agitation which keeps the waters from becoming stagnant."

And so it was.

Epilogue

In the summer of 1970 Congress passed a postal reorganization act ending the old Post Office and replacing it with a government corporation. To commemorate the passing of the old system and the beginning of the new, President Nixon, Postmaster General Winton M. Blount, and all living ex–postmasters general gathered at the Post Office Department, where the act was signed and a new insignia for the postal system was unveiled. Henceforth, the postal system, to be known as the United States Postal Service, would be identified by a bald eagle standing upon a block labeled "U.S. Mail" instead of by the pony express rider who had so long loped across the American scene.

The corporation and the bald eagle marked not only the reorganization of the postal system but also a change in postal policy that had been in vogue for more than a century. No longer was the Post Office to be the people's homespun Post Office, to be used as an instrument of government policy for whatever purposes Americans desired. Rather, it was to be a business like any other great American business. And no longer was the basic postal policy to be service first and a balanced postal budget afterward. The corporation was a victory for all those who through the Post Office's 178-year history had always believed that the Post Office should be self-supporting even if it meant less service.

The service-first policy went back at least as far as 1851, when Congress reduced the postal rates and established a new order in the postal service. Operating under that policy in the century that followed, the old Post Office had helped to bind the Union together and support its politicians; it had diffused knowledge, subsidized the nation's newspapers and magazines, underwritten the building of stagecoach, railroad, steamship, and airplane lines, and promoted business with a variety of services including cheap postage rates for advertising. So successful had the policy seemed that Clyde Kelly, a member of the Committee on Post Offices and Post Roads in the House of Representatives in the 1920s, prophesied in 1931 "that there will be no change in the service-first policy of the United States Post Office." In 1970 Kelly's prophecy proved wrong, largely because of Congress's gradually eroding interest in the postal service.

At the end of World War I, the nation's postal system had been completed. By then there was no longer a need for post roads to new settlements, and the American people had been supplied with all the principal mail services they were to have—parcel post, postal savings banks, special delivery, money orders, city delivery, rural free delivery, and airmail, all coupled with cheap postage. All that was necessary after that date was to improve the services and keep the postal system up to date so that it could efficiently process the great volume of mail generated by a bustling economy and a cheap postal service.

Unhappily this was not done with the same enthusiasm and imagination that had been used to build the service. With the service completed and the mail being delivered regularly to almost every man's door, and with the development of the telephone, radio, and television, Americans no longer sent long petitions to their congressmen demanding better mail service, and Congress, not hearing from home, tended to ignore the postal system. Besides that, the reduced importance of politics in the Post Office diminished Congress's interest in it, particularly in urban areas where so many of the postal workers were securely placed under civil service regulations.

Furthermore, as the years passed, there were more and more places for the dollars Congress was appropriating, and because the postal service seemed less important than other matters, Congress gave it low priority in the race for dollars. Finally, in the years following World War I there was no John Wanamaker, burning with energy and ideas and able to effectively propagandize Congress and stir its interest in postal affairs. Instead, postal officials in the latter years, unlike Wanamaker, became far more concerned about the postal deficit than about planning for the future, modernizing the Post Office, and developing labor-saving techniques that would improve the service, and congressmen, no longer pressed either by their constituents or by their own interests to do otherwise, usually followed the lead of those in charge of the service.

This willingness to take directions from the postal authorities was apparent during the 1930s, when the emphasis in the department was upon the retrenchment of the service in order to

Epilogue

save money and reduce the postal deficit. So severe was the retrenchment that largely because of it the volume of mail declined by 136,356 pieces between 1932 and 1940. Yet Congress did nothing to turn the program around. Aside from the construction of a number of new post office buildings almost nothing was done to improve the service for the future, and the Post Office emerged from those years and World War II ill prepared to handle the great mails that all but engulfed it after the war.

The growth of the mails between 1945 and 1970 was one of the little-noticed marvels of postwar America. In that quarter of a century the volume of mail leaped from 37,912,067,000 pieces to an almost incredible 84,881,833,000 pieces. In 1966 alone the number of pieces of mail increased by more than 3,500,000,000 pieces and by another 2,500,000,000 the next year. By 1970 the mail was flowing at the rate of 415 pieces annually for every man, woman, and child in the nation. This was more than was produced by the combined postal systems of the world and reflected the tremendous vigor of the American economy.

Neither the postal authorities in the 1930s nor Congress could have prepared the postal service for this growth in the volume of mails, of course. But a more imaginative program than concentrating on the deficits might have alleviated some of the problems that piled up on the Post Office in the 1950s and 1960s. Particularly disastrous to the mail service in these years was the dismantling of the excellent railway mail service that began in the 1930s.

This was not altogether the fault of either Congress or the men in charge of the Post Office. Hard hit by the depression and the use of automobiles, the railroads reduced the number of their passenger trains, which forced the Post Office Department to

Epilogue

do the same with the railway mail service. But so anxious were postal officials to reduce expenditures and save money, that they apparently welcomed the opportunity to curtail the expensive railway mail system. In Congress a few protests were raised against the reduction of this service, but to no avail. Once begun, the practice seemed irreversible and continued into the World War II period, until in 1969 only 54,256 miles of railway mail routes remained where there had once been 208,517.

The destruction of the railway mail service eliminated most of the railway post offices in which, since the Civil War, the mails had been sorted and distributed as the trains moved along. These were the most important facilities in the Post Office's system of distributing the mails, and their loss forced the department to develop a new plan of mail distribution. Motor trucks were used to move the mails where possible, and even highway post offices were established to take the place of the railroad post office. But the heart of the new distribution plan was the large urban post offices. To these the mails were sent and distributed to various sectional centers, which the department identified by the first three digits of a zip code it had developed in 1962.

The new distribution plan was, in effect, a return to the system which had been used before the Civil War, when the mails had been routed through distribution offices. It placed an enormous burden on the large post offices, and the fruits of Congress's long neglect of the postal service became apparent as the department struggled with the growing mails. Ninety-five percent of the large government-owned post offices had been built before World War II and many of them before World War I. Old, overcrowded, inaccessibly located by railroad depots in the heart of busy cities, they were totally unsuited to handle the gigantic mails that jammed their work spaces and overflowed into corridors and basements.

New labor-saving machines were badly needed in these post offices to lift the burden of the ballooning mails from the postal workers. But for years little thought and almost no money had been given to the development of new mechanical devices to speed the flow of the mails. Out of sheer necessity, Postmaster General Arthur Summerfield, who was developing the new distribution system, put a high priority on the development of new machines, and in time some post offices, like the one at Detroit, became highly mechanized. But it took time to develop the machines and longer still, apparently, to install them in the principal post offices. Meanwhile the mails grew relentlessly, and in lieu of machines and new methods of handling the mails, the department had to employ more and more people to stay even with the mounting mails.

More and more the responsibility for getting the mails through rested upon these employees of the great urban post offices. Let a machine break down or inexperienced workers fumble their assignments and the whole system was likely to collapse, as it did in Chicago in October of 1966, when for nearly three weeks the post office almost stopped functioning and a backlog of nearly 10,000,000 pieces of mail accumulated.

Perhaps the new system was less expensive than maintaining the old railway mail service would have been—provided this could somehow have been done—but it was not inexpensive. Inflation, salary boosts for an ever increasing number of employees, and growing costs for transportation took large portions of the postal revenues. Postal deficits went over half a billion dollars in 1949 for the first time, and over a billion in 1966, and Congress felt compelled to raise first-class postage three

Epilogue

times—from three to six cents—in a decade. That matters appeared to be getting out of hand was suggested by the fact that only once in seventy-two years before 1958 had first-class postage been raised, and that came in 1931 during the depression, when the postage was increased from two to three cents.

By the middle of the 1960s, Postmaster General Lawrence O'Brien became convinced that the Post Office was in a "race with catastrophe," and urged a major reorganization of the old institution. Following his recommendation, President Lyndon Johnson appointed a Commission on Postal Organization to "conduct the most searching and exhaustive review ever undertaken" of the American Post Office and to "determine whether the postal system as presently organized" was "capable of meeting the demands of our growing economy and an expanding population."

For more than a year the commission and its contractors examined the Post Office fore and aft and discovered what they were looking for. In four volumes and a summarized report, the commission noted, among other things, antiquated buildings and equipment, rules and regulations that stifled change and prevented managers from managing, and rising expenditures that threatened to drive the postal deficits to fifteen billion dollars in the next decade unless something was done. It pointed to the waste and inefficiency that were almost everywhere, poor personnel management, politics in appointments, an inappropriate method of setting postal rates, and an operation that needed at least $5,000,000,000 worth of new buildings and equipment.

Significantly, the commission declared that the Post Office was no longer needed as an instrument of government policy to support American politicians, newspaper and magazine publishers, and the transportation system. "The Commission concludes, therefore," ran its summarized report, "that today the Post Office is a business. Like all economic functions it should be supported by revenues of users. The market should determine what resources are to be allocated to the postal service." This meant, of course, that in the commission's view, the old Post Office was incapable of "meeting the demands of our growing economy and an expanding population," and it recommended reorganizing it into a government corporation.

The commission's report was completed in June 1968, and much of the nation's press—ironically, all things considered—propagandized ardently for the adoption of its recommendations. But there was considerable doubt that Congress would give up its control of the system. For although the commission had assured the public that the failures of the Post Office were traceable directly to "outdated and inappropriate management processes," and that only a complete break with the past such as a government corporation would provide could correct the old Post Office's problems, there were those in Congress who did not believe it. "Reform is not spelled c-o-r-p-o-r-a-t-i-o-n," said Texas senator Ralph Yarborough in 1969. To "substitute a money corporation" for the Post Office, he argued, was no reform. It would destroy the concept of service. Calling attention to the electrical failures that had occurred in New York City and the breakdown of the telephone service there, the senator reasoned that there was no assurance a corporation would improve the postal system. In his view the mail service was "still the most efficient of any type of service in America," and indeed, in spite of all its tribulations it was still doing what it was intended to do reasonably well. In 1970 it was delivering daily more than 200,000,000 pieces of mail to thousands of businesses across the country and to some 60,000,000 homes, 20,000,-000 of which had changes of address every year.

Epilogue

Even the president's commission had a hard time supporting its contention that the Post Office was a failing institution insofar as service was concerned. In its summarized report, the commission noted that it had "found a pattern of public concern over the quality of the mail service." Yet of the seventy-five national associations representing major groups dependent upon the mails whom it had invited to criticize the service, only 63 percent did so, and even they were critical only of certain aspects of the service.

Moreover, in its full report, which was not widely read, the commission included a summary of a Roper survey which indicated that 76 percent of all Americans were "completely satisfied with the postal service." In commenting on the survey, the commission pointed out that big-city dwellers were somewhat less satisfied with the service than others and that heavy individual users were still less satisfied. Not highlighted was the fact that of all Americans questioned only 1 percent were completely dissatisfied with the mail service they received. Somewhat lamely, the commission concluded: "The lesson is clear: from a distance the mail service is not bad, but the more you use and depend on it, the less satisfactory it seems."

Senator Yarborough's views of the mail service and the postal corporation represented generally those of many representatives of rural America, and when the reorganization proposal reached Congress in the spring of 1970, the lines of battle formed, as they had so often in the past, between the spokesmen for urban America who wished to accept the postal corporation and those of rural America who did not.

Rural members of Congress feared, of course, that any postal system based on the premise that the service must pay its way would mean reduced mail facilities in the countryside where they had never paid their way. Moreover, a corporation divorced from Congress's control meant the end of the congress-man's voice in appointing postmasters and rural mail carriers who would be agreeable to them and to the rural patrons. A man from Philadelphia, as one disgruntled Iowa congressman pointed out, might be appointed postmaster in Iowa! They foresaw, too, that in the effort to save money smaller post offices would be closed or their mails postmarked from a larger town and the identity of the towns those offices represented would be lost.

Urban Americans, on the other hand, seemingly had much to gain from a postal corporation. They need not fear a reduction of their postal services because under almost any system of cost ascertainment their services could be shown to be paying for themselves. Hopefully, too, they could look forward to more efficient service and a reduction of the postal deficit, which, when all was said and done, was the real reason for the whole reform movement. And finally, the corporation, not Congress, would be saddled with the burden of finding the five to ten billion dollars necessary to refurbish the old Post Office that Congress had so long refused to appropriate. The money saved here and from the mounting postal deficits could, perhaps, be put to better uses in the cities.

Urban congressmen, in fact, had only one real reservation about giving their complete support to the reorganization of the postal system, and that was the opposition of urban postal work-ers to the scheme. As matters stood, postal employees knew they could count on Congress's sympathetic, if not overly gen-erous, response to their demands. Would a corporation be as understanding? Many thought not. Some even feared for their jobs, for there was much talk about reducing the number of employees as the corporation mechanized the service. For these

Epilogue

reasons, the workers opposed the new plan, and because of their opposition, the passage of a reform bill remained in doubt until the spring of 1970, when the urban postal workers struck for the first time in the history of the Post Office.

Although the Postal Commission had reported in 1968 that the salaries of postal employees had "not only kept pace with," but had "risen somewhat more than, those in the rest of the economy," the postal workers felt in 1970 that they were overdue for a raise. Only the year before they had been denied their increase in pay because the administration wished to couple any salary raise with the postal reorganization. By March 1970 their disappointment had festered until it erupted into the strike that kept the carriers from making their appointed rounds and demonstrated the all but forgotten importance of the postal system to American life. In the flurry that followed, the postal workers dropped their opposition to the corporation in return for salary increases, and the way was cleared for the passage of the reorganization act, which finally came five months later.

So in this way the end came to the old Post Office. Tired of the responsibility of managing the postal service, unwilling to find the money necessary to rebuild the old establishment after so many years of neglect, and most of all worried about the postal deficit, which even in 1970 still did not claim nearly as much of the total government budget as it had in 1890, Congress gave up its control of the system, not even bothering to keep its veto power over increases in postage rates.

And once again, urban America had its way over rural America in the management of the Post Office. But this time there was a difference. Always before, rural America had obtained some concessions when it had acceded to the demands of urban America. In 1851, when postage had been reduced, the promise had been given that there would be no reduction in the service in rural America if postal deficits occurred. And in the 1870s and 1880s, when city delivery services were being installed, rural America eventually received rural free delivery.

In the postal reorganization act, however, there was little to comfort those who were concerned about mail facilities in rural America. To be sure, the preamble of the act paid lip service to the old postal policy. "The Postal Service," it read, "shall have as its basic function the obligation to provide postal services to bind the Nation together through the personal, educational, literary, and business correspondence of the people." And it also made specific promises to rural America with the declaration that "the Postal Service shall provide a maximum degree of effective and regular postal services to rural areas, communities, and small towns where post offices are not self-sustaining. No small post office shall be closed solely for operating at a deficit, it being the specific intent of the Congress that effective postal services be insured to residents of both urban and rural communities."

But rural legislators who looked not at the promises but the realities of an independent postal corporation virtually compelled to be self-sustaining by the fateful year of 1984 at least, were not convinced that the rural mail service would not suffer.

Important Dates

Important Dates

Important Dates

1845	Railroads classified for compensation purposes according to the size and importance of the mails carried and the speed of the railroads
1846	Postmaster general makes first contract with an American steamship company to carry the mails to Europe
1847	First postal convention with a European power made
	Secretary of the Navy authorized by Congress to subsidize steamships to carry the mails to Europe
	Use of postage stamps authorized by Congress
1851	Postage reduced to three cents for letter going less than three thousand miles
	Congress establishes policy of subsidizing Post Office if necessary to maintain service
	Books admitted to mails
	All weekly newspapers allowed to circulate in the mails free of postage within the county where published
1852	Postage on periodicals reduced to newspaper postage rates
1855	Registered letter system adopted
	Prepayment of postage made mandatory
1857	Law enacted providing for an overland letter mail from the Mississippi River to San Francisco
1860	Pony express launched by Russell, Majors, and Waddell Freighting Company
	Beadle brothers publish their first dime novel
1861	Transcontinental telegraph completed
1862	The United States mail service suspended throughout the Confederate States of America
1863	City free delivery of mail established
	International postal conference held in Paris
	Mail matter divided into three classes
1864	Money order system established
	Post offices classified into five classes according to the amount of postal business done
	Railroad post office launched on the Chicago and Northwestern Railroad
	Congress authorizes subsidizing of steamships to carry the mail to Brazil
1865	Congress outlaws the mailing of obscene matter

Important Dates

1865   Congress authorizes subsidizing of steamships to carry the mail to China and Japan

1866   Congress enacts legislation to promote competition among telegraph companies

1868   Congress declares letters and circulars relating to lotteries nonmailable

1873   Office of the superintendent of foreign mails provided for

Chief of the Division of the Office of Mail Depredations provided for

The use of postal cards authorized by Congress

Congress passes the Comstock Law forbidding the mailing of lewd and obscene material and advertisements for contraceptives and abortifacients

New guidelines for compensating railroads for carrying the mails adopted

1874   Prepayment of postage on newspapers demanded

Postage on second-class mail matter based on weight instead of piece reduced

International Postal Conference in Berne, Switzerland, establishes the Universal Postal Union

1878   *Ex parte Orlando Jackson* decision affirms that Congress can determine what can or cannot be carried in the mails

1879   Congress authorizes giving monetary rewards for the capture of mail train and stagecoach robbers

1881   Star route frauds uncovered

1883   Pendleton Civil Service Act enacted

Practice of basing postmasters' salaries on the gross receipts of their offices begun

1888   Congress declares that sealed mail is no protection for obscene matter

1889   National Association of Letter Carriers founded

1890   Sea post offices placed on certain oceangoing vessels

Congress passes stringent antilottery law allowing the postmaster general to issue fraud orders

1892   *Ex parte Rapier* decision declares that barring obscene material from the mail does not prevent publication and is therefore not censorship

Important Dates

1894	Congress begins appropriating money to reward those who aid in the capture and conviction of mail robbers
1896	An experiment in the free rural delivery of mails begun
1902	President Theodore Roosevelt issues "gag order" forbidding postal employees to lobby for their interests in Congress
	Rural free delivery of mail made permanent service
1903	Post Office scandal revealed
1908	President Theodore Roosevelt classifies fourth-class postmasters east of the Mississippi and north of the Ohio River under the civil service law
1910	Postal savings banks established
1912	President Taft classifies the remainder of the fourth-class postmasters
1913	The enlarged parcel post system begins operation
1914	Senate approves treaty to suppress obscene literature in the foreign mails
1916	Congress authorizes the postmaster general to pay the railroads for carrying the mail on the basis of space used instead of weight of mails
	Congress establishes a government corporation to construct and operate steamships
1917	The United States government takes control of the nation's railroads
1918	Postal rates on periodicals raised
	The nation's telegraph and telephone lines placed under the control of the postmaster general
	First regular airmail service begins between Washington and New York
1920	Provision made for government-owned ships to be sold to private steamship lines
1928	Congress enacts a new steamship subsidy law
1931	Letter postage raised from two to three cents
1962	The zip code developed to expedite the mails
1967	President Johnson appoints a postal commission to study the Post Office
1970	Postal workers strike for the first time in the Post Office's history
	Postal Reorganization Act passed, making the Post Office a public corporation

347

Bibliographical Essay

Of the great mass of original sources relating to the study of the American Post Office, the following are indispensable: *The American State Papers: The Post Office* and *The Annual Reports of the Postmaster General* from 1823 to the present give the year-to-year story of the development of the postal service from the administrative point of view; the debates in Congress on postal affairs, often on Post Office appropriations bills, found in the *Annals of Congress*, *The Register of Debates in Congress*, the *Congressional Globe*, and the *Congressional Record* show the development of the nation's postal policy and the importance of the postal system to various aspects of American life; the voluminous collection of *House and Senate Documents and Reports* from 1823 through World War I has the results of Post Office investigations, some of the hearings of the postal committees in Congress, and recommendations of Congress relating to the Post Office; the *United States Statutes at Large*; and the great body of postal records in the National Archives in Washington, D.C., Record Group 28, largely untouched by scholars, contains the *Postmaster General Letterbooks* and hundreds of boxes of materials on various aspects of postal history.

Bibliographical Essay

GENERAL SURVEYS OF THE AMERICAN POST OFFICE

Books on the American postal service are numerous, but few have been written by scholars. A brief scholarly work, *A Short History of the Mail Service* (1970) by Carl Scheele outlines the development of the American postal system and contains a good bibliography on postal history. Pao Hsun Chu's *The Post Office of the United States* (1932) has interesting comments on the growth of postal systems in general. Lindsay Rogers, *The Postal Power of Congress: A Study in Constitutional Expansion* (1916), though old, is an invaluable work on what happened to Congress's power to establish post roads and post offices. Short helpful essays on the Post Office appear in Leonard D. White's scholarly histories of government administration: *The Federalists* (1959); *The Jeffersonians* (1961); *The Jacksonians;* and *The Republican Era, 1869–1901* (1958). Ross Allen McReynolds, *United States Postal Development, 1602–1931: Summary and Interpretation* (1937) is an excellent but unpublished dissertation at the University of Chicago.

Interesting and valuable but not scholarly surveys of the American Post Office are Daniel Roper's *The United States Post Office: Its Past Record, Present Record, Present Condition*, and *Potential Relation to the New World Era* (1917), written by an assistant postmaster general in the Wilson administration, and Louis Melius, *The American Postal Service: History of the Postal Service from the Earliest Times* (1917).

PROLOGUE

The ancient Persian postal system was made immortal by the Greek historian Herodotus, whose *Histories* contain the most of what is known about it. A useful and interesting study of the development of postal systems is Alvin F. Harlow's readable *Old Post Bags: The Story of the Sending of a Letter in Ancient and Modern Times* (1928). *Mail for the World* (1953) by Lawrence Zilliacus is in the same category as Harlow's book but shorter.

British historians have been much more interested in their postal system than their American counterparts and have written extensively about it. J. W. Hyde, *The Royal Mail* (1899) is a popular account of the British system with quotes from original sources. Among the best and most recent accounts of the British postal service are Howard Robinson's *The British Post Office* (1948), an excellent study, and F. George Kay, *Royal Mail: The Story of the Posts in England from the Time of Edward IV to the Present Day* (1951).

THE COLONIAL POST OFFICE

Mary Wooley, "Early History' of the Colonial Post Office," in *Publications of the Rhode Island Historical Society* (1894) traces the beginning of the postal system in the English colonies in America. William Smith, who wrote *The History of the Post Office in British North America, 1639–1870* (1920), has a sharply focused article, "The Colonial Post Office," in the *American Historical Review*, vol. 21 (Jan. 1916). An often-cited and thoroughly documented treatment of the colonial and early American postal system is Wesley Everett Rich's *History of the United States Post Office to the Year 1829* (1924). In his *Autobiography* (1868), Benjamin Franklin made interesting comments on his administration of the Colonial Post Office, but Ruth Lapham's doctoral dissertation, *Benjamin Franklin and the Post Office* (1925) at Northwestern University has the full story.

Carl Bridenbaugh's *Cities in the Wilderness* (1938) cites the importance of the postal service to the colonial towns. A. D. Smith, *The Development of Rates of Postage: An Historical and Analytical Study* (1918) examines the development of postage rates in the colonies and for the later period as well. The difficulties colonial governors had in communications is highlighted in Oliver Morton Dickinson's *American Colonial Government, 1696–1765: A Study of the British Board of Trade and Its Relation to the American Colonies, Political, Industrial, Administrative* (1912).

Arthur Schlesinger, Sr., *Prelude to Independence: The Newspaper War on Britain, 1764–1776* (1958) contains passages on the importance of the mails to the newspapers. The importance of propaganda in the Revolution is covered by Phillip Davidson, *Propaganda and the American Revolution, 1763–1783*, but he has

Bibliographical Essay

little to say about the postal service. An interesting account of the colonial postal service on the eve of the Revolution is found in *The Journal Kept by Hugh Finlay, Surveyor of the Post Roads on the Continent of North America* (1867). *William Goddard, Newspaperman* (1962) by Ward Miner is the story of the man who began the "Constitutional Post" before the Revolution. The rise of an American national identity before the Revolution is suggested by R. L. Merritt in *Symbols of American Community* (1966).

Clyde Kelly, *United States Postal Policy* (1931) traces the development of the Post Office's service-first policy. Pliny Miles, *Postal Reform: Its Urgent Necessity and Practicability* (1855) contains a plea for reforms such as the establishment of money orders, delivery systems, and the elimination of the franking privilege. Joshua Levitt, *Cheap Postage* (1848) urges reduced postage upon the Post Office. *The Autobiography of Amos Kendall* (1949) gives Kendall's views of his handling of postal affairs. The efforts of the department to carry the mail to the Pacific before the Civil War are thoroughly treated in LeRoy Hafen's *The Overland Mail, 1849–1869: Promoter of Settlement, Precursor of Railroads* (1926). Edward Chapman's *The Pony Express: The Record of a Romantic Adventure in Business* (1932) is one of many accounts that have been written about this brief episode in American postal history.

Gardiner G. Hubbard, "Our Post Office," *Atlantic Monthly*, vol. 25 (Jan. 1875), finds the American postal system in the 1870s less efficient than the British and gives reasons. Daniel D. T. Leech and W. L. Nicholson, two men who worked in the Post Office Department in the nineteenth century, discuss its operation in *The Post Office Department of the United States of America: Its History, Organization, and Working, 1789–1879* (1879). The Wanamaker administration, as well as the day-to-day operations of the postal service, is thoroughly explained in *The Story of Our Post Office: The Greatest Government Department in All Its Phases* (1893) and in Herbert Adams Gibbons, *John Wanamaker* (2 vols., 1926). The development of rural free delivery of mail is covered in *R.F.D.: The Changing Face of Rural America* (1964) by Wayne E. Fuller.

Bibliographical Essay

Forrest McDonald indicates the difficulties of forming a nation among widely scattered Americans whose means of communication were poor in "The Anti-Federalists, 1781–1789," *Wisconsin Magazine of History* (Spring, 1963). *One Nation Indivisible: The Union in American Thought, 1776–1861* (1964) by Paul Nagle is a perceptive account of the ways early Americans viewed their Union. Julian P. Bretz, "Some Aspects of Postal Extension in the West," *The Annual Report of the American Historical Association* (1909), has interesting observations about the political value of the extension of the mail service to westward-moving Americans.

The controversy over the sending of abolition literature to the South has been much written about. Clement Eaton, "Censorship of the Southern Mails," *American Historical Review*, vol. 47 (Jan. 1943), has the principal points of the story. A doctoral dissertation prepared at Ohio State University, *The Controversy over the Distribution of Abolition Literature* (1930) by W. Sherman Savage, is an extensive treatment of the subject. Clement Eaton has a discussion of the growth of southern newspapers in *The Growth of Southern Civilization 1790–1860* (1961), and his *Freedom of Thought in the Old South* (1940) traces the control of southern thought after the death of Jefferson.

An unpublished doctoral dissertation at Fordham University by Roger F. Bartram entitled *The Contributions of Joseph Holt to the Political Life of the United States* (1958) deals with the controversy Holt stirred up over the restriction of the mails. Roy F. Nichols, *The Disruption of American Democracy* (1948) indicates the importance of the curtailment of southern mails as an irritant to the South.

The Confederate mail service is cursorily treated in August Dietz, *The Postal Service of the Confederate States of America* (1929). An uncritical sketch has been done by Walter F. McCaleb in "The Organization of the Post Office Department of the Confederacy," *American Historical Review*, vol. 12 (1906). John R. Reagan, the postmaster general of the Confederate Post Office, throws some light on his management of that office in his *Memoirs, with a Special Reference to Secession and the Civil War* (1968).

Bibliographical Essay

Paul Buck shows how the South was drawn into the economic net of the North in his *Road to Reunion* (1937).

DIFFUSION OF KNOWLEDGE

A readable account of the history of American newspapers is Bernard Weisberger, *The American Newspaperman* (1961). A longer study is Frank Luther Mott's *American Journalism: A History of American Newspapers in the United States through 250 Years, 1690–1940* (1941). R. C. Buley gives an interesting description of newspapers and the mail service in *The Old Northwest: The Pioneer Period, 1815–1840* (2 vols., 1950). A short study of country journalism is *The Rural Press and the New South* (1948) by Thomas D. Clark. The standard work on the history of magazines in the United States is Frank Luther Mott, *A History of American Magazines* (5 vols., 1938–57), which is mostly a cataloging of magazines.

Albert Johanson, *The House of Beadle and Adams* (1950) covers the story of the Beadles and their books. Raymond H. Shove, *Cheap Book Production in the United States, 1870–1891* (1937) describes very well the rise of the cheap book in America but pays little attention to the influence of the postal laws. Frank L. Schick, *The Paperbound Book in America* (1958) mentions the pre–Civil War postal legislation but has misunderstood the postal laws of the post–Civil War period. Robert Russell Hertel has a doctoral dissertation, *The Decline of the Paperback Novel in America, 1890–1910* (1958), prepared at the University of Illinois, which relies heavily upon *Publisher's Weekly* magazine, where most of the story is told.

Mary Noel, *Villains Galore* (1954) deals interestingly with the content of the paperback dime novels, and the trouble these and other second-class matter were causing the Post Office can be seen in a contemporary article by Eugene F. Loud, "A Step toward Economy in the Postal Service," *Forum*, vol. 24 (Sept. 1897).

GOVERNMENT BUSINESS VERSUS PRIVATE BUSINESS

American economic ideas in the nineteenth century can be traced in volumes 2 and 3 of Joseph Dorfman's *The Economic Mind in American Civilization* (5 vols., 1946–49) and in Sidney Fine, *Laissez Faire and the General-Welfare State: A Study of Conflict in Amer-*

354

Bibliographical Essay

ican Thought (1956). The transition from an agrarian to a business economy after the War of 1812 is stressed in Arthur Schlesinger, Jr., *The Age of Jackson* (1945). An unpublished doctoral dissertation by Oliver Wendell Holmes, *Stage-Coach and Mail from Colonial Days to 1820* (1956), is an excellent study of stagecoaching in America and of the role the Post Office played in the development of stagecoach routes.

The story of the railroads in America is well done in *American Railroads* (1961) by John Stover. Another important and particularly useful study for the relationship between the government and the railroads is Lewis Henry Haney, *A Congressional History of Railways in the United States to 1850* (1908). There are a number of interesting accounts of the history of the railway mail service. Among the most authoritative is the one prepared in the Post Office Department entitled *History of the Railway Mail Service: A Chapter in the History of Postal Affairs in the United States,* Senate Executive Documents, 48th Congress, 2d Session, document number 40 (1885). Other interesting works are Clark E. Carr, *The Railway Mail: Its Origins and Developments* (1909); G. G. Tunnell, *Railway Mail Service: A Comparative Study of Railroad Rates and Services* (1901), friendly to the railroad position on the subject; and C. B. Armstrong, *The Beginnings of the True Railway Mail Service and the Work of George B. Armstrong in Founding It* (1906), obviously not an unbiased account. James E. White, *A Life Span and Reminiscences of Railway Mail Service* (1910) is a firsthand story of what the service was like. Alden Hatch, *American Express: A Century of Service* (1950) has the story of the origins of express companies.

There is no study of the struggle to secure a postal telegraph, but S. F. B. Morse's *Letters and Journals* (2 vols., 1914) show how it all began. The basic work on the telegraph in America is Robert Luther Thompson, *Wiring a Continent* (1947). A short study by Edwin Walter Kemmerer, *Postal Savings* (1917), deals hastily with that subject.

EXPANSIONISM AND THE POST OFFICE

A useful study of the British mail packet service to America from the 1750s to the beginning of steam power is *The Transatlantic Mail* (1956), by Frank Staff. A careful, painstaking study of the American mail service across the Atlantic is George E. Hargest, *History of Letter Post Communication between the United States and Europe, 1845–1875* (1971).

Paul M. Seis, *American Shipping Policy* (1938) is a short but excellent treatment of the subject. *The Rise of the New York Port, 1815–1860* (1939) by R. G. Albion has a good account of the rise of the Black Ball Line and the development of American sailing ships. Arguments for the development of steamships in the 1850s may be found in a contemporary plea, *Ocean Steam Navigation* (1858), by Thomas Rainey. E. K. Collins's story is told in part by Ralph Whitney, "The Unlucky Collins Line," *American Heritage*, vol. 8 (Feb. 1957). John Haskell Kemble deals with the great steamship line on the Pacific in an article "The Genesis of the Pacific Mail Steamship Company," *California Historical Quarterly*, vol. 13 (1934).

Marcus Lee Hansen, *The Immigrant in American History* (1940) has a brief account of the influence letters had upon immigration. American ideas behind the sentiment for expansion are explored in A. K. Weinberg's *Manifest Destiny* (1935), and the idea of the American West as a gateway to the Orient is treated in Henry Nash Smith, *Virgin Land* (1950). Debates on postal steamship subsidies in Congress tend to support the expansionist thesis developed by Walter LaFeber's *The New Empire* (1963), but of course the expansionist sentiment was not strong enough to overcome agrarian opposition to postal subsidies to steamship lines.

George A. Codding, Jr., *The Universal Postal Union* (1964) is the best work on that subject.

GUARDIANS OF THE NATION'S MAILS AND MORALS

Several popular accounts of the post office inspectors have been written. Karl Baarslag, *Robbery by Mail: The Story of the U.S. Postal Inspectors* (1938) deals principally with their work in the twentieth century. John N. Makris, *The Silent Inspectors* (1959) gives an interesting account of David Parker, the first chief inspector. Ellinore Denniston's *America's Silent Investigators: The Story of the Postal Inspectors Who Protect the United States Mail* (1964) is very slight. An amusing but important story of the inspector's life is told by an inspector himself in James Holbrook, *Ten*

Bibliographical Essay

Years among the Mail Bags; or, Notes from the Diary of a Special Agent of the Post Office Department (1888). David Parker, the first chief inspector, tells his story in *A Chautauqua Boy: In '61 and Afterward: Reminiscences* (1912).

The subject of crime in the United States has yet to be studied by a historian. Frederick H. Wines, *Report on Crime, Pauperism, and Benevolence in the United States: Eleventh Census: 1890* (1895) gives the most reliable statistics on crime for that period and has interesting observations about the statistics. Thomas Byrnes, *1886: Professional Criminals of America* (1886) presents an account of crime and criminals in New York City and has an introduction on crime and on Thomas Byrnes by Arthur Schlesinger, Jr. Some aspects of crime in nineteenth-century America can be seen from James D. Horan's *The Pinkertons: The Detective Dynasty That Made History* (1967). Mark H. Haller makes an excellent beginning of the serious study of crime in his article "Urban Crime and Criminal Justice: The Chicago Case," *Journal of American History*, vol. 57 (Dec. 1970).

Fortune's Merry Wheel (1960), by John S. Ezell, is the definitive work on lotteries in America. Abortion and contraception, like crime, have been avoided by social historians. Oscar Handlin finds an explanation for the interest in abortion in the middle nineteenth century in his *Race and Nationality in American Life* (1957); David Kennedy, *Birth Control in America: The Career of Margaret Sanger* (1970) has a good survey of nineteenth-century attitudes toward birth control in one chapter. Perhaps Anthony Comstock best described the general American sentiment toward contraception and abortion in his two books: *Frauds Exposed; or, How the People Are Deceived and Robbed and Youth Corrupted* (1880), and *Traps for the Young* (1884). Heywood Broun and Margaret Leech, *Anthony Comstock: Roundsman of the Lord* (1927) is a critical study of Comstock's works. *The Search for the Obscene* (1964) by Morris L. Ernst and Alan Schwartz deals with the history of obscenity but makes no reference to the role of the mails in making obscenity a national problem after the Civil War. The Protestant background from which the drive against obscenity drew its strength is discussed in *The Rise of the Social Gospel in American Protestantism, 1865–1915* (1940) by Charles Howard Hopkins and *Protestant Churches and Industrial America* (1949) by Henry F.

Bibliographical Essay

May, though neither historian deals directly with the problem. The frustration many Americans experienced in the post–Civil War period is perceptively seen in John Higham, *Strangers in the Land: Patterns of American Nativism, 1860–1925* (1955).

Max Lowenthal, *The Federal Bureau of Investigation* (1950) has a good account of Congress's opposition to the employment of special agents for the Justice Department, and Willard B. Gatewood, Jr., *Theodore Roosevelt and the Art of Controversy* (1970) has a brief account of Roosevelt's exposé of Tillman.

POLITICS AND THE POST OFFICE

The development of the nation's two political parties in the Jacksonian period is analyzed in Richard McCormick, *The Second American Party System* (1966). Dorothy Fowler, *The Cabinet Politician* (1943) presents a thorough study of the postmaster general as a politician. Carl R. Fish, *The Civil Service and the Patronage* (1905) has much to say about the use of the Post Office by the politicians. H. J. Carman and R. H. Luthin have dealt with Lincoln's problems with the spoils system in *Lincoln and the Patronage* (1943).

One of the best accounts of the relationship between an appointee in the postal service and the congressman who sponsored him is *Politics and Patronage in the Gilded Age: The Correspondence of James E. Garfield and Charles E. Henry*, edited by James D. Norris and Arthur Shaffer (1970).

An Englishman, James Bryce, set the pattern for the interpretation of American politics in the post–Civil War period in his *American Commonwealth* (2 vols., 1888), which has generally been followed by historians of the period. A modest reinterpretation of the period can be found in a series of essays edited by H. Wayne Morgan, entitled *The Gilded Age* (1962). The politics of the period has also been newly studied by H. Wayne Morgan in *From Hayes to McKinley: National Party Politics, 1877–1896* (1969).

The civil service reform movement has been thoroughly covered in Paul Van Riper's *History of the United States Civil Service* (1958). *Outlawing the Spoils* (1961) by Ari Hoogenboom is a more perceptive treatment of the motives of the civil service reformers. A

358

Bibliographical Essay

critical view of the reformers is John G. Sproat's *"The Best Men":
Liberal Reformers in the Gilded Age* (1968).

The difficulties the postal employees had in forming their organizations have been traced by Sterling Denhard Spero, *The Labor Movement in a Government Industry: A Study of Employee Organization in the Postal Service* (1927).

EPILOGUE

The story of the Post Office in recent years is partially told by some of the men who directed it. Arthur Summerfield's stewardship of the Post Office is told by him in *U.S. Mail: The Story of the United States Postal Service* (1960). J. Edward Day, *My Appointed Round: 929 Days as Postmaster General* (1965) presents his story of how it was to run the greatest business on earth. William Doherty, *Mailman: U.S.A.* (1960) gives the postal worker's side of the story. Gerald Cullinan, *The Post Office Department* (1968) is one of a series in the Praeger Library of United States Government Departments. Carrol V. Glines has a popular account of the airmail in his *Saga of the Air Mail* (1968). Morton S. Baratz, *The Economics of the Postal Service* (1962) is a scholarly study of postal finances.

Towards Postal Excellence: The Report of the President's Commission on Postal Organization (1968) contains the summarized findings of the commission's study that laid the groundwork for the establishment of the postal corporation.

Acknowledgments

For encouragement and help in the preparation of this study I wish to thank Daniel Boorstin, who suggested it, and the administrators of the University of Texas at El Paso, who provided me with the schedules and research grants that made its completion possible. I am grateful to Carl Scheele, chairman of the Department of Applied Arts at the Museum of History and Technology of the Smithsonian Institution, for reading much of the manuscript and for saving me from a number of blunders, and to Arthur Hecht of the National Archives, who has so cheerfully assisted me through the years in the use of the postal records.

For several years students in my graduate seminar have puzzled through postal problems with me. I am especially indebted to them for their contributions, and to Mrs. Rosemary Corcoran, head of the documents division of the University of Texas at El Paso library, and her staff for their unfailing patience and help.

In some ways the writing of *The American Mail* was a family affair. I take pleasure in acknowledging the help of my daughter Jamie, who suggested numerous stylistic changes, and of my wife Billie, who read, corrected, and typed the manuscript more times than she cares to remember.

Index

Index

Astoria, Oregon Territory, 199
Atlantic (steamship), 204
Atlantic Monthly, 140
Australasia, British, 224, 230, 235
Austria, 211, 228, 229

Bache, Richard, 35, 36
Baltic (steamship), 205
Baltimore and Ohio Railroad, 158, 159, 160
Bancroft, George, 202
Bankhead, John H., 107
Banks, postal savings: arguments for, 178; aguments against, 179; attitude toward in Cleveland administration, 181; established, 183–84
Barry, William: administration of, 54–58, 60; and roads, 86; elevated to cabinet status, 286
Beadle, Erastus and Irwin, 136
Beavers, George, 321
Belgium, 210
Benger, Eliot, 25
Benton, Thomas Hart, 215
Berne Postal Congress of 1874, 213
Bertillon system, 257
Black Ball Line, 193
Blair, Henry W., 254
Blair, Montgomery, 211, 213–14, 251, 315; suspends mail service in the south, 101; and railway post office, 167; recommends international postal conference, 212; and spoils system, 292; and payment of postmasters, 298
Blood, D. O., and Company, 165
Blount, James, 224
Blount, Winton M., 331
Board of Trade, 28
Boer War, 236
Bonaparte, Charles, 278
Books: exclusion of from mails, 119, 124; cheap, 124; postage on reduced, 133; paperback, 135, 136, 252;

pornographic, 268
Boston, 26, 134, 159, 196, 219; in 1690, 17; mail routes to, 23, 26–27; as distributing post office, 167
Boston *Herald*, 145
Bradford, William, 12
Brazil, 215, 224; demand for steam mail routes to, 214; steamship lines to Baía, Pernambuco, 217; mails to, 231
Bremen, 202; steamship line to, 199; postmaster at, 201; number of letters mailed to, 209
Bremerhaven, 206
Bristow, Joseph, 144
British postal system in America: established, 21; difficulties of, 23–24; shows profit, 27, 30; involved in quarrel with colonies, 30, 32; ends 35
Brodhead, Richard, 97
Brother Jonathan, 124, 136
Brown, Aaron, 69, 98
Brown, Samuel B., 244–45
Buchanan, James, 98
Burleson, Albert, 78, 328; and rural delivery, 77; and second class mail matter, 146; and railroad compensation, 186–87; and government control of telegraph and telephone lines, 188; wars on postal union, 328
Burritt, Elihu, 197
Business: and postal service, 88; private vs. public, 163, 310; and telegraph, 177
Butterfield, John, 69, 98, 100

Calhoun, John C., 87, 92, 95, 99, 106
California, 95, 96, 290; Placerville, 96; San Francisco, 96, 179, 215, 217, 230; Stockton, 96
Campbell, James, 66, 68, 69, 292
Canada, 27, 29; Quebec, 27; post office of, 144–45, 166; New

Index

Index

Index

Index

Index

service, 197, 210; Americanization of, 134; changing nature of, 228; blamed for increase of crime, 241; influx of, 253
Indiana: Indianapolis, 86; Vincennes, 49, 242
Industry, growth of, 247
Innovations, postal, and crimes, 250
Inspectors, postal: appropriations for, 243, 245, 246, 273–74, 275, 276; special agents become, 256; qualifications of, 256; number of, 258, 276; find dishonest employees, 259; investigations of patrons, 260; and fraud orders, 263; hindered in work, 265; report on robberies, 267; and obscenity cases, 268–71; as politicians, 274; Congress's fear of, 276–77; report of published, 279; recommend fourth-class postmasters, 325. *See also* Cases, postal inspector; Special agents
International Postal Congress, 1863, 213, 221
Interstate Commerce Commission, 186, 188–89
Intolerable Acts, 33
Investigations: of Post Office Department, 51, 286; of second-class mail matter, 142; of railroads, 184; by postal inspectors, 277
Iowa, 270, 340; Clinton, 167; Dubuque, 179
Iron Age, 137
Isabel (steamship), 208
Isthmus of Panama, 96
Isthmus of Suez, 214
Isthmus of Tehuantepec, 208
Italy, 228, 229

Jackson, Andrew, 57, 91, 156, 158, 287–88, 294; and printing of inaugural address, 48; and incendiary literature, 92;

attacks railroad monopoly, 161–62; removal policy, 285
James I, 7
James, Jesse, 249
James, Thomas, 147, 311
Japan, 217, 230, 235
Jefferson, Thomas, 38, 80, 284; and route to Far East, 215; and Republican party, 238
Jenckes, Thomas, 309
Jewell, Marshall, 180–81
Johnson, Andrew, 72, 292
Johnson, Cave, 94, 172–73, 199; attacks cheap newspaper postage, 120; and postal telegraph, 174; removes special agents, 245; recommendation of on postmaster general, 292
Johnson, Lyndon B., 337
Johnson, Matthew, 28
Johnson, Richard, 56
Jones, James, 69

Kansas, 46, 72
Kasson, John A., 212
Kelly, Clyde, 332
Kendall, Amos, 59, 60, 159; takes Barry's place, 57; administration of postal service, 58–61; and incendiary literature, 92; and foreign mail service, 194
Kentucky, 49, 244; Louisville, 68, 158; Lexington, 80; Elizabethtown, 86
Key, David M., 103
King, Thomas Butler, 190, 215
King William's War, 20, 21
Knights of Labor, 254

Lakeside Library, 137
Lanier, Sidney, 220
Latham, Milton S., 216
Lee, Richard Henry, 79
Leggett, William, 163
Leib, Michael, 284
Letters: mangled in mail, 47; carried outside the mail, 62; registered, 70; drop, 71;

Index

Index

Index

Index

Index

Postmaster (*cont.*)
340; political role of, 291, 294;
compensation of, 297–99,
306; classification of, 299;
inefficiency of, 315. *See also*
First-class postmasters;
Fourth-class postmasters;
Postmasters general; Presidential
postmasters; Second-class
postmasters; Third-class
postmasters

Postmasters general: work of,
46–47, 51, 52, 119; restriction
of powers of, 78, 328; and second-
class mailing privilege, 138, 139;
advertisements for bids to
carry mail, 150; and railroads,
171; contract for steam vessels,
199; and postal conventions,
200; and steamship subsidies,
233, 235; protect mail, 240; issue
fraud orders, 263; appointment
power of, 283, 291; cabinet
status of, 286; politicized, 291;
political role of, 292–93;
review postmasters' salaries,
299. *See also* Bache, Richard;
Barry, William; Blair,
Montgomery; Blount, Winton
M.; Brown, Aaron; Burleson,
Albert; Campbell, James;
Creswell, John A. James;
Dennison, William; Franklin,
Benjamin; Granger, Gideon;
Habersham, Joseph; Hazard,
Ebenezer; Hitchcock, Frank;
Holt, Joseph; Howe, Timothy
Otis; Hubbard, Sam; Jewell,
Marshall; Johnson, Cave;
Kendall, Amos; Key, David
M.; McLean, John; Meigs,
Return J.; O'Brien, Lawrence;
Pickering, Timothy; Randall,
Alexander; Reagan, John;
Spotswood, Alexander;
Summerfield, Arthur; Vilas,
William F.; Wanamaker, John;
Wickliffe, Charles; Wilson,

William L.

Post Office, American: established,
34; during Revolution, 35, 36;
during Confederation period,
37–39, 40–41; uniqueness
of, 42; as bond of union, 81;
as means of diffusing knowledge,
110, 134; unlike European,
148; as test for economic
theories, 149; as government-
owned business, 182–83, 188;
competition with England,
197; useful to expansionists, 221;
and American expectations,
238; and changes in American
life, 248; used to protect morals,
254; underwrites democracy,
289; becomes United States
Postal Service, 331

Post Office Department:
investigations of, 51; and
Treasury Department, 53;
building burned, 58; reorganized,
58, 59; and problem of
transporting printed matter, 117;
and problem of second-class
mail, 132–33, 134, 137,
141; and mail contractors,
157; early relations with
railroads, 159–61, 166; and
express companies, 163;
prevented from entering private
business, 171; and telegraph and
telephone lines, 187; and foreign
mail, 194, 211, 212; and
steamship mail lines, 217, 223;
completes parcel post
conventions, 231; and merchant
marine, 237; and spoils
system, 288

Post offices: number of, 49,
74, 75, 77, 82, 96, 103–4, 112,
248; distributing, 167, 168, 335;
sea, 227; robberies of, 240,
246, 249, 265; inspection of, 258;
as political centers, 296;
fourth-class, 318, 319; and
politics, 322, 326; railway, 335;

374

Index

Index